Standoff At Tiananmen

How Chinese Students Shocked the World with a
Magnificent Movement for Democracy and Liberty that
Ended in the Tragic Tiananmen Massacre in 1989

Eddie Cheng

www.StandoffAtTiananmen.com

Sensys Corp.
Highlands Ranch, Colorado

For updates, errata, and more resources,
visit the book web site at
www.StandoffAtTiananmen.com

ISBN: 978-0-9823203-0-3

Library of Congress Control Number: 2009902350

Library of Congress subject headings:
China–History–Tiananmen Square Incident, 1989
Democracy–China
China–Politics and government

*To those who lost their lives during the night of
June 3, 1989 and the days after*

To those whose lives were forever changed

To the memories

Contents

Preface

I started to think about writing this book in 2004, when the fifteenth anniversary of the 1989 student movement once again rekindled interest in the online Chinese community as well as the general public in the west. Inside China, of course, all discussions were censored and forbidden. It occurred to me that the real story of that glorious movement had yet to be told.

I entered Peking University in 1980 as a student majoring in physics, just in time for the "election campaign" described in the first Chapter. In the mid-1980's, the school's Physics Department became a hotbed of exciting happenings. I was fortunate enough to personally witness and participate in some of the student movements which helped to till the soil for the drama in 1989. I left China in 1986 but was kept apprised in the adventures of my formal classmates, including the emerging student leader Liu Gang. In that spring of 1989, I watched the events unfolding in Beijing on *CNN* like millions of people worldwide. It was an extremely frustrating and hopeless experience. But over time, I realized that the distance also afforded me a degree of necessary emotional detachment and objectivity in telling this story.

Many books have been published to document personal accounts of the massacre. Others provide insights on various facets of the movement.[1] Personal recollections are also scattered in magazine and Internet articles. Buried underneath this myriad of anecdotes, however, is a fascinating story of human experience.

Almost all materials presented in this book are publicly available, most of which are only in Chinese until now, but it is the first time that the story is being told as a narrative history. When possible, I also had personal conversations with some of the characters to clarify misconceptions and rectify some of the factual errors and contradictions in the existing literature.

I chose to tell the story from the perspective of the student collective who is indeed the main protagonist. I hope this approach could help to re-create the students' experience and provide a proper background and atmosphere in their emotional state and decision-making process. How and why the government made its own decisions is certainly a subject of great interest, but is beyond the scope of this book.[2] Similarly, this book does not provide in-depth analysis of students' motives or their influences and impacts.[3]

Although intended to be a comprehensive and definitive historical account, this book is nevertheless limited by the current availability of material. Some of the main

Preface

characters have since disappeared from public scene and are unwilling or reluctant to provide more detail on their accounts. The story-telling in this book inevitably focused more on those who had written substantial memoirs and recollections and might have neglected some who chose to be less vocal. On the other hand, in the interest of not confusing readers with too many foreign names, many others who had made significant contributions were omitted or presented without specific names. We have to bear in mind that a movement like this one, after all, is not a product of only a few leaders.

Many leaders and participants of the movement did offer me their unique insights and clarifications. These include Feng Congde, Huang Haixin, Li Jinjin, Liu Gang, Peng Dechun, Wang Chaohua, Wang Dan, Wang Juntao, Wu Renhua, and a few who wished to remain anonymous.

During the course of this project, many people have provided me with help and encouragement. Sam Fleishman helped on an early draft of the first three chapters. Chen Jie, Chen Ying, Dong Jielin, Gong Xiaoxia, He Shaoyi, Jim Hansen, Huang Yishu, James Mayer, Joel Mulhern, Jeffrey Pan, Jeff Pantazes, Valerie Ricotta, Wang Chenguang, Jerry Wang, and Wang Zhengan read early drafts and offered many valuable comments and suggestions as well as editorial help. Jim Hansen also took upon himself the daunting task of painstakingly going through the manuscript a second time to correct the numerous errors I had made in English language and made the book a much improved product. Alfredo Ocampo and Alma Oliva spent hours of their own time to design the cover for this book. James Mayer is also the source of help whenever I run into trouble in the composition and layout with the LATEXsoftware.

Although a picture is worth thousands of words, none is included in this book mainly for copyright concerns. There are numerous pictures and video clips of the movement available on the Internet, some of which will be categorized as additional resources on the web site for this book, along with maps, songs, and other artifacts. For these and regular updates and errata, please visit

www.StandoffAtTiananmen.com

Eddie Cheng
March, 2009

Main Characters*

- **Chai Ling**, *23*, graduate student at Beijing Normal University.

- **Feng Congde**, *23*, graduate student at Peking University.

- **Li Lu**, *23*, senior at Nanking University.

- **Liu Gang**, *28*, former graduate student in physics at Peking University.

- **Shen Tong**, *20*, junior at Peking University.

- **Wang Chaohua**, *37*, graduate student at Chinese Academy of Social Sciences.

- **Wang Dan**, *20*, sophomore at Peking University.

- **Wang Juntao**, *30*, intellectual and activist.

- **Wuer Kaixi**, *21*, undergraduate student at Beijing Normal University.

- **Xiang Xiaoji**, *32*, graduate student at University of Political Science and Law

- **Zhang Boli**, *26*, "authors class" student at Peking University

---

*All information is as of 1989.

Power comes from the barrel of a gun.

Mao Zedong

Prologue

SUNDAY, June 5, 1989, was a clear day in Beijing. The early summer sun was casting a layer of warmth over the streets of this ancient capital of China. Yet the city looked amazingly empty. There were none of the buses, bicycles, or pedestrians that made up the usual weekend traffic. The emptiness was particularly profound along Chang'an Avenue, the main thoroughfare of the city. This magnificent boulevard was designed to carry eight lanes of vehicular traffic plus two wide lanes dedicated for bicycles. There were little signs of life. It was a gigantic slab of gray concrete flooded by uninterrupted sunlight.

There were traces of black smoke in the distant sky. Along Chang'an Avenue, burnt buses and other debris dotted the roadside. Bloodstain could be spotted in some areas, a contrast to its recently cleaned surface. Occasional sights of tanks and armored personnel carriers indicated that this was not a normal morning for this city.

A column of tanks slowly emerged from Tiananmen Square. On the wide and empty Chang'an Avenue, the tanks cruised right in the middle of the road. One block east of Tiananmen Square, however, the column came to an abrupt halt. A lone and slim figure appeared from nowhere and stepped right into the path of the lead tank. Upstairs in the nearby Beijing Hotel, foreign reporters crowded into several balconies overlooking the street. They could not believe what they were seeing but kept their video cameras rolling and took still photographs with their long lenses.

The reporters saw the man from his back. He was wearing a white shirt and dark pants. He was holding a jacket in his left hand and a

1

small plastic bag in his right. He was probably about twenty years old and appeared to be a typical college student or a young office worker. But there he was in the middle of Chang'an Avenue, standing alone and still, facing a column of advancing tanks.

As the lead tank stopped right in front of his body, the young man whipped his right arm in a forceful gesture as if to tell the tank to get out of the way. A tense pause ensued as the man and the tank stared down each other. Smoke emerged behind the lead tank as it started its engine again. The tank moved gently to the man's left. Without hesitation, the man stepped over to block the path. The tank then turned to the man's right. Behind it, the entire column of tanks were also veering left and right like a long snake. The man moved along. He was not yielding an inch.

As the tanks stopped again, the man made his boldest move yet. He climbed on top of the lead tank. He looked up and down the turret trying to find a way to see the soldiers inside. He was not successful. So he climbed back down. Just then, several civilians rushed in and dragged him away to the sidewalk. The column of tanks continued on their path without further incident.

NOBODY knew who that man was.* His age indicated that he was a member of the generation that had staged one of the most dramatic historic events of the nation which eventually ended with the tanks being in the streets of the capital. Less than two days earlier, in the evening of June 3, hundreds of thousands of troops armed with automatic assault rifles and machine guns and accompanied by heavy tanks and armored personnel carriers had shot through crowds of civilians to take over the city. Hundreds, if not thousands, of students and residents lost their lives to their own army.

Most likely, this man had received his elementary and middle school education in the 1970's. Undoubtedly he had been drilled on a particular impending threat to his country during his school years. The American John Foster Dulles, the Secretary of State under President

---

*Although it was widely reported that the man's name was Wang Weilin, there has never been any evidence of his identity or whereabouts. It is likely that his identity will never be certifiably established.

Prologue

Dwight Eisenhower, had predicted the demise of communism by its own "peaceful evolution." He said, as all pupils in China were repeatedly told, that by the third or fourth generation, the children of communism would lose their ideological zeal and turn against the system. That meant the generation of this man who stood in front of a column of tanks.

By the year 1989, the doctrine of preventing "peaceful evolution" had already faded into history. Yet a "peaceful evolution" almost happened, perhaps unexpectedly and inadvertently. In that spring, tens of thousands college students marched on streets to demand freedom and democracy or simply an equal dialogue with their own government. On May 13, hundreds of these students staged a hunger strike in Tiananmen Square, the holy center of the nation, that lasted an agonizing week. Martial law was declared on May 20. Yet its enforcing troops were blocked at the outskirts of the city by residents. The students continued to occupy Tiananmen Square until that bloody evening when soldiers finally fought into the city with tanks and machine guns.

Nobody knew if the man who stood in front of a column of tanks had been a hunger striker himself, or one of those who placed their bodies in front of military trucks during the night of martial law, or had witnessed the senseless killing of unarmed civilians during the night of June 3 and the day of June 4. It was clear that he had seen enough, heard enough, and felt enough to make a stand of his own.

T HE foreign reporters in Beijing Hotel scrambled to hide the valuable footage they had just captured. It would take a couple of days before they were smuggled out of the country and headlined through the mass media all over the world. This scene of one man against tanks would become the most recognized symbol of the 1989 student movement in Beijing and what became known as the Tiananmen Massacre. It was a fitting symbol of an unyielding standoff, a story that had not yet been fully told and understood.

In the meantime, some of the reporters could not help to wonder what had transpired during the few months in this magnificent capital. Or a few years before it—for just a short decade ago, the city and the country was a place of hope and new beginnings.

The voice of our generation has been ignored for too long, too long...

Hu Ping

1

The New Generation

ACCORDING to the Chinese zodiac, 1980 was the "Year of the Monkey," symbolizing an active, exciting, and opportune time. Indeed, an almost euphoric excitement was in the air, accompanied by the joyous and upbeat tune of a popular song that could be heard through radios and public loudspeakers everywhere, all the time:

> *Come to meet, all young friends,*
> *Let's row our boats and feel the breeze,*
> *Flowers are blossoming, birds are chirping,*
> *Lose yourself in this wonderful spring.*
> *Let our songs and laughter fly through the clouds.*
>
> *Ah, dear friends,*
> *To whom does this beautiful spring belong?*
> *It belongs to you, it belongs to me,*
> *It belongs to all of us,*
> *The new generation of the Eighties!*

The mood of this ancient nation was very different just four years earlier. Mao Zedong, the founding father and undisputed leader who

4

had ruled communist China for almost thirty years, had finally passed away. The country sank into a state of deep sorrow and despair. For the young, the "Great Leader Chairman Mao" was the God, or the communist equivalent, they had worshiped all their lives. Since kindergarten, they had been chanting the omnipresent slogan "Mao Zhu Xi Wan Sui!" It literally meant that Chairman Mao would live on for ten thousand years. His death was therefore as unthinkable as the end of the world.

In reality, the nation was stuck in the turmoil of the decade-long Cultural Revolution launched by Mao Zedong to purge liberal-minded leaders and intellectuals. The economy was in shambles, society in chaos, and people in fear. There were hardly any goods to sell in stores. Every daily necessity, from food to cloth to watches to bicycles, was strictly rationed. Every man wore the exact same blue or gray, featureless "Mao Suit" and sported the uniform crew cut. Women did not look much different from the men either, except for slightly longer hair or braids. It was very dangerous to be different, whether in appearances, behavior, or thoughts. Those who had carelessly complained in their private correspondences or personal diaries often found themselves in prison or labor camps.

Perhaps there were few who secretly celebrated Mao Zedong's death and hoped for a fundamental change, but in public, everyone cried and grieved, more so than for the passing of their own loved ones. For some, it was genuine sorrow. For most, it was perhaps more of an emotional inertia from decades of worship and conformist instinct. For yet a few, it was simply a matter of survival. Everyone took the most solemn oath to defend Mao Zedong's legacy and carry on his will. Nothing should change a tiny bit and nothing would.

Change came much more quickly and dramatically than anyone could have imagined or hoped. Within a month of Mao Zedong's death, his closest allies including his own wife were arrested in a palace coup. The so-called "Gang of Four" was swiftly condemned for being responsible for every crime and policy failure since the Cultural Revolution. Chairman Mao's legacy, meanwhile, was preserved by the new leadership.

Standoff At Tiananmen

When the dust settled, the new leader of China turned out to be a diminutive figure who had been purged by Mao Zedong twice during the Cultural Revolution but somehow survived the ordeals. Less than five feet tall, Deng Xiaoping was known for his strong will and intelligent prowess. Born in 1904 to a rural peasant family in the remote Sichuan Province, he had studied abroad in Paris and Moscow as a teenager and became a communist activist. By the time he was thirty years old, he was already working within the inner circle of the Chinese Communist Party, then a rebellious group being suppressed by the Nationalist government. During the war era, he helped to command the largest army in the communist force as a political commissar and was instrumental in several important campaigns. Therefore he enjoyed a solid reputation within the military brass.

Unlike Mao Zedong, however, Deng Xiaoping was a pragmatist at heart. His favorite idiom was the "cat theory," which posited that the value of a cat was not whether it was black or white, but whether it could catch mice. Such merit-based measuring criteria did not fit well with Mao Zedong's ideological standards. When Deng Xiaoping was purged, his "cat theory" was widely ridiculed as an example of his lack of ideological standings. However, rather than humiliating him, the adverse publicity probably helped endear Deng Xiaoping to the general public, even during the Cultural Revolution years.

After Mao Zedong's passing, Deng Xiaoping crawled back from the political abyss and set the country onto a new course. While continuing to pay lip service to Mao Zedong's legacy, he put the nation on notice that the number one concern should now be in economic development and productivity.

"Don't be afraid to let some people get rich first," he advised, breaking from the rigid socialist ideal of equality. "To get rich is glorious," he expounded to encourage people to seek their own ways to enhance their standard of living and pursue happiness. His "cat theory" became a political cover, often with his own blessing, for liberally-minded local officials to experiment with various un-socialist means to enhance productivity.

The results were immediate and astonishing. "Experiments" with limited privatization in the countryside led to such a liberation in farming productivity that an unprecedented harvest was reported nation-wide in 1979. In the cities, the young and previously jobless took up unfamiliar entrepreneurship and busied themselves in peddling all kinds of goods according to market demand. Almost overnight, it seemed that one could find anything from private street vendors and makeshift farmers markets without the need of rationing coupons. The "Mao Suit" slowly gave way to jeans, leather jackets, and skirts. Brave fashion pioneers started to grow long hair and sport curly hairdos to the scorn of their elders and envy of their peers. The status symbol of the time was a pair of oversize sunglasses with its trade-mark label intact as a proof of being a genuine item imported from Hong Kong. Never mind that the label did nothing but hinder the view. Smiles, along with a new hope for a bright future, returned triumphantly as the arrival of a new decade, the 1980's.

FUNDAMENTAL changes were occurring everywhere but most especially on college campuses. These were the most prestigious institutions in a nation where education and intellectuals were highly respected, but it had all come to a halt during the Cultural Revolution. Mao Zedong's personal disdain of intellectuals, whose loyalty was always in question, led to a complete shutdown of all institutes of higher learning. Professors and intellectuals alike were forced to move to rural farms and reform their minds through physical labor. High school graduates, deprived of the opportunity to go to colleges, were sent down to the countryside as well to be re-educated by peasants. For many years, the lives of these youth seemed to be stuck there with no end in sight. When universities gradually reopened, students were selected by a "recommendation system." They were chosen for their political aptitude and personal connections, even when they were practically illiterate.

In August 1977, barely a year after Chairman Mao's death, the newly reinstated Deng Xiaoping made one of his first decisions of strategic importance: an immediate return to the traditional nationwide scholastic tests to select college entrants. News of the reform exploded through the whole country like a shock wave. Millions of youths suddenly saw their abandoned dreams reawakened. Even more parents and relatives scrambled to find old textbooks, study materials, and any helpful tips for their children. Those who had spent years in the countryside knew that this was their "last train" to pursue a more civil and enlightened life. They were determined to earn a ticket. During two consecutive exams held at the end of 1977 and then summer of 1978, about twelve million tried their hands for the coming school year. Only about five percent of them were lucky enough to be accepted into colleges, from top universities to two-year technical schools. This had to be the largest scholastic exam ever conducted in human history. It had been ten years since the last one before the interruption of the Cultural Revolution. There were a whole generation's worth of high school graduates who were desperate.

The social impact of these exams could not be exaggerated. Through the prospective students and their families and relatives, it affected every single family. When there was not enough paper to print test sheets for this huge turnout, Deng Xiaoping diverted supplies destined for printing *Mao Zedong's Works*, underscoring a fundamental shift in priority. More than anything else, the exams established the working of an objective standard. The slogan "everybody is equal before exam scores" became a battle cry for those who had grown up in politically oppressed families. A new kind of equality and a new sense of social justice were awakened within the society.

When the lucky few of that generation walked through the campus gates, they found a strange scene. The existing students who had come through the "recommendation system" were enrolled in classes taught barely at middle school levels. They deeply resented the new arrivals. Shell-shocked by the Cultural Revolution, professors were in constant fear of saying the wrong things and unsure of what to teach. The new students were certainly not a typical freshman class. Their ages were much closer to thirties than twenties. Many were married and some already had children. Except for the few crazy months before the exams, they had not touched a book for years. Desperate as they were to be admitted into college, they actually knew little about college in general or their chosen majors in particular. However, they were also a hardened group, molded by years of life's struggles. They were determined to redouble their efforts in studying so that they could "gain

8

back" the years they had wasted in the countryside.

Even before these "old" students could settle into a comfortable college life, however, it was clear that the look of campus was about to change before their very eyes. A new generation of students was already arriving.

By 1980, the Year of the Monkey, with the happy *New Generation of the Eighties* tune blasting, those who marched through the same campus gates were almost all current high school graduates. Between sixteen and eighteen year old, these "kids" had never been sent down to experience life in the countryside. They were lucky enough to spend their entire youth in classrooms. Indeed, they were regarded as "God's favored sons" by the society at large, enjoying a social status much higher than their contemporaries. Their natural innocence and enthusiasm seemed almost foreign to the older students. Through their parents and older siblings, however, the new kids clearly understood that they had Deng Xiaoping to thank for their good fortune. When Deng Xiaoping reinstated the national entrance exam, they were still in high schools. Overnight, their future was assured. It would be college instead of the countryside and they would be reading books instead of wielding hoes.

But before leaving the campuses to this new generation, the elders had something of their own to show.

IN the summer of 1920, Dr. John Leighton Stuart, a son of American missionaries and the president of the private Methodist Yenching University, was looking for a new site for his school in Beijing, or Peking, as it was called then. He chose to purchase the country estate of a former imperial minister about ten miles northwest of the city. The site was conveniently located between Yuanmingyuan and the Summer Palace, both once magnificent imperial gardens. By 1926, he had secured two hundred acres of land and commissioned the architect Henry Killam Murphy to design a new campus in harmony with its natural surroundings. All office and classroom buildings were finished with raised wings on roofs and colorfully decorated beams and eaves. Near the main building group and surrounded by hills and willow trees was a man-made lake artfully named the "Unnamed Lake."

Standoff At Tiananmen

In the middle of the lake there was an island that could be reached by an arched walking bridge. A majestic thirteen-story pagoda sat on a hill by the lake. It was built as a replica of the ancient Tungchow Pagoda and named Boya, or "Learned and Elegant," yet the pagoda was designed to serve the very practical purpose of supplying water for the campus. The scenic campus was dotted with many antique artifacts "rescued" from the nearby Yuanmingyuan ruin, providing even more of a feel of an imperial garden.

Decades of development and consolidation followed. The picturesque campus eventually became the site for the most prestigious school in China, the Peking University. With strong liberal arts and natural science programs, the school was unofficially crowned as the "Highest Institute of the Land." Every year, it consistently attracted the best and brightest students throughout the country.

One of those older students who beat out millions of his peers to enter Peking University in 1978 at the mature age of thirty-three was Hu Ping. Although born in Beijing, Hu Ping was raised in Sichuan Province, Deng Xiaoping's hometown. The Cultural Revolution, which started as he was finishing high school, forced him to spend five years laboring in the countryside of the neighboring Yunnan Province. Later, he lingered on as a worker in local factories for a few more years. His undesirable family background appeared to be an insurmountable obstacle to any realistic prospects—until the opening of the college entrance exam. In fact, he was so confident of his intelligence and years of self-taught knowledge that he took the exams for graduate school directly, skipping college. Without hesitation, he chose Peking University and was accepted as a graduate student in philosophy.

Unlike most of his new classmates, however, Hu Ping had more than books in mind when he came to this school. Besides its strong academic reputation, Peking University was even better known for its political activism or "student movements," massive protests that stemmed from young students' desire for democracy and freedom. Several large student movements, when students marched on streets to protest government policies, had played significant roles in the course of modern Chinese history. After the communists took power, they took credit for the movements and praised them as an indication of early popular support for communism. In the official version of history, student movements were patriotic, progressive, and democratic undertakings. It became something of a holy grail. Since young students harbored few materialistic desires or self-interest, the doctrine went, student movements could not be wrong. During the Cultural Revolution, Mao Zedong proudly proclaimed that "student movements are naturally reasonable [and correct]" as he unleashed a round of massive student movements of his own. Historically, almost every significant student movement was initiated and led by Peking University students.

The student movement that played the most important role in China's modern history was the "May Fourth Movement." On May 4, 1919, at the end of the World War I, students in Peking University learned that the integrity of China's territory had been sacrificed to Japan in a deal reached in the Paris Peace Conference despite China's status as a victor in the war. Thousands of outraged students rushed out of their old campus near downtown to Tiananmen Square and staged a demonstration.* It was a violent protest. Radical students marched to the residences of government officials to demand answers. In one instance, they beat and severely injured a minister and then burned down a house.

Protests continued for a month. When some students were arrested for the violence, the chancellor of Peking University resigned in protest. A class boycott spread to other parts of the country. By early June, a general strike in China's nascent manufacturing industry broke out in support of the students. The crisis was elevated to an unprecedented and dangerous level. Finally, the government was forced to yield under the pressure. They released the arrested students and refused to sign the Paris peace resolution.

The "May Fourth Movement" had a lasting impact. The Communist Party credited the movement for giving birth to the Party itself two years later. After they seized power, the date of May 4 was designated as the "National Youth Day." The tradition of student movements was

---

*Tiananmen Square as we know it today did not exist at the time. The demonstration was carried out largely near the entrance of the Forbidden City behind Tiananmen.

taught to generations of pupils as a positive force in bringing about social changes. The violent nature of the movement was glossed over and
even praised for its revolutionary spirit.* Jumping on the bandwagon,
Peking University decided to dedicate May 4 as the official anniversary
date for the school—never mind that the school was founded decades
before the movement.

With that history in mind, Hu Ping believed that Peking University
would be the place where he could find more liberal and independent
minded people like himself. Having personally experienced the prej-
udice and oppression through his young life, Hu Ping had been trying
to find the key to change the system. Now, at Peking University, he
believed that he finally had found it. As early as 1975, he started to
write a treatise titled *On Freedom of Speech*. Citing the famous procla-
mation by Archimedes on the power of the lever, "give me a place to
stand and I will move the earth," Hu Ping wrote confidently that freedom of speech was precisely the place to stand so one could "move"
the seemingly insurmountable system. For a young man with no college education and minimal reading material, his treatise was an as-
tonishingly comprehensive analysis of the importance of freedom of
speech and its justifications from philosophical, political, psychological, and even practical perspectives.† Of course, he could not have it
published. But encouraged by the ongoing reform, he thought that he
might finally find a way in Beijing or at Peking University.

His timing was ideal. Accompanying the dramatic political change,
an active "Democracy Wall" movement was happening right at the
nation's capital. A temporary power vacuum existed following Mao
Zedong's death and with Deng Xiaoping not yet in full control. Taking advantage of this opportunity, young activists gathered in Beijing
to publish their ideas through "Big Posters," written in big characters
with brush pens, on a wall in the downtown area a couple of blocks
from Tiananmen Square. Pasting Big Posters on walls in public spaces
had been a common propaganda method. It was also the only way

---

*Also ignored was the fact that the May Fourth Movement was largely led by
the emerging Nationalist Party at the time.[4]

†He did have a copy of John Stuart Mill's *On Liberty* from which he drew much
of his inspiration.

12

to publish one's ideas without official sanction. During the Cultural Revolution, Big Posters were hailed as a significant tool in practicing "Big Democracy" for the working class. This time, however, the "Democracy Wall" evolved into a steady forum to condemn the Cultural Revolution itself and advocate policy and leadership changes. In fact, the pragmatic Deng Xiaoping was the favorite hero of these activists. Much of their debates and articles were designed to help him defeat the remaining Maoists and regain power.

Hu Ping found the "Democracy Wall" very much to his liking. He plunged in and became an editor for the *Fertile Soil*, one of several emerging makeshift mimeographed magazines. It was in that magazine that Hu Ping published his *On Freedom of Speech* for the very first time. The reaction was muted however. His fellow activists were too busy practicing free speech to be interested in a philosophical discussion of it.

As the activists started to organize and more articles argued systematically for the need for democracy and human rights, Deng Xiaoping's patience began to run out. Having consolidated his power, Deng Xiaoping was ready to put a lid on this unauthorized free forum. Demonstrating that his pragmatism had a strict limit, Deng Xiaoping formulated his own doctrine of "Four Cardinal Principles" as the supreme guide of China's politics: 1. the principle of upholding the socialist path; 2. the principle of upholding the people's democratic dictatorship; 3. the principle of upholding the leadership of the Chinese Communist Party; 4. the principle of upholding Marxism, Leninism, and Mao Zedong Thought. In short, these principles predetermined that all speech and actions in China must conform to the communist ideology and the Party's unchallenged rule. Deng Xiaoping stressed that the "Four Cardinal Principles" were a matter of life and death for the Communist Party.

Not everyone was persuaded. On December 5, 1978, Wei Jingsheng, a twenty-eight year old electrician and former Red Guard, published a powerful article on the "Democracy Wall" titled *The Fifth Modernization: Democracy*. It argued that the more important modernization task for China was that of her political system, or democracy, than the officially stated goals of "Four Modernizations."* Sensing that the days of the "Democracy Wall" were already numbered, Wei Jingsheng went on to publish an even more provocative essay *Democracy or New Dictatorship?* In it, he singled out Deng Xiaoping by name and warned that, lacking any reform in the political system, Deng Xiaoping was becoming a new dictator himself not that different from the late Mao Zedong.

Although a lowly electrician at the time, Wei Jingsheng was not the typical uneducated worker of his peers. He was raised in a prestigious family of high-ranking officials. When he was an infant, his family had lived next door to Mao Zedong. He received the best education from elementary to high school when it was interrupted by the Cultural Revolution. He became a zealous Red Guard with his fellow offspring of high-ranking officials. But soon the Red Guards were cast aside and they were sent down to the countryside for re-education through labor. For the first time, Wei Jingsheng got a close view of the horrid conditions of peasants living under the socialist system and transformed himself into an activist.[5] At the "Democracy Wall," he found his voice and could no longer contain himself.

That was the last straw. Wei Jingsheng was promptly arrested and, six months later, sentenced to fifteen years in jail for the crimes of "counter-revolutionary" activities and leaking state secrets.[†] Several more activists were subsequently arrested and sentenced to lengthy prison terms when they assisted Wei Jingsheng's defense efforts and protested his case. The "Democracy Wall" itself was physically removed and Big Posters were declared illegal except in designated areas.

With the movement crushed, Hu Ping spent the summer in his hometown. It was in Sichuan Province when he realized that the year of

---

*The "Four Modernizations" was a long-standing goal for China to achieve before the end of the twentieth century. It included modernizations in agriculture, industry, science and technology, and defense.

†During an interview with a foreign reporter, Wei Jingsheng had mentioned the names of army commanders in the on-going Sino-Vietnam border war. Although such information was not public, it was apparently well known in the rumor mill. Wei Jingsheng refused to name his sources.

The New Generation

1980 was, in fact, an election year.

As a People's Republic, China's election system was modeled after that of the Soviet Union. Local representatives were elected by citizens every three years. These representatives chose delegates to the provincial congresses, which in turn selected the delegates for the National People's Congress. In reality, it hardly meant much since elections, if held at all, were merely a formality. While the laws allowed any citizen to declare candidacy, all elections had to be conducted in the "official" manner, in which a pre-approved slate of candidates was dutifully elected. Candidates were expected to be quiet and modest. The very idea of campaigning was regarded as self-promotion and symbolic of the "phony Bourgeois democracy."

The local elections of 1980 were not going to be the same however. It was, after all, the era of reform and new ideas.

It started over the summer in provinces like Sichuan. In some local colleges, a few brave students declared themselves as independent candidates and launched small scale and tentative campaigns. Local officials, already confused by Deng Xiaoping's reforms, were at a loss as to how to deal with this new phenomenon. When officials in a university in Hunan Province attempted to suppress campaign activities, thousands of students marched off campus to protest. For the most part though, the campaigns were tolerated as yet another "experiment" of the reform. One official newspaper, *China Youth Daily*, ran a positive report on the election activities in Shanghai. It amounted to a tacit official endorsement.

When Hu Ping returned from Sichuan to Beijing that fall, he found some of his fellow "Democracy Wall" veterans already plotting for a coordinated election campaign in Beijing, where elections were scheduled for December. Since many of them were now college students, they decided to launch the campaigns on the campuses. They should be able to expect the largest and most receptive audience there. Chen Ziming, one of the key organizers in the "Democracy Wall" movement, took the leadership role. Peking University would of course be the central focus. Hu Ping was assigned to be an adviser to a much younger Wang Juntao who would spearhead the campaign there as a candidate.

Among his fellow activists, Wang Juntao was quite an odd figure. His father was a loyal military officer who would eventually rise to the rank of a general. His childhood was spent in a protected environment with luxury and prestige. Growing up, he had access to many books that were not available to the general public. He took full advantage of this privilege and became an avid reader when he was still very young. On April 5, 1976, a spontaneous memorial service broke out in Tiananmen Square to commemorate the recently deceased longtime premier Zhou Enlai and to protest the then Maoist regime. Wang Juntao, who was not yet seventeen years old, led his high school class to join the movement and posted two of his own poems. In the ensuring crackdown, he was jailed for almost a year until Deng Xiaoping regained power and reversed the verdict for the movement. Overnight, Wang Juntao became a young national hero for what came to be known as the "April Fifth Movement." His pictures, poems, and deeds were plastered all over the press. He was made an alternate member to the Central Committee of the Communist Youth League and designated a potential future leader.

But just then, the young Wang Juntao abandoned the path of great promise and chose to join the rebellious "Democracy Wall" movement. Despite his young age and inexperience, he became the deputy editor of a major movement magazine *Beijing Spring* founded by Chen Ziming, another "April Fifth Movement" hero. Wang Juntao's energy and resourcefulness turned *Beijing Spring* into the best produced magazine on the scene. Its namesake also became a synonym to the "Democracy Wall" movement itself. Compared to its peers, however, *Beijing Spring* was a moderate and cautionary voice and it generally supported Deng Xiaoping's policies. But when Wei Jingsheng was arrested and many scrambled to distance themselves from his radical moves, it was *Beijing Spring* that took up his case in protest. After Wei Jingsheng's sentence, *Beijing Spring* published its very last issue which contained a passionate plea on his behalf. It also published an inside report written by Wei Jingsheng himself describing the secretive and notorious Qingcheng prison dedicated to top political prisoners. A decade later, Chen Ziming and Wang Juntao, along with many leaders of the 1989 student movement, would pay their own personal visits to Qingcheng.

Wang Juntao was also one of the lucky youths who passed the college entrance exam to become an undergraduate student in Peking University. He chose to major in applied physics with a belief that a systematic science training could help him to understand social and political issues and would be most beneficial in his intellectual development. As with Hu Ping, Wang Juntao understood the value of Peking University's tradition of independent thinking and student activism. Physics was certainly not his main concern.

FOLLOWING the traditional designs of Chinese gardens, the campus of Peking University was divided into several different zones. Surrounding the famous "Unnamed Lake" and the Boya Pagoda at the north side were picturesque classroom buildings and the central library. The student dormitories, on the other hand, were clustered at the south end in nondescript barracks-style five or six story buildings. Every morning, students woke up in their rooms and headed north to spend the entire day studying in classrooms and libraries. They usually would not return to their rooms until late at night. Without exception, they ate their meals in one of the several massive dining halls. The quality of the food was dismal, but there were few complaints from these students who only cared about catching up on their studies after the hardships they had suffered in the countryside.

Every morning and evening, heavy traffic, on foot and bicycles, passed through the center of campus between classrooms and dormitories. Right there, a tiny strip mall served as a town center with a post office, a small general store, and an even smaller bookstore. Outside, there were a few permanent bulletin boards for the school authorities to post their official notices and host occasional art exhibits. Time and again, students also put up their own Big Posters to publicize their lost items and petty complaints. These unauthorized postings were removed quickly by the facility crew.

The area was affectionately known as "The Triangle" for its geometrical shape by everyone associated with Peking University and beyond. It was not only where everybody passed through in their daily routines but also the place to find out the latest happenings in campus

previous democratic
activities 1580s

life.

On November 3, 1980, the first day of the official election period, Wang Juntao announced his candidacy with a Big Poster at The Triangle. There were two seats available for his district, which comprised the entire student body in the school. He soon found that he was not the only self-proclaimed candidate. Two other students declared their candidacies on the same day and more followed within the next few days. Election campaigning, which no students had experienced previously, quickly brewed into a feverish pitch. Candidates organized their own rallies and town-hall style sessions that were attended by hundreds. Their debates filled auditoriums to capacity.

It was even crazier at The Triangle. Candidates, along with their supporters and detractors, regularly published theories and opinions with Big Posters which spilled over to cover all the reachable walls of the stores and a nearby dining hall. Independent opinion polls and makeshift newsletters seemed to spring up everywhere daily to help drive the frenzy.[6] The school authorities chose to stand aside and allow the Big Posters to remain on walls and cover each other several layers deep.

Indeed, Hu Ping became so optimistic of the prospect of this campaign that, just a few days later, he decided to leave Wang Juntao's camp and declare his own candidacy. He reasoned that the two of them could have enough drawing power to take both seats. All told, a total of eighteen candidates participated. Among these were several women who were seen as an oddity in the male-dominated political arena. In an attempt to refute a sexless image inherited from the era of Cultural Revolution, one female candidate raised a curious concept of "oriental beauty" as a model for young Chinese ladies, triggering an overheated discussion that could be the very first debate on feminism in this traditional and communist nation.

Hu Ping understood that this election campaign had turned out to be a big free forum for new ideas rivaling the "Democracy Wall." It was crystal clear that it had little to do with the local district seats. Hardly any local issues were raised and little interest was drawn when someone talked about education funding, cafeteria food, dormitory conditions, and so on. Rather, all Big Posters, speeches, and debates

18

were centered on the "big issues" that dealt with China's past, present and future. To capture the significance of this historic movement, Hu Ping opened his campaign announcement with an emotional line, "The voice of this generation had been ignored for too long, too long..."

In Big Posters and mimeographed pamphlets he once again published his *On Freedom of Speech* as his main campaign document. The thesis was extremely well received this time and ignited a debate on the prospects of democracy and liberty in China. A group of law students went on to draft the nation's very first press law which would allow independent publications. When the draft was circulated on campus, thousands signed on in support. Above all, Hu Ping's maturity, intellect, and sharp oratory skills left strong and lasting impressions. Not only did he easily establish and maintain his status as the leading candidate, he also became known as the thought leader and a symbol of the entire campaign itself.

Wang Juntao, on the other hand, chose a somewhat different strategy. The then twenty-one year old junior did not care as much about the prospect of being elected. Rather, he viewed the campaign even more as a platform to publicize his views. The opening sentence of his campaign announcement clearly displayed a rebellious spirit: "The Chinese people had just witnessed and experienced ten years of darkness, corruption, and cruelty of political tyranny and four years of convoluted and complicated thinking, debating, and struggling. Now, we finally obtained our rights to election!"

Words like these could have landed him in jail at the time, but Wang Juntao was just getting started. Almost every single week, he picked a theme to give a big speech and/or publish a thesis with Big Posters. They ranged from criticisms of the Cultural Revolution, to his views on key historical events in the People's Republic, to roles and responsibilities of the (rubber-stamp) National People's Congress, and to the reform of the education system. He even chimed in on the "oriental beauty" debate and published his own preferences in choosing his future wife.

Finally, just a week before the voting, Wang Juntao released a promised bombshell: a long and provocative essay titled *Was Mao Zedong a True Marxist?* He argued that Mao Zedong was not a Marxist in the ideological sense but a "mere revolutionary" who had changed China according to his own likings. Such a frontal attack on the sacred legacy was unheard of. Although most students at least partially agreed with his assessment in the essay, many also felt that he had acted immaturely and was enjoying argument for argument's sake. It was widely believed that Wang Juntao's bombshell, released against the advice of Hu Ping, cost him many crucial votes.

For a month, the fever and chaos of the campaign completely took over the campus. The Triangle was no longer just a traffic intersection but a permanent meeting ground. Every day, students braved the bitter cold to stand outside with their lunch in hand, while they read the most recent Big Posters. They debated with each other passionately. Often, they scribbled their own comments on the Big Posters. Candidates' speeches and debates drew thousands every evening. Daily opinion polls, rumors, personal attacks, and claims of conspiracies further fueled the fire. One could not help but wonder if anyone was still going to regular classes.

In a remarkable show of independence, when candidates were polled on the counter-revolutionary case of Wei Jingsheng, almost everyone believed his fifteen-year sentence was "too harsh." A few, including Wang Juntao, stated that it was a wrongful case that should be overturned. On the other hand, when asked if China should uphold the leadership of the Communist Party, one of Deng Xiaoping's "Four Cardinal Principles," almost everyone, including Hu Ping, answered "yes." Wang Juntao hedged a little bit by claiming the word "leadership" was ambiguous.[7]

The first-round voting commenced on December 3. It was remarkably orderly and fair. The top three vote getters, Hu Ping, Wang Juntao, and Zhang Wei, the president of the official student union who favored a more moderate view, were established as the official candidates for the two seats in the final round. Wang Juntao was unquestionably the most controversial choice. The debate over Mao Zedong had by now completely dominated the entire campaign. Despite a strong backlash, however, five former candidates bravely endorsed Wang Juntao.

The New Generation

The official election was held on December 11. Over ninety percent of eligible students cast their ballots. Hu Ping received a majority of the votes and was officially elected. Neither Wang Juntao nor Zhang Wei received a majority of the votes. In the ensuing runoff, Wang Juntao led Zhang Wei by a wide margin. But he was still about fifty agonizing votes shy of half. It was decided that Hu Ping would be the sole representative from Peking University's student district.

The election was deemed a success not only by the enthusiastic students but also by the tacit officials. Elsewhere in the capital, Chen Ziming and his sister Chen Zihua had no problem winning on their respective campuses. So did a couple more of "Democracy Wall" veterans. At Beijing Normal University, a student named Liu Yuan surprised everyone with his candidacy. His father Liu Shaoqi was once the president of China and official successor to Mao Zedong. But the latter launched the Cultural Revolution to depose Liu Shaoqi and cruelly left him to die alone and anonymously in a prison cell. Liu Yuan's personal story as a child of the most privileged, and then the most despised, drew attention to the reality of political inequality in China. Although Liu Yuan led the polls most of the way, he failed to receive a majority of the votes to win a seat.

Of course, the daring display of independent thinking did not earn favors for Hu Ping and Wang Juntao. When Hu Ping graduated with his master's degree, he was denied a job for more than two years. He had to get by on his wife's meager earnings. Wang Juntao fared a little bit better. With a Bachelor's in applied physics and perhaps helped by his family background, he was assigned a job in a defense institute near Beijing. Hu Ping was proud to personally take the heat for the campaign movement. He believed that one of the biggest successes of the movement was that there was no large scale crackdown after the dust settled. One of the most important aspects of protest movements, he liked to say, was that its leaders must be willing to shoulder the consequences so that the mass of followers could be spared punishment.[8]

Nevertheless, the 1980 election campaign did not appear to achieve the lasting impact the participants had predicted and hoped for. People outside of campuses were pretty much ignorant and indifferent to it. The freshmen and sophomore classes, or the new generation, while in

21

awe of the new ideas, did not share the deep social concern. When the next election cycle arrived in 1983, after the Hu Ping's and Wang Juntao's had departed, hardly a ripple was felt in Peking University. Only the officially appointed candidates appeared on ballots and were duly elected. No campaigning was necessary. The fever of 1980 faded into history and became a fable only recalled, fondly, when juniors and seniors tried to impress newly arrived freshmen.

To the older guys, the new generation was just too happy in their own good fortune and the limited success of Deng Xiaoping's reform to challenge the authorities. But history would soon prove otherwise.

We must uphold the Four Cardinal Principles!

Deng Xiaoping

2

The "Bourgeois Liberalization"

BREAKING with the tradition that massive commemorations were to be held every ten years, a splendid military review and parade was planned for October 1, 1984, to celebrate the thirty-fifth anniversary of the People's Republic of China. It was an open secret that the commemoration also served as a birthday gala for Deng Xiaoping who turned eighty that year. With the way things were going, why not?

The year 1984, a date set by George Orwell as the climax of totalitarian power, was a pinnacle time for Deng Xiaoping's reform in China. After half a decade of steady progress, the vast agricultural landscape had changed dramatically. Privatization, albeit only partial ones, had taken root. Farmers could now decide what to plant and how to sell most of their own crops and produces. With productivity soaring, the rural labor force exceeded what was needed by the available land. This allowed peasants to organize small-scale co-op enterprises to produce essential goods needed in the cities. Farmers were also free to migrate into cities as day laborers to earn extra cash. During that very year, American author Harrison Salisbury was embarking on a long journey in the impoverished countryside to retrace the steps of the "Long March." He realized that what he was witnessing was a period of the greatest prosperity in this nation's long history.[9]

The prosperity in the countryside also swept into cities like a tidal wave. Rationing completely disappeared. Migrant workers liberated from their farms provided cheap labor for a tremendous construction boom that was re-sculpting the skylines of every city. Private restaurants and convenience shops sprang up on every street corner. Nannies and house maids, professions previously condemned as servitude, reappeared to the delight of city folks. Indeed, there was no reason why people would not feel happy and hopeful. All these achievements, of course, were the handiwork of the grand architect of the reform: Deng Xiaoping.

Standing in an open limousine and outfitted in the uniform of the People's Liberation Army, Deng Xiaoping reviewed the military procession along the grand Chang'an Avenue exactly as Mao Zedong had done in the past. A festive but well disciplined parade of people, arranged by their professions, followed the military processions. As the contingent of college students approached, the young men and women of the new generation suddenly broke out of their lock-step formation and became a horde of free-wheeling, hopping and dancing youths. In the midst, a large, hand-made banner was unfurled with four big characters depicting "Xiao Ping Ning Hao," or "Hello, Xiaoping." It was only a brief moment as the banner soon vanished in the surging crowd. But it was captured not only by photographers and television cameras but also by Deng Xiaoping himself on the reviewing stand atop Tiananmen. Caught by surprise, the old man smiled and waved.

The literal translation of the name Xiaoping was "little ordinary." In Chinese tradition, it was a term of endearment to refer to one's peer or younger folks as "little something." However, such terms were never applied to an older or respectable figure. Certainly, there was no denying that the spontaneous gesture from these students was genuine and heartfelt. To this new generation, the eighty-year old Deng Xiaoping was not an elder statesman, but one of their own.

IRONICALLY, at the peak of his power and influence, Deng Xiaop-

Deng's popularity in 1984 (irony, hub)

ing was now neither the head of the Chinese Communist Party nor the government. After he firmly consolidated power in 1979, he decided that the nation's leadership should be headed by younger cadres. Elder leaders should retire at a certain age rather than die in office as most high level officials usually did. To set an example, he installed two "young and upcoming" leaders, Zhao Ziyang and Hu Yaobang, to press his reforms. In fact, both Zhao Ziyang and Hu Yaobang were already in their sixties at the time. Zhao Ziyang, who as the head of Deng Xiaoping's hometown Sichuan Province had spearheaded a successful reform effort in the countryside, was to be the Premier. Hu Yaobang was in charge of the Party itself as the General Secretary. Deng Xiaoping, meanwhile, did not retire entirely. He took hold of the critical post of Chairman of the Central Military Commission. As the supreme commander of the nation's military force, he would be able to step in and assert his control at any time notwithstanding the heads of the Party or the government.

This strange power-sharing arrangement worked perfectly through the early 1980's. With Deng Xiaoping staying behind the scenes, Zhao Ziyang proved to be an effective administrator of the reform. Under his quiet leadership, the economic reform was steadily widening and deepening. He was also happy to leave ideological ambiguities, an inevitability for the reform effort, to the Party leader Hu Yaobang.

Hu Yaobang joined the Communist Party in 1929 when he was only fourteen year old. He became known as a leader of the Party's youth front who had sometimes organized boys to assist the war efforts. After the founding of the People's Republic, he served as the head of Communist Youth League for many years and built a power base from the younger generation. When Deng Xiaoping was making his historic comeback, Hu Yaobang was instrumental in securing the support of intellectuals and young people including the "Democracy Wall" activists. His tireless efforts to rehabilitate officials who had been prosecuted during the Cultural Revolution also won him many friends among the newly powerful elites. For his open mindedness, his liberal views, and his willingness to deviate from strict Marxist doctrines, Hu Yaobang became one of the few friends of intellectuals within the Party leadership. As General Secretary, Hu Yaobang pressed hard for people to be receptive of new and different ideas and for an acceptance of unorthodox but pragmatic means to improve the society and further the reform. He encouraged youth participation in social dances. He led the leadership into a fashion reform by abandoning the nondescript "Mao Suit" and adopting western suits and neckties as formal attire.* He even suggested that the nation gave up eating with chopsticks, blaming the habit as a health hazard with shared dishes. To the conservative elders, however, the most damning of all was when Hu Yaobang publicly stated that Marxism did not have all the answers.

Unquestionably, such spontaneity and candor caused him no end of trouble. For example, in November 1983, during a visit to Japan, Hu Yaobang surprisingly announced that three thousand Japanese youths would be invited to visit China in 1984 as a way of easing the historical tension between the two countries. Such an expensive gesture, paid for by the Chinese government, was beyond the understanding of China's youth whose lives had just started to emerge from poverty. Indeed, when the Japanese government failed to reciprocate, resentment grew.

Hu Yaobang's personal style was often mocked by the new generation of youths. Even shorter in height than the diminutive Deng Xiaoping, Hu Yaobang was often seen as a cartoonish figure who, when excited during his speeches, bounced in his chair with his legs dangling in the air. Nevertheless, the younger generation viewed him as an endearing though sometimes annoying and comical character who genuinely cared about their concerns and well-being.

MEANWHILE, good fortune kept coming to the happy-go-lucky generation of college students. By the mid-1980's, their attention turned abroad.

Along with the internal reform, China had been gradually opening herself to the rest of the world. Initially, a few students and scholars carefully selected by the government were sent to the United States and western Europe to study modern science and technology. But these opportunities were beyond most students' dreams due to the scarcity

---

*With the noted exception of Deng Xiaoping, who continued to wear the "Mao Suit."

of foreign currency reserves. Then, Tsung-Dao Lee, the renowned Chinese-American Nobel Prize winner and professor of physics at Columbia University at New York, helped to open another route. He informed China that there was an abundance of scholarships available to science majors in graduate schools in the United States. Chinese students could apply for them and fund their own studies. Professor Lee founded and painstakingly managed a pilot program that accepted a few selected physics students to the U.S. each year. American professors quickly recognized the intellect and ability of these students and the program proved to be a huge success.

Even as Tsung-Dao Lee's program expanded and similar ones were implemented in other science disciplines, an even more fundamental change was occurring. Students discovered that they could independently apply for American graduate schools without the help of either the Chinese government or official programs. Suddenly, previously unknown acronyms like TOEFL (Test Of English as Foreign Language) and GRE (Graduate Record Examinations), basic requirements for admission to American graduate schools, became common greeting terms in daily conversations. With good scores in these tests, a reasonable undergraduate transcript, and a few easily obtained recommendation letters, admission to a good American university was more than likely. They would no longer have to please any authority or suffer through ridiculous tests on the official version of history and politics. It was just that easy! In addition, the dollar value of the scholarships offered by American schools seemed astronomical. "They would pay us to study there!" Life could not be better or the future any brighter.

During the long hot summer of 1985 the opportunities in American universities were on the minds of some second-year graduate students in Peking University's physics department. Only a year earlier, they saw many of their classmates flying off to America through Professor Lee's pilot program. From letters describing a different life on the other side of the Pacific Ocean, they understood that TOEFL and GRE were far more important than their studies at hand. Now, in addition to exchanging information about American universities, they spent much of their time learning obscure vocabularies and tricky grammar subtleties of the English language. And, of course, with more time to spare, they also talked often about politics and current affairs.

On one hot afternoon, these students noted the coming fortieth anniversary of the end of the World War II. China was one of the Allied Nations in that war but her victorious status was always overshadowed by her horrible sufferings under the long and cruel occupation by the Japanese Imperial Army. That part of the history seemed to have faded by now. But the students felt otherwise. A few months ago, Yasuhiro Nakasone became the first Japanese prime minister to pay an official visit to the Yasukuni Shrine, whose enshrinees included convicted war criminals in World War II. It was an act condemned in the official press as an insult to Chinese people. Instead of celebrating as a victor, it might be wiser to remember how China became a helpless victim to the much smaller Japan.

As the chatter heated up, an idea for action was hatched. The anniversary of the "September Eighteen Event" was just one week away. On September 18, 1931, the Japanese army attacked and occupied the northeastern region of China, foreshadowing an all out war between the nations a few years later. The students decided that they should call attention to that anniversary instead. September 18 should be a day of national commemoration and never to be forgotten.

So, on September 13, a Big Poster was pasted at The Triangle. Titled *How Should We Commemorate September 18?*, it bore the signature of the graduate student association of Physics Department. The short but emotional prose reminded readers of the shame China had suffered at the hands of Japanese army and that Japan might still be trying to revive her imperialist ambitions. It called on the National People's Congress to establish the anniversary as a National Day of Shame and commemorate it annually. It had all the appearances of youthful innocence that was well-intentioned.

As usual, the poster did not survive the night. Irritated, the students posted up another, more emotional, poster the next day. Besides condemning the cowardly removal of the first poster, it also proposed a more concrete action. It called on students to commemorate the millions who died in the war by going to Tiananmen Square on September 18 and laying a wreath at the foot of the Monument to People's Heroes there.

The next few days saw The Triangle area flooded with posters, banners, impromptu speeches and debates, a scene that had not been seen since the election campaign of 1980. Both the physics students and the school were caught off-guard by such an enthusiastic and emotional outbreak. Viewing it as an expression of patriotic spirit by this new generation of students, the school offered to support and help organize the laying of a wreath at Tiananmen Square.

Yet the pledge of support vanished as soon as the school became aware that, by coincidence, a National Congress of the Communist Party was scheduled to convene on exactly that date in the Great Hall of People adjacent to Tiananmen Square. Occasions of Party Congress were always presented in a festive atmosphere with colorful flags, flowers, and balloons decorating the entire Square. Certainly, the students could not be allowed to stage a contrasting remembrance ceremony. Furthermore, there was a rumor that the students' actions might be targeting General Secretary Hu Yaobang, who had been working to improve the Sino-Japanese relations.

Words of trouble spread. The scheduling of the Party Congress was the perfect proof that history had been forgotten. As angry Big Posters flooded The Triangle, the physics student leaders feared for a disastrous escalation. They conducted a series of negotiations with the school and reached a compromise. The school promised to organize an on-campus rally to commemorate the anniversary and the student leaders called off the plan for Tiananmen Square.

THE morning of the September 18 started peacefully as most students planned to attend the official on-campus rally in the afternoon. By noon however, many noticed that the campus gates were locked up.* Lines of policemen were standing guard outside. Obviously, the authorities were not taking any chances. Hundreds of outraged students gathered around with flags and drums. They appeared to be ready to storm the gates. But after a couple of hours of standoff, per-

---

*Like every other "unit" in China, every college campus was walled off from its surroundings like a gated community. Passages were only allowed through guarded gates.

suasion prevailed.

A group of about three hundred students did make their way to Tiananmen Square in late afternoon. They found the Square sealed off by policemen. Just as they started to gather and walk around the police picket line, they were given impromptu permission to enter. The students followed instructions and laid a wreath at the Monument to People's Heroes peacefully.

If the school had hoped for the whole thing to go away with the passing of the anniversary date, they were disappointed. Angered by the campus lock down, a graduate student in constitutional law put up a new Big Poster the day after. His provocative essay asserted that the campus lock down was unconstitutional and a blatant violation of students' civil rights. For a good measure of defiance, he proudly signed the poster as "Chen Xiaoping, member of the Chinese Communist Party." With that, the commemorative activity turned into a public discourse on liberty and democracy. Not since the 1980 election campaign had the students seen such an open and direct challenge to authority. The excitement was obvious and immediate. Once again, posters, banners, and debates flooded The Triangle. The debate was centered on constitutional rights, or the lack thereof, in practice and reality.

It took five years, but the spirit of the 1980 election campaign was now revived in Peking University. Classes of the still younger undergraduates received their first taste of the "student movement" tradition of the school. It would not take as long for them to make their own grand entry.

Chen Xiaoping was threatened to be expelled from the Party but eventually received only lesser punishments. The physics graduate students were visited by various authority figures but were spared of any real consequences. They quickly moved on, busy with their TOEFL, GRE, and other more urgent matters. Within a year, most of them would be on airplanes over the Pacific Ocean. During all the commotion, however, few of them had noticed a quiet and reserved classmate of their own.

Liu Gang was one of the older ones even in this class of graduate students. He was born in 1961, in Liaoning Province of northeastern

China where people were known to be open, straightforward, and kind. In 1977, when the national entrance exam for colleges was reinstated, he was not yet a senior in high school. But he took the test anyway and was admitted to the University of Science and Technology. After graduation, he spent two years working before becoming a graduate student in Peking University.

When Liu Gang arrived at Peking University in 1984, he knew he had come to a school with a profound tradition of "student movements." He just did not know he would witness one so close and so soon. As events unfolded in that September right before his eyes, he knew that he was in the right place. Yet as an outsider, he observed quietly but intently. When he had the urge to join, he posted his essays at The Triangle anonymously, unknown even to his own classmates.

Pretty soon, though, Liu Gang came to the conclusion that there was nothing mysterious about "student movements" and the roles played by so-called "student leaders." A student movement, like this one, could start from nowhere quite innocently. If it struck a nerve in the public emotion, it would naturally gain momentum. While the leaders could initiate and steer the events in the early stages, their control of the movement was limited at best. Nevertheless, he was very disappointed when his classmates reached the compromise with the authorities and bowed out. He viewed it as a cave-in. In a poem he posted anonymously to mourn the spiritual death of the leaders, he expressed his frustration at having been awakened and then abandoned, leaving him to find his own way in order to carry on. But that was exactly what Liu Gang had decided to do. Carry on!

M EANWHILE, the reform was hitting a snag by 1986. Social discontent was bubbling up everywhere in China. Along with a freer economy, people were forced to confront two phenomena they had not experienced under the communist rule: inflation and corruption. Centuries-old Chinese wisdom held that social stability could only be achieved through uniformity: "Never mind poverty, but do mind inequality." The socialist ideal of equality meshed perfectly with such traditional beliefs. In Mao Zedong's China, the government was most proud of its ability to maintain a "stable" economy, in which wide-spread corruption did not exist and wage differences were minimal. With central planning, inflation became a distant memory. Indeed, prices of common goods, along with wages, stayed the same for decades. When production could not meet the demand, a condition that existed all through the Cultural Revolution, severe rationing was imposed. But prices nonetheless stayed the same despite empty shelves and long lines. The absence of inflation and corruption was critically important to the people as they could take comfort knowing that life was fair even though it was harsh.

When Deng Xiaoping started his reform by advocating the pragmatic policy of letting "some people get rich first," he ran up against these norms of society. As the reform shifted from the countryside to cities, where lives were dominated by state-run industries and bureaucracies, resistance grew out of fear. While very few opposed the idea of the reform, most were angry that "wrong people" were becoming rich first. The initial risk takers who responded to Deng Xiaoping's call and plunged into private enterprise tended to be those who had lived on the edge of society and had little to lose. They also had to be daring and resourceful in finding legal loopholes to operate in the gray areas of tight regulations. In the eyes of the majority who worked diligently in their assigned jobs and followed the rules, these entrepreneurs were cheaters and hooligans who bribed officials for profits. But now, these "bad elements" were getting fabulously rich and arrogant to the great contempt of those who lived by their wages.

College students were still enjoying their ivory tower lifestyle largely isolated from the social changes. While they were aware of complaints about inflation, the mundane economic details did not provoke them as much as the forceful speeches of Professor Fang Lizhi, a fifty-year old astrophysicist. In his younger years, Fang Lizhi used to be a top physics student at Peking University. Even then, his outspokenness got him in trouble early and often. In 1957, the twenty-one year old Fang Lizhi was already expelled from the Communist Party when he was branded as a "rightist" during the "Anti-Rightists" campaign. He was forced to spend a decade performing manual labor in the countryside. Deng Xiaoping's reform fundamentally changed his fortune. Fang Lizhi soon found himself back in the Communist Party. He was appointed a professor at the University of Science and Technology and became a vice president of the school. He also enjoyed opportunities to travel abroad for his scientific endeavors. The more he traveled, however, the more he realized the importance of democracy for China.

In 1986, Fang Lizhi returned from a four-month stay at the Institute of Advanced Study at Princeton, U.S. In that summer, he went on a personal tour to give speeches at many universities in southern China. In no uncertain terms, he told students that concepts like liberty, human rights, and separation of power were real and working in the west. They were not phony smoke and mirrors described in Chinese textbooks. China, with her ideological restrictions, had fallen behind not only in material development but also in political structures and social organizations. The only way for China to achieve modernization was to move past the one-party dictatorship and reform in the political arena. In short, his speeches echoed the sentiment of the "Fifth Modernization" advocated by Wei Jingsheng who was still serving his long sentence in jail. Fang Lizhi did not make any reference to Wei Jingsheng. The young generation in his audience had no recollection of that electrician. After almost a decade, Wei Jingsheng's case, along with "Democracy Wall," had been eradicated from the public's mind if not from the official record. But Professor Fang Lizhi's status afforded much more credibility and persuasiveness to his message. Audio tapes of his speeches were duplicated and disseminated from dormitory to dormitory and from campus to campus.[10]

Fang Lizhi's speeches, echoed by a few other well known intellectuals, caught the attention of Deng Xiaoping himself. In a meeting of the Party's Central Committee that September, Deng Xiaoping strongly warned the rank and file against what he now termed a movement of "Bourgeois Liberalization." He specified the true nature of that movement as "admiring the western multi-party democracy and attempting to undermine the Communist Party's leadership; admiring the capitalist economy and attempting to undermine the socialist system; and admiring the decadent western lifestyle and attempting to undermine the spiritual health of Chinese people." In other words, they were attempting to undermine his "Four Cardinal Principles." Recognizing that his chief lieutenants of reform, General Secretary Hu Yaobang and Premier Zhao Ziyang, were not fully convinced of this danger, he vowed that he would take a personal stand on this issue, if necessary.

T HE University of Science and Technology was a relatively new school founded in the heyday of the "Great Leap Forward" period of 1950's. It was designed to be a technical institute without liberal arts programs. During the Cultural Revolution, it was relocated from Beijing to its current campus in Anhui Province. The obscure school started a new life in the early 1980's when young professors like Fang Lizhi took advantage of its remote location and pushed reforms to make it one of the most liberal campuses in the nation. Through aggressive recruiting efforts, it gradually gained an academic reputation on par with more traditional schools. At its peak, it was now competing with Peking University in attracting top talent from the annual college entrance exams.

Yet another local election cycle arrived at the University of Science and Technology in the late November of 1986. In a matter-of-fact manner, a ready slate of candidates was announced. This time, however, it did not go well with students who had been listening to Fang Lizhi's speeches. After a few days of protests on campus, students decided to march to the provincial government building in the city to publicly demonstrate their desire for open and free elections.

Fearing for a disastrous outcome off-campus, Fang Lizhi showed up in a student assembly on the eve of the march. He praised the students' enthusiasm and encouraged them with words like "democracy could not be given from above but had to be demanded from below." Nevertheless, he tried to dissuade the students from carrying out the march. In an attempt to assuage the students' fear, Fang Lizhi promised not to punish anyone after the dust had settled and defiantly proclaimed to the audience, "whoever wanted to punish any students, they would have to fire us first!" He received a thunderous applause.

But the call for a march proved harder to resist. It was December 9, another anniversary date of a famous student movement that occurred in 1935. So, on this day in 1986, thousands of students gathered in front of the school library. Some were waving flags and shouting slogans. Many others came out of curiosity but were soon overtaken by

early student demonstrations

the zeal of the crowd and joined in. At the top of the steps stood an exhausted Professor Fang Lizhi with a bullhorn in his hands. He had been standing there for a couple of hours screaming at the top of his lungs in a last ditch effort to persuade students not to take the protest off campus. But even he could not stop the momentum that was mounting. Shortly, a massive march started out and left a speechless Fang Lizhi with only a few students in an empty square.[11]

Those who marched were excited that they now had a student movement of their own. They chanted slogans such as "We Want Free Elections," "Long Live Democracy," and even "Give Me Liberty or Give Me Death."* Yet the march turned out to be uneventful. When they reached their destination, they had no idea what to do next. So, they lingered for a while until a series of buses arrived. They boarded the buses, which were dispatched by Fang Lizhi, and quietly returned to their campus. Their efforts were not a total waste however. Weeks later, in an open and peaceful election, Fang Lizhi was elected along with two other candidates not in the original official ballot.

IT was going to be a winter of unrest. Similar student protests were occurring in a few other southern cities with campuses that Professor Fang Lizhi had visited. Like the many rivers in that area, waves of discontent pushed toward Shanghai, China's industrial and financial center.

Shanghai, which literally meant "going to the sea," was a southern city on the east coast where the mighty Yangtze River ended into the East China Sea. Centuries of port activities had made Shanghai a city of commerce and trade. Her people were best known for their business acumen and especially their attention to detail.

College students in this city were not happy this fall. An American rock 'n' roll band had made a historic visit to the city during the summer, a first in China. In the rousing atmosphere and encouraged by the band, several students rose tentatively to dance on the stage. They were promptly beaten and pushed down by police who were trying to maintain order. There was outrage brewing in the city.

---

*This American slogan was well known and popular in China.

Standoff At Tiananmen

In early December, a Big Poster showed up on the campus of Shanghai Jiaotong University, a large engineering college in the city. It described what was happening at the University of Science and Technology and called upon the students to support their brave compatriots. Soon, there was a call for a large-scale protest involving all major campuses in Shanghai on December 19 at the People's Square in the center of the city. Since the mayor of the city, Jiang Zemin, was a distinguished alumnus of the school, many challenged him for a direct dialogue. To the amazement of the students, word came that Jiang Zemin had swallowed the bait.

As the mayor of China's largest city, Jiang Zemin was relatively unknown among the country's political elite. He graduated from Shanghai Jiaotong University with a degree in electric machinery in 1947 at the age of twenty one just a couple of years before the founding of the People's Republic. During his student years, Jiang Zemin had joined the communist underground and participated in several student movements himself. He spent his earlier years as an engineer in various factories, including a brief training stint in the Soviet Union, before being elevated into management positions. It wasn't until 1980 that his political career really took off and ultimately led to the mayorship in 1985. Along with his engineering background, he was known for his open mind and pragmatism. Just a year earlier, amid students' complaints about inflation and corruption, he had personally visited another campus in Shanghai to share the concerns. He was going to repeat the same feat this time.

But on this occasion, his visit to his alma mater on the eve of the planned march did not go as well. As soon as he started to speak, boos rained down on him. Students heckled and demanded that he should listen instead of lecturing.[12]

Visibly irritated, Jiang Zemin halted his speech and threatened one of the hecklers. "What's your name?" he asked. "Do you dare to come up here? Do you dare to speak up here?"

It was Jiang Zemin's turn to be astonished. Without hesitation, the student snatched the bait and jumped on stage. He took the microphone and calmly announced his name. A dozen more students followed onto the lectern and waited for their turn to have a dialogue

36

interesting

with the mayor. When one student pointedly asked, "How did you become the mayor anyway? Who elected you?" Jiang Zemin knew that it was not going to be his day.

In a curious and perhaps desperate attempt to diffuse the situation and impress the young crowd, Jiang Zemin recited Abraham Lincoln's *Gettysburg Address* in English from memory to demonstrate his knowledge of western democracy. Then he proceeded to lecture the students that China was different from the United States, that they only knew Lincoln's words but not their meanings, that China's democracy must be implemented under the total leadership of the Communist Party, and so on. When the heckling started up again, he turned grim and issued a stern warning: whoever organized protests that resulted in interrupting social order and production would have to take responsibility for their actions.

News of Jiang Zemin's failed mission spread throughout Shanghai that very night and fueled the fire that was already burning. Many students, excited and anxious about the events, had a sleepless night. They did not know what would transpire the following day.

The traffic into the city on December 19 was so bad that only a few hundred students were able to make it to the People's Square at the city center by the scheduled two o'clock starting time. But crowds continued to pour in through the afternoon. By five o'clock, with an estimated thirty thousand gathered, police sealed off the Square and allowed only those with a student identification card to enter. In the crowd, a list of demands was hastily drawn and delivered into the City Hall. Yet there was still no response when darkness fell. Students were getting hungry and cold. Just before midnight, ten student representatives were invited into the City Hall for a negotiation. The city agreed to all the demands except for one: open, candid, and positive reporting of the student movement itself in the official media. Jiang Zemin was not at all ready to go that far. Not only was such reporting unheard of in China, but the reaction nationwide might be explosive. The negotiation broke off and, despite continuous personal and emotional pleas from their school officials, thousands of students decided to sit through the night in the Square.

Finally, in the predawn hour of half past five, Mayor Jiang Zemin's patience was exhausted. Police urged everyone to leave the Square immediately. Over loudspeakers, they warned that students' patriotic zeal had been hijacked by "a small clique of conspirators who were determined to destroy the peace, production, and social order," code words indicating that the protest was now considered criminal and would be suppressed by all means possible. Fifteen minutes later, truckloads of police forces entered the Square. They kicked and dragged students onto buses to haul them away. Within an hour, the square was cleared. Most students were sent directly back to their campuses. Some were detained in police stations but only very briefly.

The next day, Jiang Zemin's personal response to students' demands was circulated on all campuses. To justify his rejection of open-reporting, he trotted out the party line that the media in China was "the mouthpiece of the Party." It existed "for the interest of people, the interest of peace and stability." So, only "news that was positive to the government policy would be reported." Finally, he warned students not to be misled by "a clique of conspirators," and that occupation of public space and interruption of traffic would not be tolerated for the interest of public good.

But on this day, students were too angered by the rough police tactics to heed the mayor's warning. About a hundred thousand students and residents crowded People's Square and all the major city throughways. With traffic completely stopped, the city was shut down. This time, police stood by and took no action. Then, totally exhausted but satisfied, students returned to their respective campuses peacefully.

The day after, in a tacit response to student's demand for open reporting, newspapers carried an official comment on the student protest marches. The city then returned to its bustling normalcy.

Nobody knew it at the time, but the events in Shanghai that December were merely a prelude to a much larger protest in Beijing in the spring of 1989. Mayor Jiang Zemin received praise for his firm but flexible handling of student movements both in 1986 and then later in 1989. He would eventually become the surprise successor to Deng Xiaoping and the head of China for over a decade.

The forty-year socialist experiment in China has failed.

Fang Lizhi

3

The Democracy Salon

I<small>T</small> was a rather curious time in Peking University during the December of 1986. An arts festival was going strong on campus and students, when not busy with TOEFL and GRE, were happily involved in singing, dancing, and attending movies and concerts. Exciting news of student movements trickled in from down south daily but there were no evident ripple effects. A group of students from the neighboring Tsinghua University marched into the campus but failed to elicit any response in support for their compatriots in Shanghai. Perhaps for the first time in China's history, a student movement was underway without Peking University in the lead or even involved at all. In fact, some at Peking University quipped, "since we didn't get to lead this time, why should we bother to follow?" When Peking University was tranquil, all of Beijing was quiet as well. The newspaper *Beijing Daily* was so amazed by the calm that they ran stories about how students were concentrating in their studies.

But in reality, the city was very nervous after seeing what happened in Shanghai. They knew all too well that if a similar protest broke out in Beijing, the impact would be far greater and might evolve into a political disaster. So, on December 26, the city council rushed to approve a ten-point regulation on public demonstrations. Organizers would have to apply for a permit in advance. Marches would not be allowed to interrupt traffic and the social order of the city. Key areas surrounding the Great Hall of People would be off limits. This appeared to rule out the symbolic Tiananmen Square. That restriction seemed utterly ridiculous, students argued, if we were not permitted to protest in Tiananmen Square, where else would we bother? The "Beijing Ten-Points," as the regulation became known, finally presented them with a cause.

A variety of challenges became evident immediately. Students sought permits to demonstrate on all sorts of issues. Some proposed to march in support of the Communist Party. Others, with a wicked sense of humor, wanted to protest the ongoing Iran-Iraq war. But instead of receiving a yes or no answer within three days as required by the "Beijing Ten-Points," they were visited by police and school officials.

Near the end of the year, a few unsigned Big Posters appeared at The Triangle with a simple message: "Let's Go March at Tiananmen Square on New Year's Day!" Other than challenging the new regulation, there appeared to be no purpose for the march. It was difficult to ascertain whether it was genuine or a practical joke. In any case, few thought a march was a good idea.

But the government was nervous enough that they put out a stern warning in the press, promising to punish anyone who dared to defy the regulations. City residents were warned not to go to Tiananmen Square on that day. The stakes for this phantom march was on the rise.

Like most in Peking University, Liu Gang was confused and unsure about the situation. Unlike in the past, there was hardly any discussion among his classmates about this call for demonstration. He saw someone running through dormitories knocking on every door and shouting "See you at Tiananmen on New Year's Day," but there was no response. Liu Gang concluded that maybe nobody cared anymore, not even his own classmates who used to be active.[13]

The New Year's Day of 1987 was heavily overcast and very cold in Beijing. Liu Gang decided to go to Tiananmen Square by himself and was surprised by what he saw. There were thousands of policemen, lined up three-deep, surrounding the Square. A large formation of Young Pioneers, the communist equivalent of Scouts, was assembled in the center. Passers-by were told that the Square was off limits for the day because an oath ceremony by the Young Pioneers was to be held. Liu Gang wandered around as more and more people arrived and gathered behind the police lines. He could tell that many of them, perhaps hundreds, were students from Peking University. Then, he started to spot his classmates in the crowd. One by one, they were all there! Liu Gang became increasingly upbeat as the morning went on.

Sensing the assembling students, the policemen became nervous and scrambled to disperse any large clusters. Although several spontaneous attempts to break through police lines failed, it was inevitable that there would be more to come. Around noon, a crowd with make-shift banners formed at the northeast corner of the Square. The leading banner was a large sheet of pink plastic cloth with a curious message: "Support Xiaoping! Support the Reform!" Whoever made that banner obviously did not want anyone to think of them as anti-government. The crowd marched around to gather up more participants and turned away from the Square, chanting slogans and singing patriotic songs. The policemen were puzzled but relieved. They could not care less if the students wanted to march somewhere else.

But the relief was short-lived. As the crowd gathered momentum, it turned around suddenly and charged back into the Square. What followed was a scene of chaos and horror. Caught off-guard, police rushed in and grabbed anyone they could reach. Those caught were thrown into waiting police vans. Others were beaten. When the crowd was finally dispersed, more than fifty students were detained with thirty-four from Peking University. Among them was Liu Gang.

The remaining students gradually returned to campus dazed and confused. When this new generation was growing up, they learned from textbooks about the glorious "May Fourth Movement" in 1919. They knew vividly how that rotten government arrested patriotic students and how the movement escalated from it. Never did they imagine that they would be at the same Square and witnessing their own classmates brutally handled and taken away by the "people's police." What

41

had just happened? And what should they do now?

The evening news reported that hundreds of "hooligans" tried to engage in disruptive behavior at Tiananmen Square that day and were "taken away from the scene." They were careful not to declare those students as arrested or even detained.

Angry shouts could be heard through the campus of Peking University that night: "They took our classmates! They took our classmates!" A stream of students marched to the residence of the school president who was not at home. Students were told that he was already in the office working on the case. So they marched to the office building and found their president frantically contacting higher authorities. They demanded immediate action. If their classmates were not returned, they chanted the various actions they would take: "Boycott Class!" "Sit-in!" "Demonstrate!" And even a few "Hunger Strike!"

It was almost midnight. Snow was falling and the temperature dropped below freezing. To keep warm, students decided to march around the campus while they waited. It drew more students out of their dormitories. Pretty soon, virtually every student and many young faculty members had joined in, singing patriotic songs in the dark. When they reached the southeast corner of the campus, they saw a thick picket line of policemen blocking the road to the city. Surprised, they stopped right in front of the police line, chanting "No Violence" and "Return Our Classmates." They did not know what to do next.

The heavy feeling of nerve and anxiety did not last long. The thousands of students who were coming up from behind had no idea what was happening. They pressed forward and the momentum carried everyone charging into the picket line. Remarkably, the police did not offer much resistance. Following the momentum, students turned and headed toward the city. As they marched on, They chanted "Long Live Democracy," "Long Live Freedom," and "Happy New Year, Police Comrades!"

Along the way, a vice president of the school was riding in a police car to provide an update on the progress in securing the release of detained students. The march persisted. They were determined to continue until every detainee was released. Finally, at about three o'clock in the morning, the vice president once again caught up with the procession. He frantically shouted into the cold night air: "I am the vice president of Peking University. I mean what I say. All the detained students were back on campus half an hour ago!"

The march finally stopped in an incredulous mood of disbelief, excitement, and relief. For the first time under the communist rule, the government had succumbed to people's pressure and released detained citizens. The new generation had achieved a milestone of their own in the long history of student movements!

The victory, however, did not come without a huge price. But it was not paid by the students.

ON January 12, 1987, Professor Fang Lizhi was at home cooking dinner when he received a phone call from a close friend who congratulated him for finally being able to move back to Beijing and reunite with his family there. That was news to Fang Lizhi himself. The friend told him to turn on the television. Sure enough, it was reporting that Fang Lizhi had, once again, been expelled from the Communist Party. He was also removed from the University of Science and Technology and reassigned to a staff researcher position at the Beijing Astronomical Observatories. Well, not too bad, he thought, at least he could still work on his science.

In fact, the entire leadership at his university was sacked and replaced by bureaucrats dispatched from Beijing. A period of "reorganization" had befallen the school. Through that cold January, as exhausted students turned their attention to final exams and the upcoming winter break, bad news kept coming. A couple of days after Fang Lizhi's ouster, two more intellectuals, writer Wang Ruowang and reporter Liu Binyan were also stripped of their Party memberships. Like Fang Lizhi, this was not their first time either. Both of them were also sacked during the "Anti-Rightists" campaign in the 1950's. In a harsh speech by Deng Xiaoping that was made public in an editorial in the official *People's Daily*, the three were singled out as symbols of a "Bourgeois Liberalization" movement that must be suppressed. During his speech, Deng Xiaoping referred to the forgotten Wei Jingsheng, using him as a warning to anyone who would attempt the same challenge.[14]

Standoff At Tiananmen

The big shocker came a week later. On January 16, it was announced that the Party's General Secretary Hu Yaobang had resigned. His resignation letter was an obviously forced self-criticism. In it, the official press reported, Hu Yaobang recalled the errors he had made during his tenure. He said that he had committed grave mistakes "on matters of principles." It was then made clear that the mistakes involved not taking Deng Xiaoping's warning of "Bourgeois Liberalization" seriously enough and he was unwilling to suppress the student movements.

In the winter, when students marched on streets for democracy and liberty, most of them did it for their own excitement. None had imagined that their actions could have such an impact as causing a leadership change at the highest level. They could not help but feeling a sense of guilt about Hu Yaobang's fate. Although Hu Yaobang was not loved by the students when he was in power, he had now become a tolerant and honest father-like figure after his downfall.

There were still some silver linings in the dark cloud. Unlike deposed leaders in the past, Hu Yaobang was allowed to keep his seat in the Politburo although his influence would dwindle to less than nothing. His comrade in Deng Xiaoping's reform, Premier Zhao Ziyang, took over the General Secretary post. In a quick but risky political maneuver, Zhao Ziyang defined Deng Xiaoping's anti-"Bourgeois Liberalization" as an ideological struggle. Although ultimately important to China's future, he said, it nevertheless should not interfere with the ongoing economic reforms.

The man who succeeded Zhao Ziyang as the Premier was a technocrat by the name of Li Peng. An orphan whose father was executed as an early communist revolutionary, Li Peng was adopted by the late Premier Zhou Enlai and grew up as one of the privileged sons of revolution. He received education in the Soviet Union and steadily rose within the government ranks despite a lack of clear achievements. Yet he had already acquired a reputation as the one chosen by the conservative elders in the leadership, who were now turning their suspicious eyes to Zhao Ziyang.

EVER since being "taken away from the scene" at Tiananmen Square on that cold New Year's Day, Liu Gang found himself becoming an activist. Upon returning to the campus, he immediately led an effort to collect and publish the names of all of those who were detained. He turned it into a "watch list" and support group to make sure nobody would be singled out for any punishment in secret.

When his fellow physics graduate students threw a party celebrating the traditional Chinese New Year that winter, they invited Fang Lizhi's wife to show their support. They had a good time together. Liu Gang was already looking for opportunities to do more, which would come quickly enough in April when it was Peking University's turn to hold elections.

After the turmoil in the south, Peking University certainly did not want to see any extra-curricular activities here. But Liu Gang thought otherwise. He went to the election office and proposed to nominate Deng Xiaoping as a candidate. An official there thought his idea was interesting and welcomed it. After gaining his foothold in the door, however, Liu Gang added that he would also like to nominate Professor Fang Lizhi. He was setting up a head-to-head competition by popular vote.[15]

"You must be kidding!" said the officer in disbelief. "That of course would not be allowed."

"How so?" inquired Liu Gang innocently.

"Well, for one thing, neither Deng Xiaoping nor Fang Lizhi belongs to our district. You can only nominate someone who is either a student or a faculty member in Peking University." The officer was nonetheless patient.

"So, we can nominate anybody who is a professor here?"

"Sure, if he or she gets enough signatures for support."

"Well, then, we would like to nominate Professor Li Shuxian from our physics department. Would that be all right?"

"Of course."

What the official did not know was that Professor Li Shuxian was Fang Lizhi's wife. The two had met as classmates at Peking University in the 1950's. They shared a dreadful experience during the "Anti-Rightists" campaign in 1957. That painful episode left lasting scars in their young hearts but drew them closer together. They married in 1961 while they were forced into reforming their minds through manual labor. The only thing they could afford as a treat for their relatives and friends were some candies paid for with monies scrimped from their rations and savings. When Fang Lizhi went on to work at the University of Science and Technology, Li Shuxian stayed in Beijing with their sons and remained a low-profile professor in Peking University's physics department.

Actually, Liu Gang was not at all sure whether Li Shuxian was willing to run. It was only a couple of months after her husband's public downfall. It would be understandable if she did not want to draw attention to her family. But Liu Gang was pleasantly surprised. Li Shuxian was ready. "I could be a candidate to support you students," she said, with the condition that she would not actively campaign herself. That was fine with Liu Gang for he had planned to take care of the entire campaign himself anyway.

It did not take a whole lot to publicize Li Shuxian's candidacy. Word spread quickly that she was Fang Lizhi's wife. This alone made her the people's choice overnight. To push the candidacy through the election system, however, was a different matter. The school was now on full alert. Although they could not deny Li Shuxian's candidacy outright, they tried every possible means to block it. Under tremendous pressure, the graduating class of the physics undergraduates withdrew their nomination. Others started to waver.

Li Shuxian stood firm when she was personally pressured to withdraw. Liu Gang countered every move by the authorities. He studied the mundane details of election rules and designed tactics for each round of voting. Almost miraculously, Li Shuxian was able to gather just enough votes to get her through preliminary voting, no matter how the officials staggered the slates.

Ultimately, Li Shuxian's candidacy prevailed. She won a seat to the local district council with ninety percent of the popular vote. Students were happy with what they had achieved. After a bitter winter, they finally had something to celebrate. They were proud that they had helped to vindicate Fang Lizhi and his ideals, albeit on a small scale. Meanwhile, Li Shuxian proved to be more than a capable and courageous representative. When she was denied an office in the school to meet and communicate with her constituents, she put up a desk at The Triangle and showed up there regularly to mingle with students. Beyond being a symbol of defiance, the desk enabled her to maintain close contacts with some of the emerging student activists including an undergraduate student by the name of Wang Dan.

Liu Gang knew that this limited victory was not a goal in itself. But his time was running out. That summer, he graduated with a Masters in physics and was promptly assigned to a dull research job in Ningbo, a coastal city south of Shanghai. Many officials at Peking University were greatly relieved to see him out of the school and the city. What they did not know, however, was that Liu Gang would be back, much sooner than anyone thought.

PEKING University was celebrating her big anniversary in 1988. Ninety years earlier, the Qing emperor Guangxu was engaging in a reform of his own to open and modernize his country. He decreed the creation of a new kind of school with a charter to "take the traditional Chinese learning as the foundation, take the western knowledge as the practical, organically combine the Chinese and western skills to achieve a lasting impact." The school, originally named Metropolitan University, was the first one in China to offer science courses. Revolutions and wars often interrupted development and threatened her survival. But the school expanded through consolidations, one of which led it to absorb Yenching University and settle into its current location. There, it formally became known as Peking University and arguably the best college of the country.

Ignoring the actual date in 1898 on which the school was founded, Peking University adopted May 4 as her anniversary date to pay homage to that glorious student movement in 1919. And so it was on May 4, 1988, a lovely spring day, various activities were planned to commemorate the anniversary. It would be a festive day on campus as alumni from far and wide returned for reunions and tours down memory lane. Among the home-coming alumni was Liu Gang who came to hold his own event that day.

Liu Gang had already left Ningbo and made his way back to Beijing. He quit his job after only a few months and struck out on his own to see if he could survive as a self-sustaining laborer, providing for himself with his own hands. He traveled through China alone, going as far as the remote desert in the west and the vast grassland in the north. Eventually, he settled back in the capital city where his legend grew as his adventures became known to the small circle of student activists.

In Beijing, he continued to live an unsettled life. He moved around a lot to take up odd factory jobs here and there. He visited Peking University and other campuses frequently where he had no problem finding a bed to crash in among his former classmates and friends. He also became active in a few exclusive salons where reformist intellectuals and young entrepreneurs met regularly to discuss current affairs. These informal, and sometimes clandestine, gatherings were growing in influence. Professor Fang Lizhi was a regular and active participant in some of them. A year and half after his downfall, the taboo of "Bourgeois Liberalization" seemed to have faded already. Even high-placed government officials were attending these gatherings. But Liu Gang's interest was still fixed on college campuses. He thought the idea of salon gatherings could be extended to connect with the new generation of students.

Officially, the lasting legacy of the "May Fourth Movement" was summarized in two concepts it introduced to the old China: Democracy and Science. It was marked on the Peking University campus by a stone sculpture of intertwining letters "D" and "S." Of course, in the parlance of communist double-speak, the concept of democracy had since lost its original meaning. So, Liu Gang thought that the anniversary was a perfect occasion to launch his new salon, an open forum for people to freely discuss the school's proud tradition, especially the "D" concept. They spread the word that a meeting would be held under the statue of Miguel de Cervantes, a visible landmark near the western entrance. The bronze statue was a present from Spain as a symbol of cultural exchange. Liu Gang did not pause to think if his effort was in the same spirit of the great author's famous hero Don Quixote. He excitedly described his plan to Professors Fang Lizhi and Li Shuxian and asked if they could "just happen to walk past the area" to provide a little symbolic support.

The Democracy Salon

The statue of Miguel de Cervantes stood on top of a pedestal in the middle of a grass lawn. The sword in his right hand had long since disappeared, replaced occasionally by a tree branch. On this day of anniversary, dozens of students showed up to find out what was going on. They took turns to give a ten minute speech through a portable radio with a tiny microphone. Most reflected on the importance of democracy and independent thinking. Fang Lizhi and Li Shuxian did come by. They did not just walk past either. Li Shuxian gave a speech herself. She brought a copy of China's Constitution and told the students that the rights of free speech and assembly were guaranteed by it. However, she also cautioned them to pay close attention to what was and what was not practically possible in China at the time.

The salon took hold. They agreed that it should become a weekly event to be held every Wednesday afternoon. Ever the modest one, Liu Gang preferred to call the forum "Grass Lawn Salon," or perhaps a little more lovingly, the "Garden of Hundred Grasses." But it would become known as the "Democracy Salon," a name that implied a political agenda.

The new salon held regularly for five weeks. Liu Gang managed the gatherings with his former classmates, graduate students in physics. They brought in a guest speaker to lead the discussion each week. These speakers included some outspoken intellectuals who had been labeled as front-runners of "Bourgeois Liberalization." It became an attraction drawing large numbers of students with some from other campuses. Curious foreign journalists also showed up to snoop around. The sessions were averaging about eighty attendees and occasionally reached two hundred. Among the regular participants were a group of young undergraduate students, mostly freshmen or sophomore, who were the true "New Generation of the Eighties." Now, they stood side by side with the older graduate students to soak in the Peking University tradition of independent thinking. For now, though, they remained mostly quiet, not yet ready to assert themselves.

One of the younger students was Wang Dan, a slim nineteen year old sophomore in history.* His boyish face, decorated with a pair of

---

*He had spent his freshman year in chemistry before transferring to history.

49

thick and oversize glasses, gave him the look of a typical bookworm. When he did occasionally break his silence, he surprised people with a calm eloquence in his words. He was no stranger to the scene since his father was a professor at the school.

T HE Salon meeting on June 1, 1988 had a special attraction. Liu Gang was able to bring an unusual guest: the American Ambassador Winston Lord along with his Chinese-American wife, author Bette Bao Lord. Their presence drew the largest crowd to date. Many came out of curiosity, hoping to hear tips to gain admission to America.* That same night, a scuffle broke out near the campus and a graduate student by the name of Chai Qingfeng was killed, apparently by some hooligans from outside of the campus.

Although an isolated incident, the tragedy struck a chord with some students and ignited an unexpected wave of protests as Big Posters flooded The Triangle. They evolved quickly from complaining about the lack of security into protesting the status of human rights.† Against Liu Gang's warnings, Wang Dan and some younger friends formed an "Action Committee" to surreptitiously steer the protests. To their disappointment, however, the protest died out and the Action Committee failed to accomplish anything other than drawing unwanted attention to themselves and the Salon.[18]

The school had of course been keeping a wary eye on Liu Gang and his Salon. The death of Chai Qingfeng gave them a handy excuse to take action. They blamed the Salon for attracting people onto the campus and causing a security risk. To ensure safety, they announced, people coming onto the campus must be monitored and registered.

Liu Gang was an easy target. He was now no longer a student at Peking University and therefore had no legitimate reason for being on

---

*Winston Lord later cited meeting these students as a highlight of his stay in Beijing. But he also received a personal message from Deng Xiaoping himself that he should never meet Chinese students again.[16]

†Six "unemployed hooligans" responsible for Chai Qingfeng's death were publicly arrested and pronounced guilty before a trial. One of them was quickly sentenced to death and the rest received long prison terms. While demanding democracy and human rights, no students questioned the legal procedure.[17]

campus. The authorities tried persuasion first. They brought in his father, a police officer in his hometown, to take him home with a promise of a good job. After Liu Gang turned down the offer, they banned him from entering the campus altogether. Liu Gang soon found himself followed. When he did sneak on again, his hosts were visited and warned. It was no longer practical for him to continue managing the Democracy Salon. So he passed the baton to Wang Dan. Meanwhile, he got a job and rented a room near Yuanmingyuan just outside of the school.

Yuanmingyuan, or the Gardens of Perfect Clarity, used to be a lavish imperial summer palace built in the early eighteenth century. It was designed to provide the royal family with two features that were not native to this old capital city in northern China: a complicated system of streams and lakes with flowers and rice paddies typical of the south and huge, majestic buildings mimicking European palaces. In her glory days, the park spread over 850 acres and was deservedly referred to as "the Garden of all Gardens." However, much of the majesty and beauty were lost in 1860 when the joint Anglo-French army invaded Beijing. In a criminal act denounced by Victor Hugo, they looted the garden and set it on fire.[19] Legend had it that the park burned for three days and three nights. It never recovered from this catastrophe despite later efforts to revive it. Decades of looting by locals and subsequent invasions followed. Finally, all that was left were a few ruins of stone structures and vast wastelands. Eventually, a Park of Ruins was established to serve as a reminder of China's weak and suffering past as well as atrocities committed by foreign imperialists.

As soon as he settled down in Yuanmingyuan, Liu Gang set out to resurrect his Salon here. Playing on the Chinese name of the park, he called this new version "Cry from Deep Lake Salon." In his vision, this Salon would become the Hyde Park of China where people could gather informally and freely exchange their thoughts and give speeches on current affairs. Once again, he built up quite a following. It attracted intellectuals and students from campuses other than Peking University. They met at the south entrance of Yuanmingyuan every Friday afternoon. Plain-clothed policemen also came to videotape the scene.

Standoff At Tiananmen

Among regular participants of the Salon was Zhang Lun, a Peking University graduate student in sociology who lived in the same dormitory building as Liu Gang. Impressed by Liu Gang's talent and spirit, Zhang Lun decided to bring Liu Gang into the fold of an older generation of activists. Had you heard about Wang Juntao? Sure, Liu Gang knew the name but hardly much else.

Years after that election campaign in 1980, Chen Ziming and Wang Juntao got together and established an enterprise of their own. The Beijing Social and Economic Sciences Research Institute, situated in the western suburb, was the culmination of many years' of hard labor and entrepreneurial ingenuity. Taking full advantage of Deng Xiaoping's reform, they earned their seed capital by publishing best-selling books and providing mail-order technical training for public servants.[20] By the late 1980's, they had shaped their Institute into an independent think tank with operations in opinion polling and book and magazine publications. The Institute employed many of the "Democracy Wall" veterans and entrusted them to provide research work in China's political and social issues, directed by the steady hands of Chen Ziming. The fact that such a private and independent think tank could exist at all showed how far China had progressed in this decade. But their existence was still more tolerated than embraced. Chen Ziming continued to live under surveillance. Mainstream intellectual communities in Beijing, busy making headway inside the government, also kept a safe distance. Chen Ziming and Wang Juntao were constantly pushing the limits in safeguarding and expanding their foothold and influence through personal relations. They were also quick to identify and recruit new talent, especially those who had got into political trouble.[21]

As a free-lancer without a steady job, Liu Gang was certainly intrigued. He frequently visited the Institute and worked part-time in their polling operations. He and Wang Juntao became fast friends. They talked frequently about what was happening in Peking University and other campuses.

Although only a few years removed from his own college days, Wang Juntao now looked down on the new generation of students with obvious disdain. Typical of someone who had matured a little bit, he thought that these "kids," who had entered college straight from high schools, were socially inexperienced. The pressure of the national college entrance exams, one of the crown jewels of Deng Xiaoping's reform, had by now suffocated most high school students. Few dared to read any books that didn't pertain to the subjects of the exam. Fewer still pursued hobbies or attended social clubs. By the time these students reached college, many were already burned out and had little interest in their class work. Those who did study were focused mainly on TOEFL and GRE with the single-minded goal of going abroad. More students resigned themselves to playing cards and Mahjongg, a traditional Chinese tile game.[22] They were not at all interested in politics and other idealistic pursuits. The large-scale protests of 1988 had caught Wang Juntao by surprise, but did not change his views.

Liu Gang agreed. Despite his energetic and persistent activism, he harbored a deep pessimism about students' passion for political reforms. In private conversations, he liked to say that the only reason students were enthusiastic to engage in protests was because it provided a perfect excuse to skip classes and exams. For these students, rallies and marches were just a few activities they could do for the fun of it.

Nevertheless, the new generation youngsters did carry on at Peking University after Liu Gang was kicked out. To limit exposure, Wang Dan moved the Democracy Salon indoors to his dormitory building. They met regularly on Wednesdays and continued to invite distinguished intellectuals as guests to attract student participants, who came only by word of mouth.[23]

One of the students who had heard of the Democracy Salon was a junior in biology. Just like Wang Dan, Shen Tong was born and raised in Beijing. He grew up in a traditional courtyard house near the bustling Xidan business district. As a little boy, he had witnessed all the marches and parades along Chang'an Avenue, adjacent to his little neighborhood. In those cold winter days, his father took him to witness the funeral of the late Premier Zhou Enlai, the April Fifth Movement, as well as the Democracy Wall. Through it all, his father would tell the boy, who was not yet old enough to comprehend all the happenings, that "one needs to be concerned enough to become more educated but know enough to stay away from disaster."[24]

Shen Tong had his first close encounter of "disaster" while he was still a high school student. He spent the summer of 1985 in Peking University where his sister was studying. As he was busy making a small fortune by selling books of underground poetry, he witnessed the student movement developing out of commemorating the September 18 anniversary. His sister became one of those who reached Tiananmen Square to place a wreath. She later saw two of her friends arrested in the aftermath.[25] At home, Shen Tong was shocked when his open-minded father warned him that he should never participate in any such student movements.[26]

When he finally became a student of Peking University himself in the fall of 1986, Shen Tong was assigned to dormitory building no. 28, overlooking The Triangle. Ignoring his father's advice, he went to Tiananmen Square in that freezing cold New Year's Day of 1987 but successfully avoided trouble.[27] His luck ran out, however, during the unrest following Chai Qingfeng's death. Shen Tong was drawn in and became involved in the Action Committee, for which he was fired as an officer in the official student union and forced into writing a lengthy self-criticism essay.[28]

Disappointed, Shen Tong set up a small club of his own, consisting with close friends in his dormitory building. He called it the Olympic Institute to pay homage to the young Albert Einstein who had led a club by the same name. Unlike the Democracy Salon, the Olympic Institute was designated as non-political. They were more interested in philosophical discourses in "using rational means to approach all things."[29] Through the activities of the club, he met Wang Dan and was very excited with the prospect of joining forces with this famous student leader.[30]

T HE year 1989 was a conspicuous one for China with several important anniversaries appearing on the calendar: the two-hundredth anniversary of the French Revolution, the fortieth anniversary of the People's Republic, and the seventieth anniversary of the May Fourth Movement. It would also mark the tenth year of Wei Jingsheng's imprisonment. Yet hardly anybody remembered this electrician and his case. Memory and history could be easily erased or concealed when all media were tightly controlled.

One of the few who did remember Wei Jingsheng was Professor Fang Lizhi. Just a couple of months after he settled in the Beijing Astronomical Observatories in early 1987, a supernova was observed in the Large Magellanic Cloud near our Milky Way. It was the closest supernova in more than three hundred years and caused a frenzy in the astronomical community. Fang Lizhi took up an interest as well. But instead of skyward, he chose to look back in history.

In the thousands years of written records of Chinese history, there were several instances of observed supernovae, called "guest star" by the ancient Chinese. They were regarded as important heavenly occurrences and harbingers of disasters, war, or deaths of emperors on earth. To stave off such detrimental possibilities, emperors were advised to announce a general amnesty as a gesture to please the Almighty. Emperors, as powerful as they were in their own kingdoms, had no choice but to follow suit.

Thus Fang Lizhi found himself at an interesting juncture in space-time. The modern Beijing Astronomical Observatories was built at the exact location where those ancient astronomers had duly observed and reported supernovae and advised emperors to proclaim amnesties. Was it now his turn?

This seemingly outlandish idea persisted as Fang Lizhi spent his time writing essays on histories of supernovae. It was not until the January of 1989 when he decided to act in the auspices of the year of anniversaries.[31]

On January 6, 1989, Professor Fang Lizhi wrote down a letter to Deng Xiaoping. It was brief and to the point:

> Chairman Deng Xiaoping
> Central Military Commission
> This year is the fortieth anniversary of the People's Republic of China. It is also the seventieth anniversary of the May Fourth Movement. There will certainly be a lot of commemorative activities for these anniversaries. However, compared to looking back, far more people would perhaps be more concerned about the present. They are concerned about new hopes

open letter to prisoners
release pol prisoners

these anniversaries could bring for the future.

For this purpose, I sincerely suggest to you that, at the cusp of these anniversaries, a nationwide amnesty is called for, especially to release Wei Jingsheng and all political prisoners like him.

I think that, however one would judge Wei Jingsheng as a person, releasing someone like him who had been in prison for ten years is consistent with the humanitarian principle. It will enhance the social atmosphere.

Coincidentally, this year is also the two-hundredth anniversary of the great French Revolution. No matter how we see that event, the values symbolized by that revolution, Liberty, Equality, Fraternity, and Human Rights, have become universally respected by humankind. Therefore, I sincerely appeal to you once again to consider my suggestion, so that we can add on more respect for the future.

Best Regards,

Fang Lizhi 1/6/1989

Fang Lizhi did not have any inside channel to deliver the letter. He put it in an envelope addressed to Deng Xiaoping and dropped it in a mailbox. On the next day, he showed copies of the letter to two guests who had come to visit him. One was Liu Da, the Party boss at the University of Science and Technology when Fang Lizhi was serving as vice president. Liu Da liked what he saw and promised to deliver the letter through his connections, perhaps all the way to Deng Xiaoping himself.[32] The other guest was an American friend from Princeton, Perry Link. Professor Link translated it into English. With the help of foreign journalists in Beijing, Fang Lizhi's personal appeal suddenly became an open letter.[33]

With that, Professor Fang Lizhi broke a long public silence he had maintained since being sacked three years earlier. It was also the first time that Wei Jingsheng, a lowly electrician with no higher education, was recognized by the nation's intellectual elite.

Fang Lizhi became an instant celebrity in the small circle of foreign journalists in Beijing. They followed him around and tried to catch his next move. They were not disappointed. In a symposium with many prominent intellectuals, they caught Fang Lizhi going even further in an impromptu speech. "In the past, I have always encouraged people to join the Party and reform it from within," he said, "but now I have fully realized that it is not enough. We must also take action from outside of the system. We must force the issue in any way we can." Fang Lizhi advocated to raise the issue of human rights in China. But he got little response in the symposium, as most of the audience was shocked by his sudden outspokenness.[34]

But his rallying cry for amnesty generated significant echoes. Several supporting open letters followed in February and March, cosigned by many prominent intellectuals. It was the first time since the "Anti-Rightists" campaign in the 1950's that intellectuals in China formed a collective voice in their challenges to the government, albeit in the form of polite advising.

Having broken his silence, it seemed that Professor Fang Lizhi could no longer restrain himself. In early February, he published a provocative essay titled *China's Despair and China's Hope* in a Hong Kong newspaper.[35] In it, Fang Lizhi boldly declared that "the forty-year socialist experiment in China has failed." The root cause for the failure, he said, was in the socialist system itself. On the other hand, he pointed out that "China's hope is in the fact that more and more people are escaping from the blind hope in the government and take up the position of openly criticizing and monitoring the government's behavior." Li Shuxian brought the article to Wang Dan and Shen Tong. They immediately made copies to circulate and post as Big Posters at The Triangle.[36]

Fang Lizhi's newfound activism also received attention from far beyond the city. Much to his surprise, he and his wife were invited to attend an official banquet given by the visiting American President George H. W. Bush. On February 26, the couple took a ride with Perry Link and his wife to the Great Wall Sheraton Hotel for the banquet. A few blocks from the hotel, however, their vehicle was suddenly surrounded by a throng of police. They would not be allowed to reach their destination either by bus or on foot. Angrily, the four of them went to the Shangri-La Hotel on the other side of the city and pushed into the White House press briefing room there. A hungry and tired

Fang Lizhi lodged a strong protest in front of the world media.[37]

The next day, Fang Lizhi and Li Shuxian published an account of their experience as a Big Poster at The Triangle. The incident had made them keenly aware that they were marked persons in the eyes of the government.

T HE year of anniversaries was not lacking in indications for trouble either. The official rate of inflation was running at twenty seven percent at the time, but masked by the more than ten percent annual growth rate. Foreshadowing things yet to come, Nicholas Kristof wrote in *The New York Times* that "after ten years in which ordinary Chinese citizens were the greatest cheerleaders for change and helped tug the country toward the market, there are signs that they could switch sides."[38]

He explained: "inflation and corruption, along with fear of unemployment and resentment of the newly wealthy, seem to be fostering a reassessment among Chinese farmers and workers about the benefits of sweeping economic change. Some Chinese officials and foreign diplomats are growing concerned that the Chinese people, instead of helping the market economy along, will become an obstacle to it."

In March, a riot broke out in the remote Tibet region resulting in a bloody crackdown and martial law there. It was the first time in the People's Republic that martial law had been formally declared. The event however received little attention in the rest of China.

Wang Dan was very excited about this year of anniversaries. With a group of his classmates in his History Department, he was busy editing a makeshift student magazine *The New May Fourth*. He published its first issue, which would also become its last issue, on April 5, the anniversary of the April Fifth Movement. It was a provocative issue. Not only did it carry a preface written by Li Shuxian, it also featured an old article by Hu Ping, the winner of the 1980 election campaign, on freedom of speech. By now, Hu Ping had gone abroad and become the head of a New York-based "Chinese Alliance for Democracy," a renegade organization formed by Chinese students and denounced by the Chinese government. It was a symbolic connection between two generations of student activists. What's more, the magazine also included radical to begin w/

an essay by Wang Dan himself, commenting on what was happening in East Europe. In Hungary, the 1956 Prague Spring movement had been reinstated. In Poland, the Solidarity movement had been legalized after years of crackdown and would be challenging the Communist Party in open elections. Wang Dan wrote that "the freshness of the 1956 [Prague] Spring is once again permeating the air" and the days for the Communist Party's monopoly on power were numbered. He also pointed out that the success in East Europe was largely due to the continuous effort by the dissidents and intellectuals pursuing democracy and human rights. He was optimistic that China should be heading in the same direction in the near future.

There were other signs of an emerging undercurrent. Wang Dan and Shen Tong were visited by an activist from the south who was trying to instigate a nation-wide hunger strike campaign for human rights. After a long discussion, Shen Tong concluded that the time was not yet ripe for such dramatic action. He sent the activist away and never heard from him again.[39]

As the anniversary of the May Fourth Movement drew closer in 1989, the authorities stepped up their preventive measures. While they did not ban the salons outright, they strongly warned Wang Dan and Shen Tong to exercise the greatest caution in their activities. Speakers such as Fang Lizhi and Li Shuxian, for example, would be extremely inappropriate. However, Wang Dan would have none of it. He decided to openly challenge these restrictions. In the morning of April 3, a Big Poster appeared at The Triangle. It was an open letter to the authorities, signed by fifty-six students led by Wang Dan. It complained that seventy years after the May Fourth movement, Peking University's legacy of democracy was seriously threatened, and that academic freedom and freedom of speech were in danger.

In full defiance, Wang Dan moved his Democracy Salon back outdoors to the grass area under the statue of Miguel de Cervantes. The forum instantly ballooned from dozens to a few hundred participants. Privately, Wang Dan and Shen Tong began to coordinate the efforts of their two clubs with a secret alliance.[40] But neither they nor anyone else knew that impending events would dramatically transform the political backdrop along with their young lives.

The one who should have died did not; the one who should not have died did.

Bing Xin

4

The Funeral

IN the evening of April 15, 1989, Feng Congde bought a cake. It was the birthday of his wife Chai Ling. As they sat together watching television, they saw the news that Hu Yaobang had passed away. Feng Congde did not think much of it. As one of the students detained at Tiananmen Square on the New Year's Day of 1987, he felt sorry for Hu Yaobang and a little guilty for not being able to do anything when Hu Yaobang was disposed in the wake of that student movement. But that was about it.

The next morning, he went to his laboratory as usual. As a graduate student, he was busy with research for his Masters thesis, a study on remote sensing. But his computer crashed. Having nothing better to do, he wandered aimlessly into the center of the campus. As he had suspected, The Triangle was already being covered by Big Posters memorializing and commenting on Hu Yaobang's passing.[41]

Chen Xiaoping had learned the news from a friend even before the public announcement. He hurried back to his room at the University of Political Science and Law. By now, he had left Peking University

60

4.16

The Funeral

and settled in as a teacher in this politically conservative school. At the barracks-style dormitory occupied by many young and single teachers like himself, the news spread fast. Soon, many of them gathered in his room, including his fellow Peking University alumnus Wu Renhua.[42] The room was filled with a depressing silence until Wu Renhua burst out: "Whatever happens, I want to send a wreath to Tiananmen Square. A big one!"

"You?" Chen Xiaoping was surprised. They had known each other for a few years. Being a scholar in the obscure field of ancient Chinese literature, Wu Renhua had a solid reputation as a bookworm. In spite of his imposing physical size, he had a quiet demeanor and seemed to have never concerned himself with the present world.

But now, all of a sudden, it appeared that the "ancient relic," as Wu Renhua was known, was ready for some real-world action. He insisted that the wreath had to be huge in size to be eye-catching. He was remembering what he saw during the April Fifth Movement when Beijing residents spontaneously delivered flowers and wreathes to Tiananmen Square for the late Premier Zhou Enlai. It was a huge wreath, made by steel workers that had left the biggest impression. After a brief discussion, they decided that, indeed, they would build a big wreath the next day.

The next morning, Chen Xiaoping headed to Peking University to assess the mood there. Wu Renhua and others spent the entire day making their wreath. It was a big one: almost seven feet in diameter and covered with paper flowers and banners. As part of the Chinese tradition, Wu Renhua found a small bottle of Mao Tai, a luxury alcohol drink, and tied it on the wreath as a sacrifice to the deceased.* They placed the wreath in front of the main classroom building to attract attention. A note announced that the wreath would be delivered to Tiananmen Square at one o'clock next afternoon. There was no signature.

---

*When *The New York Times* reported the wreath in Tiananmen Square on April 17, 1989, it noted that a small bottle had been smashed at the scene as a protest against Deng Xiaoping. In Chinese "small bottle" is a homophone for "xiaoping." While smashing bottles did become a means of protest later on, it was not Wu Renhua's intention at this time.

4.17

From the very beginning Anti-Deng, and oversea attentions

61

Standoff At Tiananmen

HU Yaobang had died of a heart attack he suffered during a Politburo meeting a week earlier. At the age of seventy three, he certainly should not be considered as dying young. However, for many years he, along with Zhao Ziyang, had always appeared to be the "young" leaders who carried out the reforms of the older Deng Xiaoping. His enthusiasm, energy, and goofy postures had camouflaged his actual age. He just seemed to have died too young. In grief, the famous author Bing Xin, who was almost ninety year old herself, cried out: "The one who should have died did not; the one who should not have died did!" Obviously, she was referring to her own advanced age in comparison to that of Hu Yaobang.

Bing Xin's words made an appearance at The Triangle in a big banner and became an immediate hit. The sentiment took on a new meaning. It was without question that "the one who should have died" now referred to Deng Xiaoping, the old man who had wronged Hu Yaobang more than two years ago.

By noon of April 17 at University of Political Science and Law, Chen Xiaoping and Wu Renhua did not know how many people would show up for their wreath-laying party. School officials came by first. They told the two that buses and trucks were available to help them out. Surely, the school did not want to see a de facto demonstration march developing. Chen Xiaoping and Wu Renhua respectfully declined. At one o'clock, they headed out on schedule. Chen Xiaoping pedaled a flatbed tricycle carrying the wreath. Everybody else followed on foot. There were six to seven hundred of them, far exceeding the expectations of the instigators. The crowd carried school flags and mourning banners. They were trailed by a black car. They could see people in that car were handling cameras and camcorders.

It was the first march after Hu Yaobang's death. It was also the first public demonstration since New Year's Day in 1987. They passed through busy streets, singing *L'Internationale* and receiving enthusiastic cheers and applause from onlookers.

By the time they reached Tiananmen Square, it was already five o'clock. The procession had swelled to some five thousand. Slowly, they circled around the Square with funeral music playing on a portable radio. Then, they approached the Monument to People's Heroes and placed the wreath on its huge pedestal. Once again, they sang *L'Inter-nationale* as part of the custom mourning process.

They were not the first. Sporadic flowers and small wreaths were already present. But their big wreath dominated with its size. Wu Renhua felt particularly proud that, for once, the tiny, conservative University of Political Science and Law had beat his much more fa-mous Peking University, his alma mater, to the punch.

IT was already early evening when word of the march reached Peking University. It caused an emotional stir among the hundreds of students milling around The Triangle. The fact that the tiny and conservative University of Political Science and Law, of all schools in the capital, had taken the lead was a shock. Just about then, a big, vertical banner was unfurled out of one of the dormitory windows upstairs. It had three giant and well-calligraphed characters written on it: "China's Soul." The banner was very eye-catching and impressive. The crowd converged to the banner and grabbed its lower end. We should deliver this to Tiananmen Square, they exclaimed. Ignoring desperate protests of the banner's creators upstairs, they snatched it off and paraded it around The Triangle.

Among the crowd were Wang Dan and several of his Democracy Salon friends. They formed a vanguard of a march around the banner. As usual, they led the crowd through the campus first to gather up more students from dormitories. Then, with a contingent of thousands, they exited the campus and marched toward Tiananmen Square. It was almost midnight.[43]

The place was quiet and dark in the dim street lights. At the north side of the Monument to People's Heroes, the giant wreath from University of Political Science and Law was surrounded by many smaller ones. From a distance, they looked solemn and peaceful. In a sub-dued mood, the new arrivals did not notice a small camera crew on the side of the street videotaping their processions. Mike Chinoy, the Beijing Bureau Chief for the up-and-coming television news network *CNN*, had already gotten his fingers on the pulse of China's political scene.[44] But neither he nor the students themselves could comprehend the gravity of this moment as it was unfolding. At the Monument, a student by the name Guo Haifeng climbed up the pedestal and fastened the "China's Soul" banner up high. It flew down nicely along the pedestal and was visible from quite a distance. With their banner placed, students held a moment of silence and sang *L'Internationale.*

It was now four o'clock in the morning of April 18. Daybreak was approaching. They decided to stay till morning, in case the authorities would remove wreaths before dawn, as they had during the April Fifth Movement in 1976. They sat around and talked about what to do next. Eventually, they came up with a Seven-Point Petition, demanding a re-evaluation of Hu Yaobang, a re-evaluation of the anti-"Bourgeois Liberalization" movement, an abolishment of the "Beijing Ten-Points," and so on.[45] A student with good calligraphic skills wrote the list down on a big piece of paper like a Big Poster. They decided to head over to the Great Hall of People by daybreak and hand in their petition to the National People's Congress.

COVERING a hundred acres, Tiananmen Square was the largest open urban square in the world. It was named for the majestic gateway on its north side: Tiananmen, or the Gate of Heavenly Peace. Originally built in the 1420's during the Ming Dynasty, Tiananmen was designed as the outer-front gate of the Forbidden City, where emperors of many dynasties had lived and held court. Today, the Forbidden City, so named because all commoners were banned from setting foot in the compound, had been converted into a museum for empirical relics. Tiananmen, therefore, served only the symbolic purpose of being the center of this Middle Kingdom.

Tiananmen Square was only a grassy wasteland when the victorious communist army marched into this ancient capital. It was another idealistic generation of young students from Peking and Tsinghua universities who volunteered their labor to clean up the space so that a proper welcoming ceremony could be staged there for the new and hopeful ruler.[46]

Tiananmen Square took its current shape in the late 1950's when the new government geared up to celebrate its ten-year anniversary. On the north side, Chang'an Avenue, or the Avenue of Eternal Peace, was greatly widened to become the main east-west thoroughfare of the city. Two grand buildings, the Great Hall of the People and the Museum of Chinese History, framed the Square on the west and east side, respectively. The entire Square was paved in concrete, so that large-scale assemblies and military reviews could be easily staged.

With traditional Feng Shui in mind, the Forbidden City was built in a tight rectangular shape, with its main palaces aligned along a south-north axis. This axis extended outside of the Forbidden City to Tiananmen and Qianmen, the Front Gate, to the south. When the Square was built, more significant structures were placed along the same axis.

At the northern edge of the Square, just south of Chang'an Avenue, was the tall National Flag Pole. Everyday, the Five-Starred Red Flag of the People's Republic of China was raised on the pole by a military color guard, with the national anthem playing, at exactly the time of sunrise. The flag was then taken down every evening at sunset. The flag raising and lowering ceremonies were popular tourist attractions. It was also an occasion for young pupils to ferment their patriotic spirits.

Further south, at the center of the entire Square, was the Monument to People's Heroes, dedicated for the memory of martyrs in past revolutions. It was a symbol of remembrance and a place for public mourning. Visiting foreign dignitaries laid wreaths here as a part of the diplomatic protocol.

Mao Zedong left more than a footprint in the new Tiananmen Square himself. A giant portrait of his was permanently fixed on top of Tiananmen, looking over the Square. It was flanked by two slogans on each side, proclaiming respectively "Long Live the People's Republic of China!" and "Long Live the Unity of All Peoples in the World!" It was on top of Tiananmen where Mao Zedong had declared the founding of the People's Republic: "The Chinese people have stood up from now on!"

During the heyday of the Cultural Revolution, Red Guards rushed into the capital from all over the country to see their beloved Chairman Mao. Their wishes were granted occasionally when Mao Zedong waved at millions of crying admirers in the Square from atop of Tiananmen.

Even his funeral was staged in the Square, making him the only leader to receive such an honor. After his death, the Mausoleum of Chairman Mao Zedong was built near the south end of the Square, behind the Monument to People's Heroes, to display his preserved body. As Deng Xiaoping gradually dismantled Mao Zedong's work, the giant portrait at Tiananmen survived. From there, an expression-less Mao Zedong kept his watchful eyes on his people every day. He might not have liked what he saw.

At dawn, Wang Dan and Guo Haifeng found their crowd of students had dwindled to a mere two hundred. Many had gone to observe the flag-raising ceremony. Others decided that, after marching the whole night, breakfast was more attractive than petitioning to the government. Undaunted, they led the remaining troops onto the stairs of Great Hall of People. They sat down quietly, waiting for its doors to open. Wang Dan asked someone to call Professor Li Shuxian back at Peking University. They needed reinforcement and he only had her phone number with him.*

Through the early morning, Wang Dan and Guo Haifeng were busy going in and out of the offices in the Great Hall of People. It was not until eight o'clock that they finally succeeded in handing in their petition to receptionists of the Standing Committee of the National People's Congress. Wang Dan obtained a receipt to show the students outside and then left the scene.

By then, the ranks of the sit-in had expanded. A crowd of spectators gathered around them. They brought food and water as support. The crowd was not satisfied with a simple receipt. They demanded that the People's Representatives come and receive their petitions in person. The students were getting restless.

Li Jinjin, a graduate student in constitutional law at Peking University, had been sitting quietly in the crowd. He felt that it was time for him to step up and help out.[48] Li Jinjin had been the president of the official graduate students union at his school. But he lost the confidence of his superiors by organizing a few provocative activities in

---

*Li Shuxian posted Wang Dan's message at The Triangle. It later became key evidence that Professors Fang Lizhi and Li Shuxian were the "black hands" behind the students.[47]

The Funeral

that capacity. It was a lesson well learned. He convinced himself that he should avoid any more political trouble and focus on finishing his degree work.

Yet there he was, in the middle of a sit-in, feeling a strong calling for action. He stood up and introduced himself to the crowd and volunteered to be a representative for the crowd. Before taking any steps, however, he insisted that everyone should agree to end the protest as soon as their petition was properly received. With that promise, Li Jinjin entered the Great Hall of People himself. He had no idea what to expect inside.

The office workers told Li Jinjin that there were no People's Representatives on site. They didn't know if they could get anyone to meet the students. Besides, they were not sure if the students would disperse even if they did. Li Jinjin assured them that the students would do their part, so long as the People's Representatives did theirs. The office workers told him to wait and then left him alone. In the big hallway, Li Jinjin waited and waited. He sat there alone for two hours. Still without an official response, he walked out of the Great Hall to check on the students outside. They were still all there, sitting on the stairs. Li Jinjin told them the status and informed them that he intended to wait however long it would take. Anticipating a drawn-out battle, Li Jinjin sent off a couple of students back to Peking University with a new dispatch. Any reinforcements, he reasoned, should come with winter coats and be prepared to spend the night here. To solidify their stand and garner more attention, he arranged to have the big "China's Soul" banner moved from the Monument to the stairs of the Great Hall. Another copy of the Seven-Point Petition was produced and proudly displayed in front of them.

From the stairs of the Great Hall, they could see more and more people streaming in and out of the Square. Many of them came with flowers, wreaths and other memorabilia. They went straight to the Monument to pay their respect and admire the display. In the vastness of the Square, the crowd of a few hundred in front of the Great Hall was barely noticeable. But fortunately for Li Jinjin, a big group of students from Beijing Economics College came by after placing their wreath and joined the sit-in. More students followed. By evening, the

67

sit-in had swelled to thousands of people. But there was still no sign of any reinforcement from Peking University.

After seven o'clock, word finally came that several People's Representatives were ready to meet the students. Li Jinjin felt anxious. Since the early morning, they had been at this sit-in for more than twelve hours. Could this gesture come too little, too late? Would the thousands of students disperse when their demands were satisfied? He felt that he had to proceed with greatest caution. He spoke to the crowd and obtained their consent to negotiate, as well as a promise to end the sit-in once their petition was properly received. Then he headed upstairs.

Just as he reached the door of the Great Hall, he turned around and took a peek behind. From the top of the stairs, he got a full view of his "troops" for the first time. The sight of thousands of excited people at the gate of the Great Hall scared him. It would truly be unthinkable if something happened to trigger a riot. He decided that he needed to put an end to the protest as quickly as possible.

Inside the Great Hall, he was instructed to hand in the petition to the waiting People's Representatives. Li Jinjin wisely refused. He knew he had to do this outside in the full view of the crowd. With his insistence, they reached a compromise: The Representatives would come outside but not get close to the students. Li Jinjin would come back up from the side of students. They would then meet at the middle tier of the stairs where the petition was to change hands. It was like a formal diplomatic maneuver.

Li Jinjin came back to the students and briefed the crowd of his negotiation. Still uncertain of the outcome, he asked aloud:

"Our purpose today is to submit our petition to People's Representatives. Is that right?"

"Right!" the crowd roared in unison.

"People's Representatives have now agreed to receive our petition. Should we submit it?"

"Yes!"

"After we submit the petition, our task is completed. Yes?"

"Yes!"

"Should we keep our promises?"

petition

"Yes!"

"After the People's Representatives receive our petition, we should immediately conclude our sit-in and disperse. Right?"

"Right!"

With that, Li Jinjin headed back upstairs with their Seven-Point Petition. Along with him was Guo Haifeng with a similar petition from People's University. When they stopped at the middle tier, they saw three People's Representatives standing on the high tier waiting, as if they were wary of getting any closer.[49] Li Jinjin insisted that they come down. After more hesitation, the three representatives finally did. The petitions changed hands with only a brief conversation.

It was with a great sense of relief that Li Jinjin came back to the sit-in crowd. He told the students that their mission had been accomplished. They should immediately disperse and return to their campuses. Then, he left in a hurry, fearing that any lingering would trigger further actions. He got back to Peking University an hour and a half later. In the darkness, he saw a worrisome scene. There were groups and groups of students heading out of the campus with heavy winter coats. He realized that this was the reinforcement they had been waiting for all day. But now he could neither stop the flow nor imagine what this could lead to.

Li Jinjin had left the Great Hall of People in such a hurry that he failed to notice that not everybody in the crowd had heard his message. He also neglected to clear out the area, especially the eye-catching "China's Soul" banner. In the chaotic scene, only a small number of people in his immediate vicinity knew exactly what had happened on the stairs of the Great Hall. When they left, others assumed that they had given up the hopeless task. So, a sizable crowd continued to stay around the banner. It did not take long for someone to suggest that they ought to go directly to the government itself instead of the rubber-stamp National People's Congress.

Proudly holding up the "China's Soul" banner, the crowd marched out of Tiananmen Square and turned west on Chang'an Avenue. There, they only had to walk a mile to reach Xinhuamen, or Gate of New China. Almost at the same time, groups of students, the intended reinforcement from Peking University, arrived there from the opposite direction. They merged and gathered around Xinhuamen, which was guarded by armed soldiers.

Z HONGNANHAI, or Central-South Lakes, had long been an imperial garden neighboring the Forbidden City. In accordance with its namesake, it consisted of two artificial lakes and various pavilions and houses along the shores. When the communists entered Beijing, they chose the compound as the site for both the Communist Party Central Committee and the State Council of the government. It therefore became the nerve center of the new republic, surrounded by high red walls and sealed off from the general public.

Xinhuamen itself used to be a pavilion within Zhongnanhai but was later renovated into its main gate opening directly to Chang'an Avenue. The grand entry of Xinhuamen was always open. A big privacy wall blocked any views of its interior. The famous slogan, "Serve the People," was inscribed on the wall in Mao Zedong's own calligraphy. Normally, four members of the People's Armed Police* stood guard while ceremonially holding rifles with open bayonets. Passing pedestrians were advised to stay away from the gate at all times.

When the throngs of students came upon Xinhuamen, a band of soldiers immediately rushed out and lined up in front of the gate. They were not armed. Rather, their job appeared to be forming a human barrier to prevent students from storming the compound.

The students did not know what they were supposed to do. The ones who had brought the "China's Soul" banner and a couple of wreaths asked the guards if they could send them into the compound. The request was denied as a matter of course by the silence of the stone-faced soldiers.

Without a clear leader, the two thousand strong were a lot more restless this time. They chanted "Li Peng, Come out! Li Peng, Come out!" in unison as their demand for the Premier to make a personal appear-

---

*The People's Armed Police was a special paramilitary police force responsible for law enforcement and guarding important government offices. They wore special uniforms to distinguish themselves from the regular police force. Although they were authorized to carry heavy weaponry, as the name implied, they were usually unarmed while performing their daily duties.

ance.* Suddenly, they surged forward and pressed themselves into the guards. The guards, standing four or five rows deep with linked arms, stood their ground. During the powerful push and shove match, the "China's Soul" banner and flowers were tossed back and forth over the heads of both sides. They soon disappeared. Just as the situation was about to deteriorate into dangerous territory, a few cooler-minded adults managed to calm down the students.[50] The crowd dispersed in the wee hours of the morning of April 19 and avoided a disaster.

While the wreath-laying at the Monument to People's Heroes and the sit-in at the Great Hall of People were all peaceful endeavors, the scuffle at the Xinhuamen tilted dangerously toward violence. In the history of the People's Republic, storming Xinhuamen had only occurred during the heyday of the Cultural Revolution, when the frantic Red Guards cast aside all laws and norms of a civilized society. This new generation of students was by no means a reincarnation of the Red Guards. But they left Xinhuamen dejected. They felt that they had failed in their mission.

APRIL 19 was a day full of tension. Students were at a crossroads and unsure what to do next. Big Posters bearing the signature of an unknown "Action Committee" appeared in all major campuses calling for students to be a part of Hu Yaobang's funeral, which was officially scheduled for April 22.

It also happened to be a Wednesday. Wang Dan decided to hold his Democracy Salon outdoors at The Triangle. Posters there had already grown to multiple layers, as newer ones were continuously pasted on top of the older ones. Thousands of students were coming and going throughout the day, reading the posters and debating. It was the most natural setting for an open forum.

In the evening, just as the after-dinner rush was pouring into the area, Wang Dan set up a couple of tall stools and a portable radio with a small microphone right in front of the bulletin boards. He had lost his voice during the day so he asked someone else to be the host and

---

*Before becoming the Premier, Li Peng had served as the nation's top educational commissioner. He was not popular among students as he had instituted policies restricting the flow of studying abroad.

did not plan to give any speech himself.

Wang Dan was not the only one trying to be heard at The Triangle. Loudspeakers mounted in the area were also broadcasting that night. It was an announcement by the city government about the events at Xinhuamen the night before. Quite typically, it warned that "a small clique of bad elements, with ulterior motives" were conspiring to create social disorder by storming the Zhongnanhai compound and attacking police forces. Although the loudspeakers were much more powerful than Wang Dan's puny setup, they were no match in attracting students' attention.

The first few students who jumped onto the stools to give speeches were all familiar faces who had been involved in earlier activities following Chai Qingfeng's death. They talked about the importance of having their own leadership. When someone in the crowd suggested that they should give the official student union a chance, a mob democracy commenced: the students called for the official Students Union to stand out and lead. They yelled in unison three times. When nobody answered the call, a voice vote was held to disband the union. It was passed by a roar. In the darkness, the crowd was estimated to be three thousand, approximately thirty percent of the student population at the time. Now that they had the official union out of the way, they decided to establish a Preparatory Committee for a new student solidarity. It was agreed that whoever was willing to stand up in front of the crowd would make up the committee, in charge of working toward a more formal organization.

In these early days of the movement, it took great courage for anyone to put his or her name or face forward to represent an independent organization that was certain to be regarded as illegal by the government. Even with thousands present, there was not a rush to the podium. But stand up they did. Wang Dan and Feng Congde were among the first seven people to form the Preparatory Committee. The crowd gave them a thunderous round of applause as approval.[51]

Shen Tong had been staying behind the crowd for a while. He and his friends from the Olympic Institute were not particularly fond of what the Democracy Salon folks were doing and did not plan to get involved themselves. But when he heard the call for a Preparatory

Committee, he suddenly realized that he had to be a part of it. He pushed and shoved into the crowd but failed to reach the microphone before it was all over. As the crowd dissipated, he managed to find Feng Congde and talked his way into inclusion on the Committee.[52]

MEANWHILE, in a dormitory room on the same campus, several older folks were hatching up a slightly different approach.

Forty-two year old and already half-balding, Zheng Yi had arrived the day before Hu Yaobang's death. The famous author was based in Xi'an, the capital of the remote Shaanxi Province. He came to Beijing for a symposium honoring his latest writings. A former Red Guard, Zheng Yi had reached stardom by penning sharp-toned novels exposing the tragedies of the Cultural Revolution and the unbearable sufferings in the poor and remote western region of China. As early as 1980, Zheng Yi published *Maple*, a novel of the romance and tragedy of Red Guards caught in the horror of violence. It was the very first literature that cast the Cultural Revolution and implicitly Mao Zedong under a dark shadow. When the novel was made into a movie, rumor had it that it took Hu Yaobang himself to give the green light. Yet the movie still did not receive permission for a general distribution.

Zheng Yi had many friends in Beijing, some of whom were in Peking University, where a special graduate level class was in session for aspiring authors. One of Zheng Yi's friends in this so-called "authors class" was Zhang Boli who had just reached thirty year old. Zhang Boli had displayed his potential by traveling around the nation and writing investigative reports for newspapers. In the fall of 1988, he left his wife and their one-year old daughter in Shaanxi Province to pursue his life-long dream of studying in this famed school. So, in this evening of April 19, Zheng Yi found himself in Zhang Boli's room and could not contain his excitement. He had witnessed the scuffle at Xinhuamen the night before and thought that the students would, and should, keep on with the momentum to force the government into accepting their petition. If the government did not relent, he told the room, they ought to start a hunger strike, "which never fails!"

It was already late. Zheng Yi suggested advocating this idea directly to younger students who might be going back to Xinhuamen again. He took off Zhang Boli's white bedspread and, with black ink, wrote two gigantic characters on it: "hunger strike." Zhang Boli was impressed with his calligraphic skill. "I had lots of practice during the Cultural Revolution," Zheng Yi explained proudly.[53]

By the time they got to Xinhuamen, it was already midnight. As they had expected, hundreds of students were indeed there continuing the pushing-and-shoving game with the guards at the gate. They spread out their makeshift banner in a corner of the driveway and asked for signatures. In the chaotic scene, nobody paid any attention to them. More and more policemen were converging on Chang'an Avenue to encircle the two hundred or so students. Many more students were cut-off outside as they shouted slogans. A van equipped with loudspeakers lingered on Chang'an Avenue. It was broadcasting a statement by the city government: "Any attempts of storming the Xinhuamen or attacking the leaders of the Party and the government are absolutely not allowed!"

Surrounded by police, students began to sit down on the ground. Zhang Boli was then able to see a young man standing between the students and police. He paced up and down the line of confrontation and screamed his orders for all students to sit down. The man himself was still standing. Punching the night air with his fist, he shouted with a booming voice: "I am Wuer Kaixi from the Beijing Normal University! My name is Wuer Kaixi! We must hold on to our position here until Li Peng comes out! They must give us an answer to our Seven-Point Petition!"

The man by the name of Wuer Kaixi looked much more like a boy. He was wearing a faded yellow army uniform which had been fashionable for young lads during the Cultural Revolution. He had a full head of thick and curly black hair that bounced up and down as he spoke. His eyes were big, penetrating, and full of defiance. His posture and manner displayed a confidence in natural leadership talent. Indeed, he had gotten much of that appearance and charisma from his unique heritage. He was a Uyghur, an ethnic minority residing in the northwest of China who shared ancestors with Turkish and European people. While he was born and raised in Beijing, his family had moved to Xinjiang, the Uyghur Autonomous Region, when he was sixteen years old. The

Wuer kaixi's first appearance

The Funeral

young Wuer Kaixi spent three years there before returning to Beijing for high school. Just a little earlier, Wuer Kaixi and his classmates had been stopped on Chang'an Avenue by police on their way to Xinhuamen. That was when he jumped onto a flatbed tricycle and led his troop to their destination. It was his first experience standing up to lead a crowd. He looked natural for the part.[54]

Liu Gang was also standing in the back of the crowd. He was immensely impressed by this young fellow named Wuer Kaixi. It was one thing to participate in a big protest. It was entirely a different matter for an individual to stand out and give his name in front of the police, who were undoubtedly videotaping the scene. That was one brave young man, he thought.

Wuer Kaixi's courage had an obvious effect in everybody else as well. All of a sudden, pushing and shoving stopped. Students sat down tightly on the driveway in front of Xinhuamen facing the guards. They were quiet and confident. The impetuous atmosphere of the night before dissipated, replaced by an orderly sit-in.

This relative tranquility, however, did not last long. On this night, it was not just the students who were more prepared. The People's Armed Police guarding the gate were also determined not to allow the situation to escalate. A long row of buses showed up on Chang'an Avenue and the police sprang into action. They stormed into the students and anyone they laid their hands on was grabbed and pushed onto the buses. The sudden eruption of violence startled the students, who were not prepared for this response.* Their formation was broken up within minutes and many of them were stuffed into buses. Wuer Kaixi jumped on the flatbed tricycle again. Surveying the scene, he knew it was hopeless. So he screamed for everyone to withdraw to the Monument to People's Heroes in Tiananmen Square to regroup. But Chang'an Avenue was already full of police, who pushed the students back toward the waiting buses. In the chaos, a female student lost her cool and shouted "Down with the Communist Party!"

The high-pitched scream pieced the air and startled everyone into an uneasy pause. If there were to be any hints of "counter-revolutionary"

---

*Also caught off guard in the surge were Mike Chinoy's *CNN* crew and *NBC*'s Gary Fairman, who was knocked down and injured.[55]

So, the students were not really "patriotic" & pro-CCP

activities, this would be one of the worst. Students had been careful not to give the authorities any excuse to label their movement anything but patriotic. This one desperate outburst could ruin it all. Immediately, both the police and students rushed toward the source of the scream and tried to shout the poor girl down. She was quickly whisked away by several students.[56]

With the heavy presence of police, the students were not successful in retreating into Tiananmen Square. They had to disperse and find their own way back to their campuses. Those who had been stuffed onto buses only got the biggest scare of their lives. They were driven back to the campus area and let go without a fuss. A couple of bus windows were smashed during the mayhem and several students were injured by the broken glass. More suffered minor injuries from the kicking and beating by the police.

Zhang Boli did make his way into Tiananmen Square. He found himself alone and had to pretend to be a reporter to get through police checkpoints. Along his way, he witnessed a student being brutally beaten up by several policemen.[57]

THE next morning, Wuer Kaixi stood alone in pouring rain at the Beijing Normal University. He was shouting at anyone passing by about what happened last night. His voice was hoarse and his sentences broken. But he kept on talking. "I am a witness of police violence!" He accused the police of brutalizing students and molesting females. He repeated his message again and again with rain water streaming down his solemn face.[58]

By mid-afternoon, a few hundred students had gathered around him. With a bullhorn in his hand, Wuer Kaixi had a better command of his ad-hoc troops. He gathered them up and led them into another march to Tiananmen Square to protest police brutality. Just as they were leaving the campus, lightning struck close and the downpour became a torrent. His team scrambled for cover and shrank to only dozens in number. Wuer Kaixi was determined. He vowed to march even if he was the only one left. So, they soldiered on and paused frequently to give speeches along the way. By the time they reached Tiananmen Square, only a tiny handful was still with him.

The rain did not wash out all the Big Posters at The Triangle at Peking University. New ones were showing up throughout the day with screaming headlines: "The April Twenty Tragedy!", "The Blood at Xinhuamen!", and so on.[59] Most were calling for a general boycott of classes. With so much going on and Hu Yaobang's funeral scheduled for the coming weekend, few were going to classes anyway.

Most students from Peking University had missed the action at Xinhuamen as they focused on founding their own Preparatory Committee the night before. Now, a protest march was shaping up at The Triangle despite the constant rainfall. This contingent was much stronger than the one Wuer Kaixi had gathered from Beijing Normal University. They stopped by the University of Political Science and Law where local students treated them to warm buns and soup. A few thousand students made it all the way to Tiananmen Square. In the pouring rain, however, there was not much for them to do. Zhang Boli made a speech and then arranged for buses to take the students back to campus.[60]

ALTHOUGH Hu Yaobang had been demoted for his "serious mistakes," his funeral was planned with the protocol reserved for only the top leaders. The memorial service was to be held in the Great Hall of People on April 22. In order to facilitate the funeral possession, it was announced that all of Tiananmen Square would be closed to the public from eight o'clock that morning.

Students, excited by the protests of the last few days and upset that the government had yet to respond to their petition, formulated a plan of their own. Taking a page from military tactics, Peking University's Preparatory Committee decided to call on students to enter Tiananmen Square before the closure deadline and be part of the memorial service. With Big Posters bearing the signature of "Action Committee," they advised each school to organize their own contingents and assemble at Beijing Normal University by nine o'clock in the evening of April 21. Students should bring enough food, water, and winter coats to stay the night.

It was a daring plan indeed. Just a few short years earlier, it was unthinkable even to march off campus for a protest. This new generation of students had already broken through that milestone with ease during the wave of protests in the winter of 1986. Now, in the spring of 1989, they were pushing the limit even further by organizing a city-wide coordinated action.

For one evening, the small campus of Beijing Normal University became a center of activities. From seven o'clock, processions of students started to pour into its athletic field. Riding on a bicycle with a bullhorn in his hand, Wuer Kaixi zigzagged throughout the field like a skillful field marshal. He coerced the chaotic scene into order by guiding all the schools' flags into a formation. Then, as Wuer Kaixi would recall later:[61]

> At 9:00 P.M. sharp, in front of sixty thousand people, I climbed on top of a pair of parallel bars. The bars were shaking under my feet as I announced through a bullhorn, "Please be quiet." Then I declared that the Beijing Provisional Student Union was officially established. Thundering applause shook the air. I was thrilled but not scared. I hardly ever experience fear. I knew that every word I said was history, for it marked the emergence of the first independent self-governing political force in China. This organization was the precursor of Beijing Students Autonomous Federation.
>
> After I finished speaking I looked down and saw my father standing below the parallel bars. This was one of the more despicable things that the government did. My father was in Beijing, at the Party Academy; they put enormous pressure on him to come find me and talk to me.

His father failed in his mission to talk Wuer Kaixi out of this historical moment. But Wuer Kaixi was not entirely truthful either. After seeing his courage and leadership skill at Xinhuamen, Liu Gang had later sought him out and talked about the necessity of establishing a city-wide student union. The two of them agreed on the principle. But as Wuer Kaixi was speaking in the evening of April 21, there was no such a thing as "Beijing Provisional Student Union."

As students marched out of Beijing Normal University, it became a surprisingly organized affair. They marched under each school's flag, in five columns. On each side were picket lines made up by student marshals wearing red arm bands. The marshals held hands together, forming a pair of human chains throughout the procession. It was critically important for the student formation to remain orderly and intact and not to be mixed with non-students. They could not afford giving the authority any excuse that their movement was instigated by "a small clique of bad elements" as the government would always claim.*

It was already dusk when they turned onto the main streets in the city. They marched slowly and solemnly on the wide bicycle paths. Residents of the city cheered and applauded, especially when they spotted banners decrying official graft and difficult living conditions. Inflation, corruption, and the general hardship in their daily lives far outweighed their concerns of Hu Yaobang or democracy.

Tiananmen Square after midnight was dim and quiet. Flowers and wreaths covered the entire base of the Monument to People's Heroes. In the center, the "China's Soul" banner was long gone, replaced by a giant portrait of Hu Yaobang created by students from the Central Academy of Fine Arts. Apparently, the march had not alerted the authorities. There were only scant traffic police lazily patrolling the area. They watched the students pouring into the Square and did not interfere. The preemptive entry of the Square was therefore a smooth success. Just as on his campus earlier, Wuer Kaixi guided students into columns according to schools at the western edge of the Square facing the Great Hall of People. Student marshals set up a picket line along the perimeters. There, they would stand guard all night long and prevent anyone without a student identification card from entering the area.

There were hundreds of thousands of students inside the picket line in uneven columns. From up the stairs leading to Great Hall of People, the assembly looked like a bar chart. The columns for major universities stretched out almost completely across the entire Square. In between them were those of smaller colleges which were only a few

---

*When the government accused the student movement, the "small clique of bad elements" was almost always referring to non-students such as older intellectuals or "hooligans."

hundred people deep. All of them felt a great relief that they were there. They would be part of a memorial to which they had not been invited.

It was a bitterly cold spring night during which many were forced to leave the Square and take shelter in the underground pedestrian passages and subway stations. Those who stayed could not manage any sleep at all. They had to get up and move around frequently to keep warm. But mostly, they sat and talked. Student leaders from different schools gathered in a small circle to get to know each other and plan their strategies. It was a long night.

In the middle of the night, Wang Juntao arrived unnoticed. He had been spending this spring traveling through the rural areas of the great northwest, looking for development opportunities for his Institute. As soon as he heard the news of Hu Yaobang's death, however, he decided to drop everything and head back to Beijing. He barely caught up with what was happening in the capital when he discreetly walked around the Square and found some of his colleagues from the Institute. They were all keeping a low profile and observing the student formation in the darkness. Wang Juntao could not help having a flashback to thirteen years ago when he was still a teenager. During the April Fifth Movement of 1976, he told Zhang Lun that a crowd like this also stayed in the Square all night to guard the wreaths and flowers for the late Premier Zhou Enlai. Then, at dawn, police and paramilitary forces moved in. Tens of thousands of them. They beat up everybody. The key to avoid a repeat of that tragedy, he advised Zhang Lun, was to avoid provocation and confrontation at any cost.

Zhang Lun thought that the presence of Wang Juntao and his fellow Institute folks, most of whom had "records" dating from the Democracy Wall era, was precisely a provocation by itself. He urged all of them to leave the scene to the students. They left before the crack of dawn.[62]

SUBSTANTIAL police forces did show up at daybreak. They built up a human barrier in front of the Great Hall of People. From there they watched the students intently but otherwise showed no desire to evict them out of the Square.

The Funeral

Just before sunrise, a platoon of honor guards marched out of Tiananmen, crossed Chang'an Avenue, and entered the Square from its northern edge. It was the time for the traditional flag-raising ceremony. As they stopped at the giant National Flag Pole, the hundreds of thousands of students stood at attention. They turned to face the rising Five-Starred Red Flag,* singing the national anthem at the top of their lungs:

> *Arise! All who refuse to be slaves!*
> *Let our flesh and blood*
> *Become our new Great Wall!*
> *As the Chinese nation faces its greatest peril,*
> *All forcefully expend their last cries.*
> *Arise! Arise! Arise!*
>
> *May our million hearts beat as one,*
> *Brave the enemy's fire,*
> *March on!*
> *Brave the enemy's fire,*
> *March on!*
> *March on! March on! On!*

Originally composed as the theme song for a patriotic movie during the anti-Japanese war era, *March of Volunteers* was a rousing anthem inspired by *La Marseillaise*. Even in peacetime, the sense of grandiosity, urgency, and even desperation of the song was enough to cause one's blood to boil. Now, at the center of the nation, defying their own government, hundreds of thousands of students were singing the anthem in one voice. It was a moment of great crisis, uncertainty, and hope. Most of them had tears in their eyes. Looking at the rising flag, they wondered how this day would end.

The anthem finished just as the flag reached the top of the pole. Then, it began an agonizingly slow decent. As it settled into a half-staff position in honor of Hu Yaobang, students sang the somber *L'Internationale*. The aggressive fighting spirit was replaced by a strong

---

*The Five-Starred Red flag was the national flag of the People's Republic of China, depicting five bright yellow stars in the background of red. The large star symbolized the leadership of the Communist Party while the four surrounding small stars represented other social classes.

sense of sadness as more tears were shed.

In the crowd, Chai Ling was feeling an unprecedented sense of to-getherness. She made a mental note of how many of her friends were present. She also spotted an unexpected figure: a die-hard Communist Party member who had worked hard to prevent students from protesting. But there he was, participating in this historical event with nothing but sincerity.[63]

The sheer size and determination of the students must have impressed the authorities as well. Several officers came down from the long flights of stairs of the Great Hall to meet with student leaders in the early morning. As a good-will gesture, they allowed the students to remain in the Square for the duration of the funeral service. The service would also be broadcast live through the loudspeakers in the Square for their benefit. Predictably, however, they denied students' request to have their own representatives attending the service inside the Great Hall. Finally, the officials requested students to back away to make room for arriving vehicles. Under the guidance of Wuer Kaixi's bullhorn, the huge crowd grudgingly complied with discipline. Wishful but unfounded rumors were spreading that Premier Li Peng had agreed to meet with students after the funeral.

THE Great Hall of People was one of the cornerstone masterpieces constructed during the renovation of Tiananmen Square in the 1950's. It was designed to host mass conferences typical in the communist political scene. It consisted of an auditorium that could seat ten thousand people and many palace-style meeting halls for receiving foreign dignitaries as well as domestic visitors. Symbolically, it was also the site of the National People's Congress which met here annually in the spring. It was built with an architecture of Stalinist grandiosity and covered an area of forty three acres. A dozen solemn pillars, each eighty-two feet high, dominated the front face. They supported an expanded eave decorated with a National Emblem, establishing the building as the symbol of the highest power of the land. Underneath, a long and majestic set of stairs, divided into three tiers, led to its front gates.

The memorial service commenced inside the Great Hall as the clock struck ten. Curiously, all top officials wore traditional "Mao Suits" to bid farewell to the man who had abolished the attire. Zhao Ziyang delivered a eulogy filled with familiar and impersonal praises. As the National Anthem was played inside and broadcast on the loudspeakers outside, students sang once again. They sang with their greatest devotion and force, hoping that their collective voice could carry enough power to penetrate the granite walls of the Great Hall. Then, they bowed their heads to observe a moment of silence.

Although their voices might not have been heard, their presence was undoubtedly felt by everyone inside. Ge Yang, a prominent magazine editor, observed:[64]

> After Zhao Ziyang delivered the eulogy for Hu Yaobang, we filed past to pay our last respects. As we walked by the glass doors of the Great Hall of People, many lingered for a moment to observe the many thousands of students sitting outside on the Square. Rows of soldiers stood with arms linked to separate the students from us. I felt rage as I stood there silently watching them. The atmosphere was tense. Some of the officials feared that the students might try to force their way into the Great Hall. A soldier came over and asked me politely to move on.
>
> My driver walked up to me and took my arm. I replied, "I just want to stand here for a while. I belong to the Communist Party, and I was wounded serving the Party during the war. I have seen much, but I have never before seen such abuse of students by Party members like yourself."
>
> The soldier listened and then left.

Referring to the rows of soldiers separating the students from the dignitaries inside the Great Hall, Ge Yang noted in a poem that "a wall of brute force" had split the land into two sides. "On one side lay Hu Yaobang's body, but on the other side was his soul."

INSIDE the Great Hall, Hu Yaobang's body was lying in state covered with the flag of the Communist Party. Officials and dignitaries walked past slowly to pay their last respects. At the end of the service, as tradition dictated, the funeral procession carrying the body would exit the Great Hall, circle Tiananmen Square, and then head west on

Standoff At Tiananmen

Chang'an Avenue for the crematorium in the suburb. As funeral music played endlessly from the loudspeakers, students in the Square eagerly but patiently waited for the sight of the hearse. It was their own chance to bid farewell to Hu Yaobang.

It had been a long night and morning. As the farewell process dragged on inside, many decided that they had fulfilled their desire and mission. They trickled out of the Square for food and rest. But a few thousand persisted. They crowded toward the Great Hall of People to get a peek of the hearse.

It was after another long wait when word came that the funeral possession had already been spotted on Chang'an Avenue heading west. Along the boulevard, millions of residents lined the sidewalks to give Hu Yaobang a dignified send-off. Tens of thousands of bicycles followed the hearse on the side, ringing their bells. It was a scene reminiscent of that for late Premier Zhou Enlai in 1976. But this time, the hearse had skipped Tiananmen Square where thousands of students had been waiting.

A small chant emerged from the angry crowd and gradually grew into a roar:

"Li Peng! Come out!"

"Li Peng! Come out!"

The crowd surged forward. Soldiers, with their arms interlocked, struggled to hold their lines. At the forefront was Wuer Kaixi, still with the bullhorn in his hand, calling for Premier Li Peng.[65]

"Look," screamed Wuer Kaixi, "so many students have starved for a whole day just for the opportunity to talk to you." He shouted, "after forty years of the People's Republic, this is the first time a man has stood under the National Emblem, in front of the Great Hall of People, in front of the highest authority of the land, and demanded a dialogue with you. I protest! You are shameless!"

Wuer Kaixi's statement was not historically accurate. Calling out national leaders in front of the Great Hall of People was far from an invention of this new generation. It had happened many times during the turmoil of the Cultural Revolution. Even more recently, Chen Ziming and Wang Juntao had witnessed the same scene during the April Fifth Movement in 1976. Yet Wuer Kaixi was certainly sincere in his sentiment. The young students never had the chance to receive a proper education of this part of history and they believed without a doubt that they were making an effort that nobody had ever made before.

It did not take long for some hot heads to suggest that they could push through the soldiers and storm the Great Hall. Surveying the numbers, Wuer Kaixi thought that they had a decent chance. But fortunately, just as he was going to yell into his bullhorn, others prevailed in stopping him. After a heated discussion, they decided to send in representatives with their Seven-Point Petition, to which they still had not received any response. "If they still ignore us, we will just kneel down in front of them!" suggested an emotional Zhang Boli. Kneeling, of course, was the traditional protocol for meeting an emperor. Zhang Boli proposed the dramatic gesture as a symbolic protest.[66]

"No way! I don't want to kneel down in front of the communists!" replied a terse Wuer Kaixi.

"If you don't, I will!" Guo Haifeng, who had been a part of the previous petitions with Wang Dan and then Li Jinjin, grabbed the petition paper and headed to the Great Hall of People. Two others, Zhou Yongjun and Zhang Zhiyong, followed him. Perhaps caught by surprise, the soldiers let them sneak through.

It was about half past noon. The three of them marched onto the middle tier of the long flight of stairs. They looked around. There was nobody nearby. Down below at a distance that seemed far away, thousands of students stood behind lines of soldiers. Most of the students were not aware of the plan but their attention was fixed after spotting three figures ascending the stairs. Still ahead and higher up, the giant doors to the Great Hall of People remained closed. There were only a few guards at the top of the stairs looking down at them.

Slowly, Guo Haifeng lowered himself to his knees. On his left, Zhou Yongjun followed reluctantly but only knelt with his right leg. On his right, Zhang Zhiyong knelt down with both knees and buried his head into his chest. But Guo Haifeng looked up in defiance despite his body position. He raised both arms holding the long scroll of petition paper over his head toward the National Emblem high above.

A shock wave propagated down the stairs and through the student body in the Square. A brief silence was immediately overcome by

kneeling ...

dramatic / emotional

horrified cries and screams.

"No!" "No!"

"You can't kneel down! Stand up!!!"

Perhaps for the first time in their young lives, this new generation vividly felt that they and their government were not on the same side. The drama was so intense that nobody knew how to react to it. The three of them knelt there for as long as half an hour. Nobody came out of the Hall to receive or reject them. It felt like an eternity.

A middle-aged man suddenly emerged from inside the Hall. He was crying profusely as he stumbled down the stairs. When he reached the three students, all he could do was try to hug all of them at once. Out of breath, he repeatedly murmured, "It's all useless, it's all useless. This is not a government you could try to talk to."

The restless crowd had seen enough. Ma Shaofang, a student leader from the Beijing Film Academy pushed forward to the line of soldiers. He saw Wuer Kaixi at the bottom of the stairs. With tears all over his face, the twenty-one year old Uighur was screaming to no one in particular, "I did not kneel down! They did!! But I did not kneel down!!!" Nearby, Pu Zhiqiang, a lanky student from the University of Political Science and Law, was angrily hitting his own head with a bullhorn, causing blood to stream down his face. Quietly, Feng Congde bit his finger to write a note on his handkerchief with blood. He was not alone in that act. Passing through the chaos, Ma Shaofang made it onto the stairs and dragged the three representatives back down to the crowd.[67] Student leaders gathered around and made a quick decision to avoid confrontation for the time being. They declared an indefinite strike to boycott classes. With the University of Political Science and Law leading the way, dejected students filed out of Tiananmen Square the same way they came, school by school, following the flags. Wuer Kaixi remembered:[68]

> The soldiers began to beat us when we tried to leave the steps of the Great Hall. They really beat us, too. When we were finally out of Tiananmen Square, I fainted from hunger and exhaustion.*

---

*Wuer Kaixi might have indeed fainted. However, there were no other witness accounts of police brutality on that day.

The Funeral

The dramatic scene at Tiananmen Square was absent from most official media the next day, which only dutifully covered the official service inside the Great Hall of People. But several small newspapers in Beijing, including the *Peasants Daily*, the *Science and Technology Daily*, and the *China Women News*, broke the silence. They wrote positively of the spontaneous participation of the thousands of students and residents at Tiananmen Square and along Chang'an Avenue. There was no mention of the kneeling petition, of course.

I am Liu Gang. I believe most of you know me already.

Liu Gang

5

The Autonomous Federation

SHEN Tong was one of the very few students who did not attend the funeral at Tiananmen Square. He had a bad feeling about the new Preparatory Committee at Peking University. He and his Olympic Institute friends did not get along very well with Wang Dan and his friends from the Democracy Salon. Others in the committee had their own ideas too. If he wanted to play a bigger role in this budding movement, he figured that he would have to find his own niche.[69]

Fortunately for him, Shen Tong realized that he actually had the movement cornered, quite literally. His dormitory room on the second floor had its window overlooking The Triangle. It was the best seat to observe the crowd. People were putting up Big Posters and making impromptu speeches which were difficult to hear. A couple of students in electronics were trying to rig up an amplifier. Shen Tong invited them upstairs to set up the equipment in his room. With donated money, they purchased and installed a couple of loudspeakers outside of his window. Inside, they got amplifiers, microphones, and recording machines. All of a sudden, the student movement had its own broadcasting station, a very first for any student movement.*

Shen Tong did not stop there. In adjacent rooms, he set up mimeograph machines to print leaflets. He assigned his friends from the Olympic Institute to take charge of each area of the operations. There would be daily news broadcasts with content gathered by their own reporters. There would be speeches by important figures, which could be instantly duplicated on audio tapes. There would be newsletters as well. He had, in fact, established an independent media center for the movement.

As Shen Tong was finishing up this remarkable project, he saw students returning from the funeral. Looking at their faces, he realized that he had missed a great historical moment. It must have been an event that changed many people's opinions, emotions, and perhaps even lives. He could only imagine what the scene was like from the excited grapevine. Spotting a perfect fund-raising opportunity, the media center produced memorial buttons for sale. The money was badly needed to support the operation.[70]

On April 23, the day after the funeral, Liu Gang was walking through the campus looking for student leaders when he noticed the new broadcasting station at The Triangle. As usual, there was a big crowd and some people were making speeches. But the speakers no longer had to scream their lungs out. Rather, they stood on a makeshift platform and spoke into a microphone, which had a long wire connecting into Shen Tong's room. Just as he was passing by, Liu Gang caught a glimpse of a middle-aged man struggling onto the platform. So he paused to listen.

"My name is Chen Mingyuan. You can report me if you want!"

The man identified himself this way, referring to the presence of possible snitches. Even with the microphone in his hand, he was still practically screaming. An enthusiastic round of applause greeted the new speaker. The audience was not only cheering on the man for his courage but also reacting to the name. Like many students, Liu Gang had known this name for quite a while. Chen Mingyuan became famous during his youth by writing poems mimicking the style of Mao

---

*The station did broadcast over an FM frequency. But that was not well known. For most people, the "broadcast" simply meant the loudspeakers over the area.

Zedong. Unfortunately for him, he did it during the era of the Cultural Revolution. Therefore he was sent to jail for fabricating the Great Leader's work. In more recent years, Chen Mingyuan had established a reputation as a professor in Chinese literature and culture. Yet few students had ever seen him in person.

Chen Mingyuan obviously knew how to get his audience's attention. He proceeded to tell them that he was the man who had rushed out of the Great Hall of People to hug the kneeling students the day before. "It was a hug from China's conscience," he exclaimed, to more applause. He told the crowd how angry he had felt when Hu Yaobang's hearse was denied the opportunity of circling Tiananmen Square and how the news media was reporting the events unfairly. Then he lamented:

"Students, now the authorities' mouthpiece *People's Daily* is accusing you for instigation. I want to say that you are indeed instigating."

There were murmurs and boos from the crowd. But he continued on:

"But what is instigating? It is just like fanning. When a flame is dying off, you use a fan to fan it up again. Students, I want to thank you once again. Because you just have fanned up the dying flame of hope in my heart!"

Thundering cheers and applause erupted. But he wasn't done yet. Citing the example of an outspoken poet who was assassinated by the Nationalist government in years past, Chen Mingyuan declared:

"Wen Yiduo was killed by special agents right after he had made a speech here at Peking University. He was only forty-seven years old. I am already forty eight. When I stepped onto this campus today, I am prepared not to step out again!"

So on and on he went, delivering a rousing speech interrupted by repeated applause. Liu Gang was excited. He thought that this was a speech on par with Martin Luther King's *I Have a Dream*, although Chen Mingyuan did not possess the same kind of vocal chords and oratory skill. But he surely had more than made up for it with his raw emotions. At the end of his hour-long speech, Chen Mingyuan led the crowd into a frenzied chant:

"Give me liberty, or give me death!"

radical speech

"Long live democracy!"

"Long live freedom!"

"Long live the students!"

Feng Congde was upstairs at the makeshift media center. He could see tears on many faces down below. He immediately arranged to have several hundred audio tapes of the speech made. These tapes, and their subsequent copies, traveled through the country and inspired many students to join the movement.[71]

IN the years he spent in Beijing, Liu Gang had witnessed, participated in, and led more than his share of student movements. Looking back, he found the common thread unsettling. The movements came and went quickly, like a summer storm, with scant achievements to show for it. While students were fond at shouting noble slogans for democracy, most of them participated in the movements just to release their youthful tensions. Protests and marches, after all, were also perfect excuses to skip classes and final exams. As was often the case, a movement could lose its steam just as quickly as it had gained it.

Therefore, for a long time, Liu Gang had been dreaming of an extended and sustainable movement that could achieve some limited but concrete goals. He intended that his Democracy Salon could provide such a platform. He was happy to see some young members of the Salon playing critical roles in the Preparatory Committee at Peking University. Yet it had also become obvious that the current movement was far beyond the confines of a single campus. The University of Political Science and Law had taken the lead in marching into Tiananmen Square after Hu Yaobang's death. Wuer Kaixi, hailing from the relatively unknown Beijing Normal University, had clearly distinguished himself in organizing and leading the protests so far.

The organizational success in attending Hu Yaobang's funeral, involving hundreds of thousands students from dozens of college campuses, both emboldened and worried Liu Gang. More than ever, he felt the urgency in having a city-wide student organization he had talked to Wuer Kaixi about. That was why he was at Peking University this morning, looking for people who were willing to stand up and lead the movement.

Standoff At Tiananmen

Just a couple of hours earlier, Liu Gang was at Beijing Normal University talking to Wuer Kaixi who was busy making his own dormitory room into a headquarters for his phantom Beijing Provisional Student Union. The two of them agreed to hold a meeting that evening with student leaders they had gotten to know from various schools. Liu Gang told Wuer Kaixi to be prepared to chair the meeting as he headed out to search for other attendees.

While he was happy that Wuer Kaixi was ready to lead, Liu Gang had his reservations. He was not convinced that the twenty-one year old sophomore had the mind to match his heart. He was also worried about Wuer Kaixi's obvious charisma. The last thing Liu Gang wanted was for a single individual to dominate a new organization. If Liu Gang had his way, he would prefer a more mature character, preferably a young teacher or a graduate student. He had several candidates in mind: people like Chen Xiaoping, Li Jinjin, or Wu Renhua.

As he was walking through the campus of Peking University, Liu Gang realized he had another dilemma at hand. His alma mater had traditionally been the leader of all major student movements. It was also the school that could produce the most resources both in leadership and personnel as evidenced in the Democracy Salon and the new media center at The Triangle. Yet he was worried about the potential negative impact should a single school dominate all other campuses.

Liu Gang knew his concern was not entirely unfounded as soon as he encountered Wang Dan in his dormitory room. There were a dozen or so student leaders crammed inside having a meeting of their own Preparatory Committee. A couple of reporters from Hong Kong and Taiwan were also present, casting a glorious glow on the young faces. They did not seem particularly interested in Liu Gang's idea of a city-wide organization. Liu Gang left the room disappointed.[72]

He spent the rest of the day shuttling among various campuses, notifying student leaders of the meeting as he went. He did not have much luck in locating his leadership candidates either. The only person he was able to find was Wu Renhua at the University of Political Science and Law. Wu Renhua was supportive of Liu Gang's efforts but he had to decline the invitation. This was, and should be, a student movement, Wu Renhua reasoned. It would not be wise for a teacher like himself to get directly involved.[73]

B Y the time Liu Gang got back to Yuanmingyuan that evening, many students had already gathered around its southern gate. There was a strong feeling of clandestineness in the air. People were meandering in the twilight in small groups. They could not ascertain whether the next group was their fellow comrades or undercover agents. Liu Gang calmly led the crowd inside to a small conference room. He arranged a couple of students to stand guard. Only students with proper identification cards could be allowed in.

At seven o'clock, Liu Gang closed the door. There were about sixty students inside. They signed in with their names, school affiliations, and contact information. Once again, the University of Political Science and Law demonstrated its strength in this movement by having eight students present, more than any other school. Zhou Yongjun, one of the three who had knelt down at the Great Hall of People, and Pu Zhiqiang, who had a very emotional reaction to that scene, were among them. In contrast, only two people came from Peking University. One was Liu Gang's classmate and the other was an early leader who had just been expelled from the school's Preparatory Committee in an internal power struggle. Neither of them could realistically represent their school. This was not uncommon, however, as most of the delegates came from connections with Liu Gang himself. There had not been a proper selection process at any school.

Yet one way or another, more than twenty colleges were present. Although a couple major universities were missing, the list was sufficient for such a hastily called meeting. As the attendees wondered aloud what all this was about, Liu Gang started calmly: "I am Liu Gang. I believe most of you know about me already. For the sake of time, I will not talk too much about myself." In fact, he did not intend to draw attention to himself. His non-student status and past records could complicate things or even scare many away. He assured everyone that the place was safe and laid out his thoughts on establishing a formal inter-campus organization to coordinate and lead the current student movement. Since he was not a student, he volunteered that he would serve only as a facilitator. With that, he turned the meeting over to Wuer Kaixi, another face that was easily recognized by most in the room.

Wuer Kaixi was prepared. In a no-nonsense style, he announced that the meeting should be short. They needed to decide on a name and a charter for the organization and elect provisional leadership. That would be all.

For the name, Wuer Kaixi proposed "Beijing Students Autonomous Provisional Federation." He stressed that it was critically important to keep their movement "pure." Only students could be allowed in the organization and the movement so that they would not give the government any excuse to accuse the student movement of being used by conspirators. Hearing that, many eyes turned to Liu Gang, the only non-student in the room.

Liu Gang appreciated the irony. He also understood that it was likely the consensus of the room even though he thought it naive. The government, after all, could level that charge no matter what the students did. Nevertheless, he thought the name was weak and proposed an alternative "Youth Solidarity Union." He explained that the movement needed to create a snowball effect to involve all forces of the society. Their goal should be democracy and freedom, instead of mere self-governance for students.

Showing early signs of his leadership style, Wuer Kaixi was already impatient with the discussion. If there were no other options, he declared, let's vote on the two names. In a show of hands, Wuer Kaixi's choice easily prevailed. The delegates were not ready to embrace Liu Gang's vision.

Moving on quickly, Wuer Kaixi came up with a charter for the organization he had drafted earlier. For the most part, it borrowed verbiage from similar but officially recognized organizations. For the leadership structure, Wuer Kaixi proposed a standing committee of five individuals, one of whom would be the president.

Liu Gang did not like the plan and he could not help but inject some of his thoughts. It would be best not to have individuals responsible for the organization, he said. They would become easy targets for the government to control and punish. Since none of the delegates in presence had been properly elected or authorized by their respective schools, they would lack legitimacy if they were elected as officers. Rather, Liu Gang suggested, the standing committee should consist of schools instead of individuals. Each school could replace its representatives by its own democratic means without interrupting the organization. Furthermore, the office of presidency should be rotated among the schools in the standing committee on a weekly basis. Liu Gang hoped that, in this way, he could protect both the organization from being dominated by certain individuals and the individuals from overexposing themselves. On both accounts, he had Wuer Kaixi in mind.

Although a non-student, Liu Gang's calm demeanor and rational approach ensured his voice was heard. His proposals were adopted by consent. The election for the standing committee was then commenced. Naturally, the five biggest and most vocal schools in the movement, Peking University, Tsinghua University, People's University, Beijing Normal University, and the University of Political Science and Law were elected into the standing committee. Representatives from smaller colleges were not entirely satisfied. They pushed to expand the standing committee to be more inclusive, and two seats were added. One went to the Central College of Ethnic Minorities in a form of "affirmative action." The other went to Beijing Film Academy, representing smaller art colleges in the capital.

Although the standing committee was supposed to be for schools, the election of its first president focused unmistakably on the individuals. As expected, Beijing Normal University nominated Wuer Kaixi. Having failed to attract young teachers and graduate students to the meeting, Liu Gang now turned his attention to Pu Zhiqiang from the University of Political Science and Law who appeared to be more mature at the meeting. But Pu Zhiqiang declined in a sincere belief that he lacked leadership skills. Instead, his school nominated Zhou Yongjun, whom Liu Gang endorsed.

The two candidates each gave a brief speech. With another show of hands, Zhou Yongjun narrowly beat out Wuer Kaixi, helped by the fact that his school had the largest delegation present.[74] Secretly, Liu Gang felt a sense of relief. His worry about Wuer Kaixi's personality had been growing. Should Wuer Kaixi be elected the president, he suspected, the rotation of the presidency might not happen at all.

Wuer kaixi would be a dictator...

Standoff At Tiananmen

Liu Gang was still concerned with the lack of mature leadership. He proposed to have an advisory board consisting of prominent intellectuals. This time, he met fierce resistance. Wuer Kaixi was adamant in keeping the movement as pure as possible. Any involvement from non-students were not going to be welcomed. It was a strong sentiment echoed by most in the room. Liu Gang barely got permission to seek advice in polishing up the language of their charter.

It was getting late. Guards posted by Liu Gang frequently came inside to report that more and more unidentified people were showing up on the premises. It was time to leave. Like spies in a movie, they nervously dispersed in small groups. Many took random detours before returning to their campuses.

Liu Gang was in no mood to rest. He set out to visit his contacts among prominent intellectuals on the same night. Chen Ziming was quick to offer financial support which Liu Gang declined. He was not ready to get Chen Ziming and his independent Institute involved especially after the heated debate on the "purity" of the student movement. Instead, Liu Gang used his own savings to purchase a mimeograph machine and a few bullhorns for the new organization.[75]

At Professor Fang Lizhi's residence, Liu Gang could not contain his enthusiasm. He almost recited Chen Mingyuan's speech from memory and urged Fang Lizhi to make a similar public stand. Fang Lizhi, though, was far less interested. He felt that Chen Mingyuan might be going too far and warned Liu Gang not to act in the same aggressive manner.

MONDAY, April 24, was the first school day after Hu Yaobang's funeral. In all major campuses in the capital, no students were going to classes. The first large-scale class boycott of the movement was underway. At Peking University, the budding Preparatory Committee continued to suffer growing pains. Amid internal rifts and tension between Wang Dan's Democracy Salon and Shen Tong's Olympic Institute, they called a public meeting of all students to formally abolish the official student union and establish their own Student Solidarity. Some eight thousand students assembled in an outdoor athletic field fittingly named after the May Fourth Movement. The number easily

The Autonomous Federation

surpassed the requirement of a legal quorum. It was a gorgeous spring afternoon. Members of the Preparatory Committee stood on the stage, basking in this historical setting. Wang Dan, Feng Congde and others made speeches. But the glory did not last long. More and more people demanded the right to speak and a fight over the control of the microphone broke out. In the heat of the moment, one student leader grabbed the microphone and accused another of being a mole. The scene stunned the audience. Li Jinjin rushed onto the stage to appeal for calm. But it was too little and too late. Disgusted, the student body walked out of the meeting and left the Preparatory Committee on the stage alone and dejected.[76]

When the news of disaster at Peking University reached Beijing Normal University, students there had just finished their own election of an independent union. Naturally, the charismatic Wuer Kaixi was chosen as its president. Alerted by what happened at Peking University, the new leadership there made a conscious decision that they could not afford any appearance of an internal dispute or split. So they vowed to maintain a unified leadership under Wuer Kaixi, practically making him a dictator at his school.

It was on April 25 when the organization Liu Gang created, which came to be known as Beijing Students Autonomous Federation, held its first general meeting. This meeting was much better attended than the clandestine one at Yuanmingyuan. Most schools had by now formally selected their representatives. Wang Dan showed up to represent Peking University, which seemed to enhance the legitimacy of the meeting.

Some flavors of clandestineness persisted. Zhou Yongjun had chosen a big classroom at the corner of the top floor of a big building in his school. It was accessible only through a narrow stairway. There, each attendee was subjected to a strict identification card check. Everyone looked extremely nervous. No sooner had the meeting gotten underway than someone raised an objection to the location. The narrow stairway, while perfect for limiting access, could also become a trap should the authorities move in on them. All the delegates immediately hustled to a different room. They posted sentries outside the building. They assigned delegates to different exit points. If there were signs of

97

the authorities, they should quickly scatter into other classrooms and pretend to be studying.[77]

With the security matter out of the way, the meeting proceeded to its agenda. The smaller room was packed. People were sitting on desks and standing along the blackboard. The main agenda item was a proposal for a demonstration march on April 27 designed as a grand gesture to announce the birth of this new organization. The representatives were lukewarm about the idea. Many of their constituents were still recovering from the emotional and physical exhaustion from the overnight march to Hu Yaobang's funeral. There might not be enough enthusiasm for another march without a real purpose.

The meeting went on into late afternoon. Word came that there would be a very important news broadcast that evening. So, at six o'clock, they paused to listen. A solemn voice came on to read a *People's Daily* editorial to be published in the papers next morning:

4.25
社论
社论

> An extremely small number of people with ulterior motives continued to use the young students..., to fabricate rumors..., to vilify and attack the Party and government leaders. Blatantly violating the Constitution, they called for opposition to the leadership of the Communist Party and the socialist system... They established illegal organizations to seize power from student unions, and even took over broadcast stations. In some colleges, they incited students and teachers to go on strike, and even stop classmates from attending classes by force... They distribute reactionary leaflets, establish connections, and attempt to create even greater incidents.
>
> They wave the flags for democracy but undermine the democratic legal system. Their purpose is to sow dissension among the people, plunge the whole country into chaos and sabotage the political situation of stability and unity. This is a planned conspiracy. It is turmoil. Its essence is to, once and for all, denounce the leadership of the Chinese Communist Party and the socialist system. This is a serious political struggle confronting the whole Party and the people throughout the country.
>
> The whole party and the people nationwide should fully understand the seriousness of this struggle, unite to take a clear-cut stand to oppose the disturbance, and firmly preserve the hard-

earned situation of political stability and unity, the Constitution, socialist democracy, and the legal system. Under no circumstances should the establishment of any illegal organizations be allowed. It is imperative to firmly stop any acts that use any excuse to infringe upon the rights and interests of legitimate organizations of students. Those who have deliberately fabricated rumors and framed others should be investigated to determine their criminal liabilities according to law. Bans should be placed on unlawful marches and demonstrations and on such acts as going to factories, rural areas, and schools to link up.*

All comrades in the Party and the people throughout the country must soberly recognize the fact that our country will have no peaceful days if this disturbance is not checked resolutely. This struggle concerns the success or failure of the reform, the program of the "Four Modernizations," and the future of our government and nation...[78]

Student delegates looked at each other in shocked disbelief. Nobody wanted to break the silence that had grasped the room.

---

*"Link up" was a special term made popular during the Cultural Revolution, meaning people bypass official channels to communicate across boundaries of their working "units." It was generally regarded as an act of conspiracy.

But we marched on. We broke through every police barrier peacefully.

Wuer Kaixi

6

The Demonstration

ON April 23, the day after the funeral, General Secretary Zhao Ziyang inexplicably left the country in the midst of student demonstrations. He went on with a scheduled state visit to North Korea and left Premier Li Peng in charge of the affairs. It was Deng Xiaoping himself, however, who lost patience with this new generation of students, beneficiaries of his great reform. "This is no ordinary student movement," deplored the eighty-four year old, "this is turmoil." Thus was born the *People's Daily* editorial broadcast on the evening of April 25 and headlined in all major newspapers next morning, April 26. The editorial was written based on Deng Xiaoping's extended speeches. In North Korea, Zhao Ziyang signed off the final version in agreement.

In his speech, Deng Xiaoping emphasized two dangerous parallels in the ongoing student movement: Cultural Revolution and Polish Solidarity. Indeed, much of the language used in the *People's Daily* editorial was the same used to describe the turmoil of the Cultural Revolution. The growing influence of Solidarity in Poland had also alarmed Deng Xiaoping for a long time. He believed that the Polish Communist Party had been too soft with their struggle and would pay a hefty price for their appeasement toward the Solidarity movement. He was not going to allow a similar movement in China. He certainly had no appetite for a repeat of the Cultural Revolution either.

The silence at the Beijing Students Autonomous Federation meeting was finally broken. Wuer Kaixi was beyond furious. If students had been tired and disinterested in a new protest march, they certainly needed to wake up now! He urged the delegates to launch the biggest demonstration ever. But others were less certain. The *People's Daily* editorial was more than a signal to them. It could be a death sentence if they continued their defiance. In the history of the People's Republic, nobody had ever openly challenged any *People's Daily* editorials, the mouthpiece of the Party itself, in an organized manner. For the young students in the room, it was a scenario they had never dreamed to find themselves in. The debate was fierce and a decision was hard to come by. Finally, the march was put up for a vote. With each school casting one vote, it passed by a healthy margin of twenty-five to fifteen.[79]

Liu Gang did not have a vote. He had argued against the demonstration. Such a direct confrontation with the government was too dangerous and unwise for this organization still in its infancy. He thought that students should remain on their campuses and strengthen their independent unions which might have a chance to survive the movement itself. With the decision made, however, Liu Gang could only provide a little cautionary advice. He suggested that, when the march encountered police, students should simply sit down on the streets as a sit-in. They should avoid the pushing and shoving game of the past. Ma Shaofang, now a representative from his Beijing Film Academy, suggested that they add a few slogans to show their positive attitudes such as a cunning "Support the Correct Leadership of the Chinese Communist Party," with the operative word being "correct." These measures were readily adopted by the meeting.

In the morning of April 26, as the *People's Daily* editorial was read around the nation, Beijing Students Autonomous Federation held its very first press conference at the University of Political Science and Law. The seven standing committee members stood on the stairs of a main classroom building surrounded by student picket lines. There were not many reporters, most of whom were foreigners. As the president, Zhou Yongjun announced the founding of his organization and its missions along with the plan for their demonstration next day. The purpose of the march, he declared, was to show that the students' Seven-Point Petition was not a cause of turmoil. Wang Dan answered most of the questions. It was his first appearance at such a public scene. Yet he was calm and collected. He spoke slowly, clearly, and to the point. It was an impressive performance.

The response was quick and swift. Within hours, the city government of Beijing made its own announcement. It reiterated the Beijing Ten-Points regulation on demonstration installed in December of 1986 and proclaimed the students' planned march illegal. It called on all school teachers and administrators to do everything they could to prevent the demonstration from materializing. In the Great Hall of People, a conference of all levels of the Party apparatus in the city was held to mobilize the effort.

Rumors also started flying throughout the day. A man claiming to be the grandson of a high-up government official found Ma Shaofang at his campus in the afternoon. He had disturbing news. His grandfather had learned that the government had already decided to stop any demonstration at any cost, including the use of violence. Ma Shaofang was shocked. It was the first time the thought of bloodshed crossed his mind. He hurried to the University of Political Science and Law to look for Zhou Yongjun.

He found Zhou Yongjun in an office surrounded by several teachers. Ma Shaofang did not think twice. He burst into the room to tell Zhou Yongjun that they must convene an emergency standing committee meeting to call off the march. Calmly, Zhou Yongjun replied that it would not have the authority to overturn the decision which was made by the general meeting of representatives. Ma Shaofang insisted. His words got the attention of the teachers in the room. They were more than eager to help and quickly arranged a school van for Ma Shaofang to gather up standing committee members for a meeting. It was only after he left the room that Ma Shaofang realized that Zhou Yongjun was already in trouble.

Naturally, Ma Shaofang headed to Beijing Normal University for *efforts to cancel the March on 4/27*

Wuer Kaixi first. The latter was nowhere to be found. Just like Zhou Yongjun, Wuer Kaixi had already been confined to his school. Ma Shaofang found more trouble. After picking up a representative from People's University, they headed to the Central College of Ethnic Minorities and learned that its representative had already resigned. Next, they went to Tsinghua University and discovered a bigger mess. Just the day before, a few government officials had come to Tsinghua for a dialogue "per the invitations of the Tsinghua students." Embarrassed for being chosen in a divide-and-conquer strategy, Tsinghua students rebuffed the officials. Their newly elected leaders of the independent union resigned altogether to proclaim their innocence in this matter.

It was now almost nine o'clock. Ma Shaofang was running out of time. They hustled to Peking University where they were told that its Preparatory Committee was going to have a meeting at eleven. So they waited and discussed their options. There were only four of them at the time, barely over half of the standing committee. There was not enough time for them to have a formal meeting with the Peking University's representative. Even if they did decide to cancel the march, it was perhaps no longer possible to inform all the colleges involved. Finally, Ma Shaofang came to realize that there was little they could do despite the horrible scenes playing in his head. Should they cancel the march but fail to inform some of the small colleges, those students might end up facing much greater danger. So he persuaded the others not to cancel the march but emphasized the precautionary measures they had already agreed upon. They should have more slogans supporting the Party leadership and the socialist system. They should have stronger student marshal forces to maintain order. They should never confront the police or army when they encountered them.

The Peking University Preparatory Committee members did finally show up at eleven o'clock. Wang Dan stepped out to meet Ma Shaofang's group. After exchanging information, Wang Dan agreed with Ma Shaofang's assessment and decision. In the darkness, the two of them shook hands with heavy hearts.

That same night, in countless dormitory rooms throughout the northwest suburb, hundreds of students wrote down their wills for the first time in their young lives. These were heart-felt farewell letters to their parents as they had no material properties to settle.

THE next morning, an anxious Ma Shaofang went over to People's University to observe how the march was coming together. Before he even reached that campus, he heard loudspeakers announcing that the planned demonstration had been canceled by Beijing Students Autonomous Federation. At the front gate, a few hundred students were still gathering together with flags and banners. They were as confused as he was.

People's University was located a few blocks south of Peking and Tsinghua universities, on the way downtown. The plan was for students at People's University to wait for and join in the contingent when they came down the street. Now they were not sure if anyone would ever come. Many impatient students got on the roofs to watch northward. They only saw empty streets.

It was about midnight the night before, just after Ma Shaofang and Wang Dan reached their decision to keep on with the march, that Zhou Yongjun finally cracked under intense pressure of a day-long isolated persuasion. At the end, he simply had no answer to the question, repeatedly asked by his handlers, "would you be willing to be personally responsible for the safety of thousands of students?" At about the same time, Wuer Kaixi also capitulated under a similar circumstance. A hand-written message was rushed from Beijing Normal University to the University of Political Science and Law. On it, Wuer Kaixi suggested that Zhou Yongjun cancel the march.

Zhou Yongjun was still grabbing for his last straw. He insisted that he had no authority to overturn a decision made by Beijing Students Autonomous Federation. His handlers were not interested in technicalities. "Just write a message," they demanded. Zhou Yongjun relented. He wrote up a simple sentence canceling the march, signed his own name, and stamped with the official seal of the organization which had been hastily made during that same day. What he did not know was that his action immediately set off an operation of military efficiency. Phone calls were made to the city government which in turn notified all colleges to be on standby and assist a certain vehicle with an urgent message. Therefore, student leaders in all campuses were able to receive Zhou Yongjun's decree before daybreak. Wuer Kaixi was even chauffeured to Peking University to tell leaders there that everything would be fine as long as they remained inside the campus.[80]

The big iron gate at the southern entrance of Peking University was once again shut down. Guards were diligently checking everyone's identification card before allowing them to pass through a side door. Loudspeakers mounted on surrounding buildings were repeating stern warnings for marching out of the campus.

At The Triangle, Shen Tong's own loudspeakers countered with a repeated reading of their Seven-Point Petition. Slowly, a few hundred students lined up in formation to march toward the gate. Wang Dan and Shen Tong were at the front, each with a megaphone on hand. A giant red flag followed right behind them, on which were four big, black characters: Peking University. Two white banners flanked the red flag on each side. They read "Support the Correct Leadership of the Chinese Communist Party" and "Support the Socialism," respectively.

They walked slowly toward the south gate, hoping to pick up more students along the way. But it was still a small contingent of a couple thousand when they slowly exited the campus through the side door. It was a quarter to nine in the morning. The tentative march halted as soon as it was out of the gate. Wang Dan and Shen Tong found their route blocked by a human barrier. But it was not the police or soldiers as they had expected. It was a thick line of reporters aiming their cameras right in their faces. They also heard loud applause and cheers erupting behind the reporters. People were getting on their bicycles and fanning out. They shouted excitedly that "Peking University has come out!" "Peking University has come out!"

Only Wang Dan, Shen Tong, and a handful of their Preparatory Committee members knew that this march of theirs was supposed to be only a symbolic one.

PEKING University's Preparatory Committee had adopted a relatively independent stance in regard to Beijing Students Autonomous Federation. From the very beginning, they had doubts about that organization's legitimacy. During an earlier meeting of their own, Wang Dan and Feng Congde voted for the demonstration. But the other three standing committee members including Shen Tong voted against it. On his own initiative, Shen Tong had reached an initial agreement with the school authority. If students did not march out of the campus, they could start a formal dialogue with the school president. Shen Tong saw it as a prelude for bigger things and thought it a worthwhile bargain. Based on the vote, a decision not to participate in the march was adopted.[81]

Feng Congde, on the other hand, was very concerned about this decision. He sensed that students, fueled by the *People's Daily* editorial, would probably march out one way or another. If the leaders chose to stand in the way, they would simply lose whatever credibility they possessed. So he engineered a general meeting of department representatives and overturned the standing committee's decision by a majority vote. That was how Wang Dan was able to readily agree with Ma Shaofang to persist with the march.

Zhou Yongjun's cancellation message and Wuer Kaixi's personal visit before dawn had much less of an impact at Peking University than on other campuses. If anything, the leaders here saw an opportunity to demonstrate their own independence from Beijing Students Autonomous Federation. But now they were keenly aware that, if they did indeed march, they could be alone in the city, which was not a promising prospect. Shen Tong once again pushed for a more conservative approach. After much discussion, they reached a compromise for a symbolic march of only a few miles. As soon as they reached the Third Ring Road, just before entering the city, they would turn back. As long as they had marched outside of the campus, they figured, they would already have fulfilled the purpose of challenging the *People's Daily* editorial.

Even with that decision made, Shen Tong was nevertheless worried that Wang Dan and Feng Congde could get carried away during the march. They made Wang Dan promise that he would not deviate from this plan no matter what happened and asked Feng Congde to remain on campus for logistical support, effectively taking him out of the scene. Feng Congde, ever the team player, agreed without a second thought.[82]

The Demonstration

SOON after exiting their campus, the Peking University march found a similarly sized troop from Tsinghua University catching up on them. Joining together, they headed south toward People's University. It was right then that they spotted the very first police line. There were only a few hundred unarmed policemen blocking the way with their arms linked tightly together. As planned, the students stopped and sat down on the road. The student leaders at the forefront engaged the police in a heated but civil negotiation for ten minutes. Neither side was yielding.

This time it was the spectators who lost their patience first. Surrounding the student formation, these young city residents also outnumbered the meager police line. Taking matters into their own hands, they rushed forward and inserted themselves between the students and police. With a thunderous chant, "Get Away! Get Away," they surged forward. The police line was no match for such forces and gave way easily.

Students marched on. Their numbers started to swell. More and more students were rushing out of both Peking and Tsinghua universities to catch up with the march. Student marshals linked up their arms on the side in haste, both to keep their troop in formation and to prevent the excited residents from mixing into their rank. Although they had joined into the protest by clearing the way for the march, residents were still not accepted by the students. The "purity" of the movement was too important to give up.

Students at People's University had received the news from messengers on bicycles minutes after Peking University students exited their campus. The exciting news spread across the campus and a march formation was quickly formed at their front gate. As students on the roof spotted the approaching flags, they decided not to wait. Instead, they marched out and headed south on their own, ahead of the thousands from Peking and Tsinghua universities. No longer at the forefront of the march, Shen Tong found himself the only person still thinking about turning around. He knew that their compromise had been hopelessly lost. He marched on, alongside of Wang Dan, toward downtown. Far ahead of them, the red flags of People's University were leading the way.[83]

When the news of Peking University coming out of its campus

reached the University of Political Science and Law, students there were having a standoff of their own. They were not facing police either. A row of old professors led by the school president lined across the gate and begged for students not to proceed with their march. With tears running down his face, the school president repeated hopelessly, "If you go out today, there will be bloodshed. I will be personally culpable to you, to our school, and to your parents."

His plea was falling on deaf ears. Almost in his face was a huge banner held up high by a few students. It declared, "Defend the Honor of the Constitution to Death!" The character "death" was overlaid with red ink as if blood was dripping from it. With their adrenaline boiling, it was easy for the students to brush aside the sincere advice from their president and professors.

As they marched out, a gigantic wooden board, carried by a dozen people, elegantly glided in the middle of the formation. On it, printed in neat calligraphy, were some of the most significant articles from the Constitution of the People's Republic of China pertaining to the rights of citizens to free expression and assembly.[84] The board was the handy work of Chen Xiaoping and Wu Renhua with monetary support from Chen Ziming. Chen Ziming and Wang Juntao had also spent the previous day on campus. They reviewed slogans and plans for the march behind the scenes.

Pu Zhiqiang, who at six feet and three inches was taller than most, was waving the school flag at the forefront of the formation. He noticed that students in the nearby College of Posts and Telecommunications were still confined within its campus. He led the march in a detour over to that campus and drew in more students with the momentum of his troops. Soon, they found the contingent from the College of Aviation merging into their formation. They headed toward Beijing Normal University.

At Beijing College of Chinese Medicine, students were particularly angry that their school had just been singled out by *People's Daily*, which praised them as the only college in the city not boycotting classes. With their campus gates locked, students scaled the walls to join the march.[85]

Over thirty colleges of various sizes covered in a wide area of the northwestern suburb of Beijing. In many smaller colleges, students were more confused than ever. Their only news came from runners on bicycles who were crisscrossing the area with different and often conflicting reports of what was happening. Without strong organizations, these students chose to sit along streets and wait. They were more than ready to join in as soon as any marching troops arrived nearby. This same scene repeated again and again in many intersections, like numerous streams merging into a roaring river. A flash flood was fast developing.

At Xizhimen intersection, or Gate of Straight West, on the northwest corner of the Second Ring Road, two main rivers of students merged. Students led by Peking, Tshinghua, and People's universities from the west met up with those led by the University of Political Science and Law and Beijing Normal University from the east. Expressions of joy appeared on students' faces for the first time as they spotted friends all around. As they proceeded along the perimeter of the city, they had become much better organized. Banners and flags indicated each school in succession. The main troop marched in the middle of the street in a formation of about a dozen people across. Each block of the formation was led by a couple of students with whistles and megaphones. They repeatedly led their block in shouting slogans in unison. On each side was a picket line, linking hand in hand, to make sure nobody could get into the formation. As the procession advanced in a random pattern of stop and go, the students on the picket lines had to alternate in standing still and running like crazy to keep their lines from breaking up. When it did, however, students in the march immediately stepped in to fill the gap.

There were also occasional non-students in the march. At the front of the Tsinghua University block, several old professors marched with a particular display of dignity. Their silver hair danced in the sunshine as they proudly held up a sign: "[We have been] kneeling for too long, [now we] stand up and walk a little." The sign was referring both to the students' kneeling petition and the sufferings these professors had endured under the decades of communist rule.

There were many police barriers along the way. At each major intersection, police forces, still unarmed, stubbornly stood across the street. They linked their arms together in extremely tight formation, sometimes as deep as a dozen rows. To spectators, this looked familiar. In many movies and television broadcasts of the people's army rushing to help in flood disasters, they had seen soldiers jumping into surging water and linking their arms in the same way to block the torrent with their bodies so that breached dams could be repaired behind them. On this day, however, they were facing a flood of a different kind.

As students marched on, they were able to talk police lines into relenting on some occasions. At other places, they sat down and rested. City residents, who had been following along the students, swirled in. From all sides, they pushed and shoved police lines into oblivion. The police did not put up a serious fight either. As their lines were broken up, many smiled with a sense of relief. Some saluted the students as they streamed by. Others flashed V-for-victory signs discreetly. Just like that, the march pushed through six major blockades to reach the main boulevard ringing the city, the Second Ring Road. It had been a glorious, non-violent day for everybody.

T HE Chinese phrase "You Xing" was used for either a protest march or a celebration parade depending on its context. For generations who grew up in communist China, this was a very familiar activity. In the heyday of the Cultural Revolution, large-scale "You Xing" became a frequent affair, held all over the country whenever the central government felt the need to celebrate the publication of a new quotation from Mao Zedong or to protest against "bad elements" both international and domestic. As such, a "You Xing" could be organized and staged within the matter of minutes, typically with flags, banners, slogans, drums, firecrackers, cymbals, and gongs. For kids, "Let's go You Xing" was one of the most exciting rallying cries.

As the students turned the corner at the northwest of the city onto the Second Ring Road, their "You Xing" transformed from a protest march into a celebration parade completely. On the night before, with rumors of a military crackdown stirring, hundreds of them had written up their wills in anticipation of bloodshed. When they marched out of their campuses, ignoring teary pleas from their professors and even parents, they were solemn, apprehensive, but determined. All that anxiety, however, evaporated as soon as they saw what was ahead of them.

Residents of Beijing had come out in millions. They lined sidewalks and crowded onto overpasses. They were out there with their own banners, shouting their own slogans, laughing and cheering as if they were welcoming a liberating army. As students passed under the overpasses, loaves of bread, bottles of water, and packets of popsicles rained down on them. At one intersection, the text of a giant billboard advertising traffic safety was altered to wish the students "get back home safely." By now, the student procession had stretched over six miles in length. It was a steady current that seemed to have no end.

Residents were also rewarded by the presence of a myriad of new banners in the march which addressed issues closer to home: inflation, graft, corruption, bureaucracy, etc. Students were no longer just making abstract and empty cries for freedom and democracy. They were, as it seemed to residents, voicing the concerns of common people.

It was at Chang'an Avenue when the advancing students caught sight of regular army troops. Military trucks could be seen along the wide boulevard, carrying soldiers toward Tiananmen Square.[86] Some of the soldiers were carrying automatic assault rifles. On the street itself, unarmed soldiers were forming ever bigger human barriers just as the policemen had tried before. Students were no longer afraid. They had come to realize that, on this day, nothing could stop them. They were also aware that the possibility of a violent confrontation had already diminished.

The march slowed down and finally came to a halt in front of a wall of soldiers. The number of soldiers here was so overwhelming that the students were not sure if they could push through this time. Yet they saw the faces in front of them and knew the young soldiers were much more anxious and afraid than they were. Happily and mischievously, students sang familiar army songs and shouted "The People Love the Army! The Army Loves the People!"

Around them, spectators were in action again. They slammed their fists onto traffic signs, fences, and anything that could make noise and launched into a rhythmic chant: "Go Away! Go Away!" It was deafening. As the masses converged into the soldiers from all directions, the human barrier melted away.

Far ahead of the march, however, Tiananmen Square resembled a war zone. Thousands of soldiers had assembled there and appeared ready to defend this historic landmark from an invasion. Wreaths and flowers at the Monument to People's Heroes had been cleared after the funeral. There were no tourists or even residents. The air was tense as the students approached from the west. Soldiers and policemen flooded toward the north edge where they would make a last stand blocking the march into the Square.

The disciplined student marshals appeared first. They came in advance of the main troop and set up their own picket lines just in front of the wall of soldiers. With their guidance and under the intense stares of curious soldiers, the main troop of students marched on along Chang'an Avenue to the east. They marched past Tiananmen and bypassed the Square altogether, leaving the soldiers in a state of complete amazement and relief.

Just five short years earlier, during that National Day celebration in 1984, college students had paraded under Tiananmen waving the endearing "Hello Xiaoping" banner. As a high school student in Beijing, Shen Tong was dressed as a Taiwanese national and paraded in a dance formation for that celebration. This time around, Shen Tong and his fellow students were marching on their own. As they passed Tiananmen, the Gate of Heavenly Peace, its reviewing stand high above was ghostly empty. There were no leaders up there waving at them in larger-than-life poses.

It was already getting dark when they reached the Jianguomen intersection east of Tiananmen, Wang Dan ran up the overpass himself to get a full view of his troops. In the twilight, it was a scene that would be burnt into his memory for the rest of his life. From Jianguomen, the Gate of Founding the Nation, the entire Chang'an Avenue extended into the far horizon. For as far as he could see, the boulevard was filled with people. It was a sea of flags and banners. It was as joyous and glorious as anything his young mind could have ever imagined.

Jianguomen was the eastern end of Chang'an Avenue near the Beijing Railway Station. For the numerous "You Xing" organized by the

Unexpected Momentum

government, this was the assembling spot. Millions and millions of people had gathered here and either marched or paraded, in strict formations and with fancy floats, down Chang'an Avenue toward Tiananmen Square and beyond. Today, the new generation of students were marching in the opposite direction, literally, with nothing but their sincerity and enthusiasm.

And what a force this was. It took the entire student procession an hour and forty-five minutes to pass through Tiananmen Square. An estimated two hundred thousand marched with more than a million citizens cheering and supporting them.

At Jianguomen, they turned north. Following the Second Ring Road, they still had a long way to walk before they could get back to their campuses. As they continued, news and rumors were being passed around. In Shanghai, Mayor Jiang Zemin had shut down a popular newspaper *World Economic Herald.* The paper was guilty of publishing the proceedings of a symposium in which prominent intellectuals expressed sympathy to Hu Yaobang.[87] Its chief editor was dismissed. In the evening, as tired students trudged along the streets on their way home, they heard a surprising official broadcast from a State Council spokesman:

> We welcome the request of students to hold dialogues. Our Party and government have always advocated direct dialogues with the masses. But dialogues need to be done in suitable atmosphere and appropriately.

Taking it as a sign that the government had finally agreed to hold formal dialogues with them, students erupted into cheers all along the procession. "Victory!" "We won!" Tears of joy streamed down many cheeks.

It was close to midnight when students finally returned to the Peking University campus. The glorious and arousing *March of Volunteers* was blasting in loudspeakers to welcome their triumphant return. Feng Congde had spent this day alone on campus. He tidied up their media center and made sure that dining halls were prepared to provide late suppers. Showing his resourceful side, he also arranged school vans to go out and pick up those who could no longer walk back. These students had been on their feet for sixteen hours. They had covered close to thirty miles.

T HE morning after the greatest spontaneous demonstration ever seen in China was mixed with excitement and exhaustion. Most students slept in. When they finally woke up, they discovered that the small *China Women News* had broken ranks and reported their action in a positive tone. With its feminine perspective, the paper highlighted a banner in the march: "Mom, we are not Wrong!" expressing a cute facet of the students' feelings.

Shen Tong was witnessing the power of the media of his own. The broadcasts out of his dormitory room was drawing in all sorts of people who assumed that it was the center of the student leadership. Even the Preparatory Committee decided to hold its meetings there so that they could be close to all the action.

It was then Wang Dan saw a man in his seventies walking in gingerly. Like everybody else, he appeared to be looking for student leaders. But he did not say anything. Rather, he sat down himself and broke into an awful cry which persisted for a long time. Wang Dan and his committee members looked at each other and did not know what to do. The scene of an old man crying his heart out was not something these youngsters knew how to handle. When the old man eventually regained his composure, he told everyone that, many years ago, he had been a member of the communist underground in this very school. He had led student marches to protest against the then Nationalist government. This march by the new generation of students, he said, had awakened a feeling that he had not felt for decades. For the forty years under the rule of his own Communist Party, his feeling had been suppressed so hard that he did not even realize how depressed his life had been. Seeing the demonstration yesterday, he proclaimed, it was the first time in forty years, he felt happiness.[88]

Meanwhile, a new round of Big Posters covered the entire bulletin board downstairs at The Triangle. Students celebrated with essays and poems. Some drew detailed maps and retraced every step of this historical march. Others referred to the government's promise of a dialogue as the biggest capitulation by the authorities in the history of the People's Republic. Look at the masses on the streets of Beijing, they

114

proudly exclaimed, this could not possibly be the work of "a small clique of conspirators." The *People's Daily* editorial had been proved wrong. There was no turmoil. So, let the dialogue begin!

ONE and half years earlier, in his keynote speech to the Thirteenth Congress of the Chinese Communist Party, an optimistic and complacent General Secretary Zhao Ziyang declared that the Party would make its decisions and resolve any conflicts through "consultation and dialogue with the masses." He had not expected that it would be young students who would, in such a dramatic manner, call his bluff.

The delegates of Beijing Students Autonomous Federation met at the University of Political Science and Law again in the late afternoon. The success of the demonstration, despite the last-minute cancellation decree by its president, put them in an ultra-excited mood. Without much dispute, they summarily deposed Zhou Yongjun from the presidency for his ill-fated "unilateral decision." With a show of hands, the charismatic Wuer Kaixi was installed as the new president. It appeared that most delegates were not aware of the role Wuer Kaixi had played in the cancellation decision. Also lost in the quick shuffle was the fact that the presidency was intended to belong to a school, not an individual. The technicalities of the charter, designed by Liu Gang, could not stand the test of reality.

The dramatic eleventh hour maneuvering in the night before the demonstration also claimed another victim. Ma Shaofang resigned out of exhaustion and perhaps a degree of ambiguity for his own role. With another expansion of the Standing Committee, a graduate student from the Chinese Academy of Social Sciences joined in. Already thirty-seven year old, female, and married with an infant son, Wang Chaohua had a distinctly different appearance among the student leadership. She was raised within a family of intellectuals. Her father was a prominent professor of Chinese literature at Peking University.

Only a couple of days old, Beijing Students Autonomous Federation had already evolved into something with little resemblance of what Liu Gang had designed that night at Yuanmingyuan. Despite his wishes, it had become a committee of individuals, some of them with questionable dedications. Wang Dan seemed to be absent most of the

chaotic
organization

115

time. Wuer Kaixi was displaying a strong tendency to show off in front of reporters. He was far less interested in the mundane details of managing the organization. There were endless meetings without agendas. Representatives came and went as they pleased. No decision was ever made. If this new organization hoped to be successful, Wang Chaohua decided that they needed people who were willing to do the grunt work. So, she took her own initiative and went to Peking University to get Feng Congde involved and fill the void left by Wang Dan's absence. From a few brief encounters, Wang Chaohua had come to admire Feng Congde's ability and resourcefulness in making things happen behind the scenes.

That night, Wang Chaohua and Feng Congde attended yet another meeting with almost a hundred delegates. Wuer Kaixi opened the meeting but left immediately, claiming that he had an urgent private matter to attend to. He asked Wang Chaohua to chair the meeting. Wang Chaohua seized the opportunity. She introduced Feng Congde to the conference and set an agenda of her own. Following the great victory of their demonstration, she said, the focus for each school should be on democracy within its campus. At her invitation, Feng Congde gave a briefing on what Peking University was doing. At that campus, Feng Congde reported, efforts were underway on many levels to disband the official student unions following legal procedures defined within their existing charters. We could not be satisfied by mob democracy, he said. We had to do things by the rules.[89]

It turned out that Wuer Kaixi's private matter was actually quite public. Shortly after he left the meeting, he and Wang Dan showed up unexpectedly at the Shangri-La Hotel near downtown. There, facing blinding camera flashes and dozens of eager foreign reporters, the two of them answered questions about themselves and Beijing Students Autonomous Federation. Then, they declared that their lives were now in danger and they had to go into hiding. With that, the two disappeared into the night.[90]

Feng Congde, on the other hand, was extremely upset. At Peking University, one piece of wisdom the intellectual Chen Mingyuan had dispensed to the young leaders was to be careful about talking to reporters. Wei Jingsheng, he reminded them, was jailed largely for doing just that. The students were already aware of a different kind of danger as well. They knew that publicity could easily inflate the egos of some individuals. So, the Preparatory Committee at Peking University passed a rule that no leaders, unless designated as spokespersons, could talk to reporters. Beijing Students Autonomous Federation adopted a similar rule of their own. But in just a couple of days, that rule was already broken. Feng Congde knew that this would not be the last time.

Dialogue was of course on top of everyone's mind. They did not know how to proceed but to wait and see. And they did not have to wait long. On April 29, barely two days after the demonstration, a dialogue took place and caught everyone by surprise. It was hosted by Yuan Mu, Spokesman for the State Council, with several high ranking officials on his side. The invitations for students were distributed to official student unions in each school. These student unions, most of which were in the process of being impeached by their own constituents, were instructed to invite some "ordinary students" along with the officially appointed leaders. A few of them took bold initiatives to invite independent student leaders emerging from the movement. Guo Haifeng attended from Peking University. Wuer Kaixi, while still in hiding in his Beijing Normal University, also received an invitation. He appeared at the site of the dialogue but insisted that he would participate as a representative of Beijing Students Autonomous Federation. Failing to secure that recognition, he walked away.

The dialogue was broadcast live, a rare occurrence in China. But the proceedings were not what the students had hoped for. A seasoned bureaucrat, Yuan Mu dominated the meeting by opening with a lengthy party-line speech. Each student was then allowed to speak only once in the form of a question. Those from official unions timidly asked their soft and leading questions. Yuan Mu dished out predictable statements at ease. His frequent smirks betrayed a satisfaction that he was firmly in control. It was not so much a dialogue than a press conference.

Suddenly, a slim young man rose to break the dullness. He decried that this so-called dialogue was invalid. Rather, the government should have equal dialogues with the new autonomous organizations. Yuan Mu's smile disappeared. He tersely replied that those were illegal organizations and they would never be recognized by the government. But he did allow that future dialogues between the government and students could occur "in various forms, with various attendees, and at different levels." Before the young man could follow up, he was cut off as he had already used up his allocation. Disgusted, several students walked out of the room in protest. Most remembered the young man's name: Xiang Xiaoji, a graduate student from the University of Political Science and Law.

ON April 30, Peking University's graduate students achieved something that had never been done before. They followed the exact procedures specified by the official student union's charter and voted to disband the graduate student union in a general meeting. An elated Feng Congde briefed Beijing Students Autonomous Federation of this development right away. He was hoping more schools could follow the example.

Meanwhile, however, both the Federation and the Preparatory Committee in Peking University were in different states of crisis. Wang Dan and Wuer Kaixi did not take their own plans of hiding too seriously. They continued to stay in their respective campuses but moved around dormitories at nights. But they were not formally participating in the activities of the organizations either. With Wuer Kaixi's absence, the Federation elected Feng Congde to be their third president. The presidency was being rotated much faster than its charter specified.

Yuan Mu's statement that Beijing Students Autonomous Federation was illegal and would never be recognized by the government caused dreadful reactions. While defiant, delegates also felt that they could not become an obstacle in the effort to achieve a meaningful dialogue. They passed a resolution to organize a separate and independent Dialogue Delegation whose mission was to seek and conduct dialogues with the government. Maybe they could have better luck than the Federation itself.

Infighting continued to rage within the Preparatory Committee at Peking University stemming from personality conflicts. Members of its standing committee kept changing on a daily basis.[91] Shen Tong was feeling particularly low. He had been busy working with his media center which continued to grow.[92] They were doing regular broadcasts on loudspeakers every day from dawn to dusk. The mimeograph printing operation was churning out thousands of leaflets each day which were distributed in the many campuses in town. There were more than two hundred volunteers working on tasks of news gathering, editing, recording and printing. They were all crammed in a few tiny dormitory rooms on his floor. They even added a newspaper, named *News Herald*, edited by Zhang Boli from the "authors class".[93] Caught at the center of the storm, Shen Tong nonetheless felt that his efforts and achievements were taken for granted by the busy-work Preparatory Committee. He was not sure what role, if any, he could play in that committee. He was seriously contemplating a resignation.

The First of May was the International Workers' Day, a holiday celebrated in China. City streets and parks were decorated with flags and flowers. At Tiananmen Square, a subtle change in its festival display escaped the attention of many. The giant portraits of Karl Marx, Friedrich Engels, Vladimir Lenin, and Josef Stalin, the patron saints of communism, were no longer part of the exhibition as they had been in the past. The government explained that only Chinese heroes would be displayed from now on. The disappearance of these icons, however, was also a sign of the times.

On this day, Shen Tong left campus to procure a typewriter donated to his media center.* Upon his return he learned that the Preparatory Committee had had yet another reelection and he was no longer a member. He felt relieved at first. But that nice feeling did not last long. Soon he found out that he and Wang Dan had been tied for last place before he lost out during the runoff, most likely because he was not present in person. But he was never informed of the meeting in the first place! Feeling slighted, he went to Feng Congde to complain. Feng Congde calmed him down and told him not to worry about it much. He suggested that Shen Tong check out the new Dialogue Delegation. Shen Tong was intrigued.[94]

---

*In 1989, personal computers were not available to students. Chinese language typewriters were also very hard to come by. Almost all student newsletters and leaflets were handcrafted mimeographs and printed as handbills.

Standoff At Tiananmen

Shen Tong made up his mind after he attended a Beijing Students Autonomous Federation meeting with Feng Congde that night. The meeting, as usual, was chaotic and without any agenda. People were talking over each other but no serious discussion was held, never mind any decisions. Feng Congde was embarrassed when Shen Tong characterized the group as a bunch of amateurs. Shen Tong left determined more than ever to stay away from leadership bodies such as Beijing Students Autonomous Federation or the Preparatory Committee. If the new Dialogue Delegation wanted to have any success at all, he thought, it must be shielded off from the Federation. [95]

THE Federation, on the other hand, had its own ideas. On May 2, before the Dialogue Delegation was formed, the Federation compiled a lengthy list of dialogue conditions of its own. With fanfare, Wang Dan and Wang Chaohua delivered them to the government offices. It was a very ambitious and demanding petition, ranging from equality and delegate safety to the details of speakers' time limits. What's more, it demanded that the government respond within a day, by noon on May 3. Otherwise, it declared, students would launch a big demonstration a day later on the anniversary of May Fourth Movement. It was an ultimatum. The success of the April 27 demonstration had greatly emboldened these students.

They were shocked when the government responded in the very morning of May 3. In a press conference, Yuan Mu bluntly called the students' conditions unacceptable. While the government was willing to have dialogues with students, he said, it was not going to be threatened by an ultimatum. More damningly still, the angry Yuan Mu warned that the government would not allow students to impose themselves as an equal party in any dialogues. He continued to characterize Beijing Students Autonomous Federation as illegal and insisted that the government would neither recognize nor talk to them.

The paternalistic tone in Yuan Mu's speech was not surprising. For years, the Party and the government had been preaching that they were the guardians of the masses in the same way as local court officers were the parents of the governed in the feudalistic tradition of Chinese society. It was all right for the government to have a dialogue with the

120

masses, but it would be entirely a different matter if the other party of the dialogue could regard themselves as equals.

AT the first meeting of the Dialogue Delegation, Shen Tong saw to his dismay many familiar faces, ones who were involved in Beijing Students Autonomous Federation. Feng Congde gave a brief introductory speech and encouraged the delegates to work independently of the Federation. Then a tall and handsome man stood up and introduced himself. It was Xiang Xiaoji. Almost everyone in the room remembered that name from the previous staged dialogue with Yuan Mu. They gravitated toward him for leadership. Xiang Xiaoji did not shy away from the attention. As a matter of fact, he had come prepared.

Immediately Xiang Xiaoji proposed an agenda. The Delegation should be divided into three groups with each responsible for one issue area of the upcoming dialogue, namely,[96] 1. the nature of the student movement; 2. strategies for future economic and political reform; 3. people's constitutional rights.) Every group should spend time on thorough research and become true masters of the issues. They should not take their tasks lightly, he said, they would be representing the student body on a big, public stage. The dialogue should be done with facts, logic, and reason, instead of emotions.

It was the best meeting Shen Tong had ever attended. He looked around the room again and realized that most attendees appeared older and more mature. Indeed, he learned that they were, like Xiang Xiaoji, graduate students. As a junior, the young Shen Tong felt that he found a new home for himself. He rose and asked the delegates to avoid being involved in Beijing Students Autonomous Federation work. They needed to keep a low profile and do their quiet leg work separately from the raging emotions outside, he proposed seriously.

The delegates readily elected Xiang Xiaoji and Shen Tong to be the co-organizers. Although not officially named so, they would become known as the chairman and vice chairman, respectively, of the Dialogue Delegation.[97]

Although we are too young for death, we are ready to leave you. We must go. We are answering the call for Chinese history.

Hunger Strike Manifesto

7

The Hunger Strike

M AY 4, 1989, the seventieth anniversary of the glorious May Fourth Movement, was finally here. It was a date Wang Dan, Shen Tong, and Professor Fang Lizhi had been eagerly anticipating for months. Yet how the times had changed.

This new generation of students had already had their own movement, which climaxed with the great demonstration on April 27. In the aftermath of that marvelous day, the anniversary all of sudden seemed to be an afterthought. Should they march again? They could not possibly top what happened on April 27. Another long day on their feet did not sound all that appealing.

Students were not the only ones who were not in the mood for the anniversary celebration. Peking University canceled all its planned activities on campus, a measure of significance for a school that had adopted this date for its own anniversary. Zhao Ziyang, who had finally returned from North Korea three days earlier, was set to deliver a keynote speech in an official commemorative conference at the Great Hall of People attended by hand-picked youth leaders. Even this traditional event was being overshadowed by another conference that same day: the opening session of an annual meeting of the Asian Development Bank. This conference had brought many foreign bankers, financial ministers, and other regional dignitaries to town, including an official delegation from Taiwan. It was the first time that any people from that island, considered a renegade province by the mainland, visited here in their official capacities. There was strong anticipation of what Zhao Ziyang would say to his distinguished guests. Having been absent for so long, it would be his first public statement since the student movement began.

Beijing Students Autonomous Federation had already painted itself into a corner. The government called their bluff on the ill-advised ultimatum for dialogue. They could not fade away as they had been advertising a "big event" on May 4 as a retaliation. Their delegates considered a few alternative ideas such as holding a local rally or creating a human chain along the Second Ring Road, the beltway of the capital. The former was too low profile and the latter was a logistical nightmare. After much debate, the Federation settled on holding another traditional, multi-college march on the day of the big anniversary.

The tired delegates neglected to discuss a more important issue: what was next? By now most students were tired and exhausted. Many felt that it should be a time to declare victory and end the movement. Calls for resuming classes persisted. In fact, classes had already resumed in many smaller colleges. At larger campuses, student marshals were sometimes needed to picket against their fellow students attending classes. Although the issue had indeed been brought up repeatedly, the delegates failed to reach a formal decision.

FROM the get-go, the demonstration on May 4 was more of a parade than a march. Indeed, it felt like a victory lap. The suspense of terror and anxiety had completely disappeared. So did the soldiers. At Xidan, policemen linked up their arms in another feeble attempt to block the march. Wuer Kaixi, holding up a big red flag and riding on the shoulders of his classmates, led the charge with a big grin on his face as if they were playing a war game at summer camp. The barrier easily collapsed. They marched on with nothing but joy. Many students chose to skip the march itself. They rode bicycles or buses to Tiananmen Square for the festival.

Residents cheered along the way again. They shared the optimism of the students. Shen Tong was particularly excited when he led the Peking University contingent by his own house with his neighbors cheering him on by name. His father, however, was less than amused. Working in the city government, one of his father's duties was to monitor the video feed streaming from the numerous cameras mounted on traffic signs along Chang'an Avenue. It was with great mixed-feelings that he watched his own son leading the march. Yet when his colleagues inquired why his son was so fearless, he stated reflectively: "It must be because we, the people of our generation, have been cowards for too long."[98]

The students also had company this time around. Young workers and residents joined in, despite efforts by student marshals. Indeed, they outnumbered students at some points of the march. In front of the official Xinhua News Agency was a group of young journalists staging their own protests. They had been following the movement for weeks only to see their stories denied for publication. The shutdown of the *World Economic Herald* in Shanghai hit close to their hearts. On this day, they proudly displayed banners and flags, made for them by Shen Tong's media center volunteers in Peking University,[99] demanding press freedom. It was also the day that student movements heated up outside of the capital. In all major cities across the nation, demonstrations broke out en masse with twenty thousand or more marching in Shanghai.[100] The holiday provided a convenient time and occasion for them to catch up with Beijing and express their own enthusiasm and support.

Even with important meetings being held at the Great Hall of People, students in Beijing found Tiananmen Square wide open. They poured in and celebrated their victory. Zhou Yongjun rigged up a few makeshift loudspeakers. A *May Fourth Declaration*, drafted by Wang Chaohua with the help of the "authors class" for the occasion, was read aloud but received little attention. Caught in the happy mood, Zhou Yongjun proudly announced the conclusion of the march as well as the city-wide class boycotts. He told students that they had achieved a tremendous victory and it was time for them to go back to classes starting the next day. The announcement was received by an enthusiastic round of applause.

Around Zhou Yongjun, however, other leaders of Beijing Autonomous Students Federation were stunned.[101]

THE Asian Development Bank meeting opened inside the Great Hall of People as students were celebrating outside. Wearing a western suit with a tie, Zhao Ziyang appeared calm and relaxed. As his audience eagerly waited for his assessment of the student movement, Zhao Ziyang did not disappoint them. In his keynote speech, he started with a confident assertion that there was no, and would not be any, turmoil in China. He praised the students for their enthusiasm. The vast majority of them were not seeking to overthrow the communist system, he explained. They only wanted the government to do a better job. His tone deviated obviously from that of the April 26 *People's Daily* editorial which he did not mention at all. He emphasized that they would resolve the issues within the framework of democracy and the legal system, with calm, reason, tolerance, and order. It would not take long, he added optimistically.

With all his confidence, Zhao Ziyang certainly did not overturn the verdict in that editorial either. Technically, he did not even contradict it. While the editorial was blaming "an extremely small clique" for conspiring to overthrow the government, Zhao Ziyang stated that the "vast majority" did not have such motives. Nonetheless, it was more than a game of language gimmicks. Zhao Ziyang was changing the official attitude from confrontational to conciliatory. He also hinted that a real dialogue with the demonstrating students was possible.

Students found the speech refreshing and welcome. Along with Zhou Yongjun's announcement to resume classes, they felt this movement was indeed coming to an end. It was another ambiguous ending of course, but much better than all the previous movements. They had held the biggest demonstration ever in open defiance of the highest pressure. They had received wide support from city residents. They had established their own organizations and independent media oper-

feeling Movement to an end

125

ations. Certainly, there was no guarantee that any of those would be allowed to survive. But they also had a Dialogue Delegation who was going to work on these issues, hopefully constructively, with the government. In short, they had pushed the envelope much further than ever. With Zhao Ziyang's blessing, perhaps, they hoped, they could keep the achievements as status quo going forward. They could always ask for more in another movement down the road.

The Dialogue Delegation, meanwhile, enjoyed smooth sailing under the leadership of Xiang Xiaoji and Shen Tong. With Shen Tong's desire to stay non-political, they had practically broken off contact with Beijing Students Autonomous Federation and the rest of the movement. They hoped such a stance could help them become more acceptable to the government. Taking in the lesson learned from the Federation's brash ultimatum, the Dialogue Delegation decided to start from scratch with a much more moderate tone: they would welcome any kinds of dialogue with the government, at any level, without preconditions. On May 6, Xiang Xiaoji and Shen Tong walked to the government offices to deliver their first petition. They were followed by dozens of very interested journalists. It was a simple request for a dialogue. There was no deadline for the government. When the two of them went back two days later for a status check, they were politely received. Although there was not a formal response, officers encouraged them to keep preparing for a dialogue. The attitude was indeed changing.[102]

IN the morning of May 6, people in Beijing woke up to something they had never seen before: photographs and reports of student demonstrations splashed all over major newspapers. *China Youth Daily* went as far as to report demonstrations in at least eleven cities outside Beijing and portrayed them as patriotic actions. An article in *People's Daily* quoted a student's banner declaring that "as long as there is corruption, this country will never be stable." The articles also quoted Zhao Ziyang saying that corruption was partly due to a "lack of openness in the system of work," hinting that more openness would be on the way.

Indeed, Zhao Ziyang appeared ready to embark on a grand experi-

positive media reportage

ment in media openness, one of the key demands of the students. With this one stroke, he was gaining much needed credibility. On May 7, *People's Daily* reported the request from the Dialogue Delegation as a matter of fact without ridicule or rejection. It also quoted Zhao Ziyang as saying that it would be beneficial for the government to have dialogues with students.[103] On May 10, the same paper announced that a regular meeting of the National People's Congress Standing Committee would convene on June 20. The agenda for that meeting included hearings on student demonstrations, reevaluation of the demonstration laws, and consideration of government corruption issues. These were all parts of the demands made by students in their earlier Seven-Point Petition. Zhao Ziyang was clearly on the move.*

Students felt more hopeful than ever. By Monday, May 8, most schools had returned to their normal class schedules with the noted exceptions of Peking University and Beijing Normal University. At Peking University, thousands of students continued to gather at The Triangle day and night to emotionally debate their cases for and against resuming classes. They were worried that, should all classes resumed, they would lose all leverage against the government in a dialogue. Someone had to keep the pressure on, they argued. On Monday morning, the students' loudspeakers announced the results of a campus-wide vote. It approved a continuation of the class boycott. So, the strike carried on at Peking University. A Big Poster summarized five conditions for Peking University to resume classes which included the retraction of the April 26 *People's Daily* editorial and the recognition of the independent student organizations.[104] Beijing Normal University, led by Wuer Kaixi, followed suit and continued its own boycott to show solidarity.

Aside from their students' tough stand, the Preparatory Committee at Peking University went into a state of hibernation for a lack of urgent matters on its agenda. The situation was not much better at Beijing Students Autonomous Federation. Angered by Zhou Yongjun's unauthorized announcement on May 4, they formally expelled him the

---

*Zhao Ziyang's actions during this period would later become one of his crimes as he was accused of encouraging the student movement after it had already died down.

next day. Now that Wuer Kaixi had returned from hiding, he took the position of presidency back from Feng Congde as a matter of course. But it was still Wang Chaohua who was doing the real work. She was having an increasingly difficult time locating representatives from many smaller colleges. Most of them had resigned or simply dropped out.

Feng Congde was not happy at all, but not because of Wuer Kaixi's return. He was sad about the drifting state of the movement. Beijing Students Autonomous Federation seemed to remain a superficial organization without real grassroots support and legitimacy. The movement itself had lost its purpose. He turned his attention to his own affairs. He was scheduled to graduate with a Master's degree soon with a thesis defense scheduled in June, merely weeks away. Even though classes had not resumed at Peking University, he thought it was time for him to get back to his thesis work. So, on May 6, he resigned from both Beijing Students Autonomous Federation and Peking University's Preparatory Committee. In his resignation letter, he observed dejectedly: "The fact that this movement had to be led by people like me, who had neither received any systematic training in politics or law nor gained much knowledge of society, is a historical sadness."[105]

In terms of having dialogues with the government, it was the young journalists who tasted the sweetness of success first. On May 10, they publicly submitted a petition of their own with more than a thousand signatures. They got a quick response from Hu Qili, the youngest member in the Politburo who was in charge of the Party's propaganda work. Originally a long-time ally of Hu Yaobang, Hu Qili had now solidly aligned himself with the new General Secretary. With Zhao Ziyang's blessing, Hu Qili had already been spearheading the effort in dismantling the press censorship this week. The day after the petition, Hu Qili met representatives of the reporters and therefore became the highest-ranking official to participate in a dialogue with the masses. His involvement was much welcomed for his reputation as a reformer and an ally of Zhao Ziyang, in sharp contrast with conservative figures such as Yuan Mu. Students at Peking University were so excited by this development that thousands of them rode bicycles and wore green headbands inscribed with "Free Press" and "Equal Dialogue" to support the journalists.

"Dialogue" was in vogue. Everyday, high-ranking officials were going to factories and communities to talk with workers and residents in all walks of life. They showed remarkable sincerity and openly discussed the thorny issues of graft, corruption, and inflation. Curiously, however, nobody engaged with students. Xiang Xiaoji and Shen Tong were visiting government offices every day. There were no signs of any dialogue with them or any other students. Perhaps it was because students had insisted on having their own independent organizations, a situation that Zhao Ziyang was not ready to handle. Perhaps it was because the bureaucrats in charge of education and college affairs were dominated by conservatives within the government. Students were left out waiting, with no clear openings in sight.[106]

Many grew impatient. During a press conference at Peking University on May 11, reporters were asking questions about how long the class boycott could last and also, pointedly, "What is it that you students really want?" Frustrated, Shen Tong grabbed the microphone and bravely laid down his own vision:[107]

> We see the movement in three stages. The first is to gain attention so that the people of China understand our concerns. The second is to make our campuses democratic castles and strengthen our commitment to democratic reform while giving students in other cities and those in other sectors of society, workers, peasants, and journalists, the time to gain their own political awareness. And third, after this has been achieved, we will probably hold a nationwide pro-democracy movement in the fall, to educate people as to what democratic reform is all about.

It was not clear how many students shared Shen Tong's vision. But his was a fairly accurate account of what had been developing so far. What was going to happen in the fall was anyone's guess. With 1989 being the year of conspicuous anniversaries, they could be looking forward to China's National Day on October 1, when the People's Republic celebrated her fortieth birthday, as an occasion for something big again.

Not everyone had the patience to wait.

concern about "秋后跳账"

Some had other reasons to worry. There was an old saying in China: "to settle the accounts after the fall [harvest]." Stemming from agricultural roots, the phrase had come to mean that one would wait till the time was right to punish his opponents. It was a feared tactic practiced by the government many times in the past. Right now, as the movement was strong and enjoying public support, the government was afraid to confront students directly. But once the momentum died out, it would be easy to pick out the leaders individually. Consequently, the debate was whether a movement should be sustained for the "selfish" sake of its leaders' safety.

ON the same day as Shen Tong made his speech at The Triangle, a Big Poster showed up there. Signed by "a few graduate students," it called for an immediate hunger strike. It did not provide specific rationale for the proposal but it mentioned that the Soviet leader Mikhail Gorbachev was coming for a state visit within a week. So, it would be a good time to stage a protest at Tiananmen Square for the biggest impact.

The idea of a hunger strike was, of course, nothing new. Within every student movement in the past, the cry of "Hunger Strike" had always been heard, together with "Protest," "March," "Boycott Class," etc. But it had always been more of a menacing outburst than a serious proposal. Yet, this time it felt different.

More than a week earlier, the famous author Zheng Yi had found himself with a roomful of young, exhausted, and angry students who had just returned from Hu Yaobang's funeral. Having failed his earlier attempt in calling for a hunger strike at Xinhuamen, Zheng Yi found this audience, which included Wang Dan, Guo Haifeng, and other active student organizers, more receptive to his ideas. With a flare of drama from a seasoned writer, Zheng Yi laid out his personal experience during the Cultural Revolution:[108] "Hunger strike is the most powerful and tested weapon in a mass movement." He advised the younger generation, "Should the government impose martial law, should they disallow Big Posters and demonstrations, you could immediately declare a hunger strike." He painted a vivid picture of how a hunger strike would develop: "As soon as there are dozens of people

power of hunger strike taught to student leaders

declaring a hunger strike, there will be hundreds joining in to support. Thousands will gather and watch. There will be donations and great attention paid to hunger strikers' petitions. In twenty four hours, the weaker ones will start to faint. Within forty eight hours, many will collapse. Seventy-two hours will be a critical juncture, there will be ambulances taking strikers to hospitals every minute. The shuttling ambulances will be the most dramatic scene in the city. The whole society will erupt!"

Zheng Yi did not say anything about what would happen after the seventy-two hour limit. The strikes he had experienced were resolved within that time frame. It did not occur to the students to ask that question either. They were the new generation, the best and the brightest, and the future of the nation. There could be no way for the government to allow a hunger strike to go past seventy two hours, when their health could be seriously compromised. Surely a dialogue would have commenced by then. Besides, there was an international law that required a government to intervene in a public hunger strike within seventy-two hours, or the government would be considered illegitimate.*

The student leaders were excited about the possibilities. But, at the time, they were not fully convinced that the situation had warranted such a dramatic tactic. It should be attempted only as a last resort.

Three weeks had passed since that night. Their patience started to run short. At Beijing Normal University, Wuer Kaixi had also been talking about a hunger strike as early as May 8 to give the stalled movement a new push.[109]

LIU Gang had been having the nagging feeling that he had overstayed his welcome in Beijing Students Autonomous Federation, the organization he had founded almost single-handedly. As a non-student, he knew his presence was awkward. So he stayed behind the scenes as much as possible and worked hard in providing logistical support for the endless meetings. When he needed to advance an idea, he relied on friendly delegates as surrogates. But more and more, he felt that his words, along with his presence, were being ignored. On the

---

*It's hard to pinpoint an origin of this belief. But many students and residents believed that such and similar international laws and norms existed.

eve of the April 27 demonstration, he had strongly advised students to stay inside their campuses. The huge success thereafter, in the eyes of exuberant student leaders, had proved his conservative attitude wrong. The movement, although only weeks old, was slipping out of his grasp.

As the idea of a hunger strike was gaining traction, Liu Gang made a strong case to stop it. The Federation agreed with him this time. But the debate got so heated that it deteriorated into a shouting match. Ma Shaofang, who had come back from his earlier resignation, pounded on tables and claimed that he had confirmed intelligence that the "reform wing" in the government was hoping for an escalation of the student movement. A hunger strike should help the reformers at the top to gain the upper hand.[110] He was not convincing enough. Wang Chaohua cautioned that they should not base their decisions on unfounded rumors. With a vote, the Federation reached a resolution that, based on the government's softened attitude toward the Dialogue Delegation, they would not organize any large-scale event in the near future. Rather, it instructed schools to follow the guideline of "denouncing the April 26 *People's Daily* editorial and supporting Zhao Ziyang's May Fourth speech."[111]

The idea of a large-scale hunger strike, however, was too tempting for some to pass on. Right after the Federation meeting, Wuer Kaixi, Wang Dan, Ma Shaofang, along with several other delegates, went along for dinner at a little restaurant near Peking University. Over the meal and after much persuasion, they made their own decision to go ahead with a hunger strike. They would launch and lead it as individuals unaffiliated with Beijing Students Autonomous Federation. The federation, they were sure, would have to come around once they had the momentum going.[112]

They were not alone. That same evening, Chai Ling reached the same conclusion on her own. She came to see her husband Feng Congde in a very excited mood. She could not stop talking about a chat she had with Zhang Boli and his classmates in the "authors class." They had mapped out a strategy to pursue a hunger strike. With a mischievous smile, she said that they planned to sneak in bread and chocolate once they got started. It was, after all, just a show to pressure the government. It was not that serious of a deal.[113]

Chai Ling had already left Peking University a year earlier and was now a graduate student in psychology at Beijing Normal University. But living with her husband, she continued to spend most of her time at Peking University rather than her new school. Both of them got involved in the Preparatory Committee early on. Although not a central figure herself, Chai Ling had been in charge of the organization's secretarial work.

In the early morning of May 12, Wang Dan found Chai Ling at Peking University and they immediately joined forces on the hunger strike. But the Preparatory Committee, the leadership in the school, was not on board. Just as Beijing Students Autonomous Federation, the committee had decided several days earlier that it was not time for hunger strike. However, the committee did not want to, and could not, stand in the way of Wang Dan and Chai Ling as they were taking the initiatives on their own.

Wang Chaohua, on the other hand, was furious when she found that Wang Dan and Wuer Kaixi, the public faces of Beijing Students Autonomous Federation, had signed on to a hunger strike as individuals despite the resolution they had passed. Yet she was also keenly aware of the predicament she was in. If a hunger strike did take place and her Federation chose to oppose it publicly, it might be the end of the Federation itself as a student leadership organization. With great reservations, she agreed to organize student marshals to protect the hunger strikers per their request. Without a strong picket line, the dozens of hunger strikers could be easily hustled away by police.

Wang Chaohua still had hopes for personal persuasion. She thought she could talk some sense into the hunger strikers. But it was Chai Ling who sought her out first to question the Federation's stand. Their conversation turned sour immediately. Chai Ling spoke emotionally and made it abundantly clear that the hunger strike would go ahead with or without the Federation's support. A strong sense of helplessness submerged Wang Chaohua.[114]

T HE hunger strikers decided to formally launch their action in Tiananmen Square the next day, two days before the scheduled visit of Mikhail Gorbachev. It should give the government enough time to respond.

Standoff At Tiananmen

The stakes would be too high for the government not to.

The Soviet Union and China, two giants in the communist block, famously broke up their brotherly alliance amid an ugly spat of verbal barrages, accusations, and ideological confrontations. It culminated in a long freeze interrupted only by small-scale border battles between the two armies. It was only after Gorbachev's glasnost and perestroika and Deng Xiaoping's reform in their respective countries that they found a reconciliation possible and necessary. It would be the first summit of these neighbors in forty years to normalize the relationships between the two communist parties and the two nations. It had been billed as one of the crown jewels in Deng Xiaoping's reform.

The public enthusiasm for the hunger strike was however less than anticipated even at Peking University, the hot spot of the movement. During the day, only forty students signed up. Other campuses fared much worse, as their numbers failed to reach double digits.[115] By dusk, hundreds of students crowded The Triangle as usual. They were debating the merits of a hunger strike and the opposing voices appeared to prevail. Above all, nobody was able to come up with a solid reason for this desperate action.

As darkness fell, Chai Ling got hold of the microphone. It was the very first time she gave a public speech. Her voice was low but determined. Her flow was frequently interrupted by emotional chokes and tears. The spontaneous speech jumped randomly from one train of thought to another. Yet somehow it was a gripping voice that demanded everyone's full attention. As she went on, The Triangle, always a rowdy locale, fell into a silence it had never experienced before.

Chai Ling started with her own personal story. Like many other students, she had plans to go abroad to study and was feeling a deep sense of guilt and confusion. She was not sure if going abroad at this time of the student movement could constitute a traitorous act. On the other hand, she could not decide if it was worthwhile to stay in China either. Seemingly getting carried away by her personal struggle, she framed the hunger strike as her last ditch effort to see if China, as a country, still had any hope at all:[116]

> For several years, we have had student movement after student movement, but we got nothing. Why? We ask for democ-

134

racy and freedom from the government. But why could we never get it? We chant "Long Live the People" all the time. But why do people always run away when the police come? We chant "Police Love People" all the time. But why do police always beat us up? Why should we go on a hunger strike? Because we want to use this method, the only freedom we have left, to see the true face of our country and the true face of our people. I want to see if this country is worth our sacrifice and contribution.

We are fortunate to have parents who raised us to become college students. But it is time for us to stop eating. The government has time and again lied to us, ignored us. We only want the government to talk with us and to say that we are not traitors. We, the children, are ready to die. We, the children, are ready to use our lives to pursue the truth. We, the children, are ready to sacrifice ourselves.

We want to fight to live. We want to fight to live with the resolve of death.

Upstairs in his room, Shen Tong had turned off the lights and tried to catch some sleep after a long day at the media center. As he lay in darkness, Chai Ling's voice, out of the loudspeakers just outside of his window, penetrated his ears and into his heart. As the co-leader of the Dialogue Delegation, Shen Tong was against the hunger strike and had argued with Chai Ling during the day. But this night, Chai Ling's voice hit him hard. He found tears rushing out of his eyes, the first time he had cried during the movement. He could not stay in bed any longer. He rushed downstairs. He wanted to get closer to Chai Ling but an equally emotional crowd was in his way.[117]

Indeed, most in the crowd were crying, including grown up teachers and graduate students. Among them was a writer by the name of Bai Meng from the "authors class". With tears streaming down his face, Bai Meng rushed out of the campus and bought dumplings for Chai Ling. He made Chai Ling write down her spontaneous speech as much as she could remember. Bai Meng would spend the whole night polishing it off. An "official" *Hunger Strike Manifesto* was thus born.[118] Meanwhile, the tally of hunger strikers swelled past a hundred. It was a sleepless night for many students.

Standoff At Tiananmen

Two hours past midnight, Xiang Xiaoji, Shen Tong and other Dialogue Delegation members were simultaneously and quietly informed that the government was now ready to have a dialogue with them, six days after their petition.[119]

Stop the dialogue! There is no live broadcast!

Wang Chaohua

8

The Dialogue

Lı Lu made the decision of his young life after hearing the broadcast of the April 26 *People's Daily* editorial. He was in Nanjing, a metropolis on the southern bank of the great Yangtze River, six hundred miles from Beijing. Nanjing had been the capital city of China at various periods in history, most recently during the rule of the Nationalist government before it was overthrown by the communists. It was during that spring of 1949, with the People's Liberation Army poised to cross the Yangtze River to liberate Nanjing and chase the Nationalists off the mainland, when Mao Zedong famously wrote his *Farewell, Leighton Stuart* to laugh off the man who had procured the campus now housing Peking University. John Leighton Stuart was by then the American Ambassador to China. Unlike other western diplomats, he was staying in Nanjing hoping in vain to make positive contact with the advancing communists. Victory in his hands, Mao Zedong had no interest in the American imperialists.

Li Lu was in his senior year at Nanjing University. A couple of years earlier, as he was learning the ropes of college life, he had fol-

137

lowed Professor Fang Lizhi's call for students to join the Communist Party and reform it from within. He became a Communist Party member and dove head-first into reforming the official student union at the school. His efforts, however, led him into a close encounter with official corruption which left him totally dejected.[120]

Yet Li Lu was not a typical student of his generation either. His grandfather had died in prison during the "Anti-Rightists" campaign. During the Cultural Revolution, his parents were forced to leave the infant Li Lu in boarding schools and foster families while they endured hard labor in the countryside. In 1976, Li Lu and his family survived the devastating Tangshan earthquake in which all members of his foster family were killed.[121] In the hot summer of 1986, the freshman Li Lu decided to travel around the country alone. He acquired the unusual skill of traveling without spending any money, which he had little. He dodged conductors by hiding in lavatories on passenger trains. He slept in train stations and public parks. He even begged for food from friends, whom he might have just met minutes earlier. When he was caught by police, he pretended to be a know-nothing country boy running away from home. For that purpose, he traveled without his identification card, a rare and dangerous thing to do in China.[122]

His travel sparked a deep desire to understand the country better. So, in his sophomore year, he switched his major from physics to economics. After Hu Yaobang's death, he helped organize marches in Nanjing until the *People's Daily* editorial put an end to it. It was then and there he decided that he needed to go to Beijing where the real action was.

He took off the very next day. As he had done before, he departed without any money, luggage, or identification. All he had with him were extra items of underwear stuffed in his pockets. Arriving at the Beijing Railway Station, he calmly presented himself as a student from Peking University to a guard checking for tickets. He was waved off immediately. To his puzzlement, the guard actually smiled at him.[123]

In fact, Li Lu found the capital entirely different from what he had expected. With the frightening *People's Daily* editorial hanging in the air, he had boarded the train imagining the worst. But there was not a single trace of doom and gloom. Rather, people were happy and excited. They treated him like a hero. It was April 28, the day after the most glorious march by students in Beijing.

Li Lu hopped from campus to campus and crashed in dormitories of a few friends he knew or had just made, trying to get closer to the emerging student leadership. At Peking University, he was stopped from approaching the Preparatory Committee for lacking of any proof of identity. True to his form, Li Lu bluffed his way into an adjacent room where a meeting was taking place. He sat down discreetly and observed,[124]

> I noticed a girl who looked a bit different from the others. She was listening seriously to whoever was speaking. She was quick to respond to people's comments. She was amazingly unkempt and unattractive: her face was dirty, her jacket was rumpled and loose, and she wore a pair of wrinkled jeans. She looked like a boy. When she talked, she hardly opened her mouth. But she was clearly a sincere and kind-hearted person.

That unattractive girl was Chai Ling, the head of the secretariat for the Preparatory Committee. During a break, Li Lu cornered her in the hallway and found that, to his pleasant surprise, Chai Ling was receptive to whatever he had to say. Unlike others, Chai Ling never asked for his identification. The two of them struck an instant rapport. Finally, Li Lu became a part of the movement he had dreamed about.

THE area near the southern entrance of Peking University was decorated in the morning of May 13. Having agreed to provide logistic support for the hunger strikers, the Preparatory Committee arranged a festivity to send them off. One big banner, made by the "authors class," was particularly eye-catching. Stretching along the sidewalk, it proclaimed, "Our Warriors are Taking Off, We Await their Return." The phrase was altered from an ancient tragedy in which an assassin was sent off on a suicidal attack on Qin Shihuang, China's first Emperor.* The banner stirred up solemn sentiments. One by one and in groups, hunger strikers had their pictures taken under it while proudly flashing their V-for-victory signs.

*The original phrase stated "Our warrior is taking off and shall never return."

Standoff At Tiananmen

The school now had more than a hundred and sixty hunger strikers. They were surrounded by another three hundred volunteers who would serve as marshals, guards, and publicity personnel and do whatever they could to take care of the hunger strikers. In the late spring sun, most hunger strikers wore only T-shirts and shorts. Everyone had a white headband. On them were words like "hunger strike", "democracy", "human rights", and so on.

At half past ten, Chai Ling read aloud the barely completed *Hunger Strike Manifesto*. Then, led by two hunger strikers, everyone repeated an oath with their utmost sincerity and determination:

> I swear, for the purpose of improving the democratization of our
> motherland, for the purpose of the prosperity of our motherland,
> I will fast willingly. I will absolutely obey the leadership of the
> Hunger Strike Brigade. We will not stop until we succeed!

The so-called "leadership of the Hunger Strike Brigade" did not officially exist. But nobody was paying attention to this detail. There was no confusion as who was in charge. Most hunger strikers had been inspired by Chai Ling's voice to join this crusade.

A hearty "last meal," paid for by young teachers, was served to the hunger strikers in a little restaurant nearby. Some indulged. Others could not force down many bites. With tears on their faces, teachers and students lined up along the narrow passage from the restaurant to the gate to cheer on the hunger strikers. A flatbed tricycle carrying several hunger strikers holding a big red Peking University flag led the way. The rest of them rode bicycles slowly and silently. Off they went.

They did not get very far when Chai Ling spotted Li Lu on the sidewalk walking his bicycle with his head down. Chai Ling was happy to see him. It had been only a couple of days but Chai Ling had developed complete confidence in this good-looking young man who had a demeanor of an extremely able and resourceful person yet with the touch of mystery of an outsider. Although from out of town, Li Lu had convinced Chai Ling that he had inside connections with high-ranking officials in Beijing. So, she called him over and eagerly asked for a briefing. Li Lu just shook his head and murmured, "never mind, never mind, never mind."

"What happened?"

140

"Well, my sources got information from people close to Deng Xiaoping. If there had not been a hunger strike, they would have allowed Zhao Ziyang to resolve this whole thing peacefully and get it over with. But now, it has changed."

Chai Ling reacted incredulously to this news, "Why didn't you tell me this earlier?" Li Lu explained that he was in the crowd the previous night when Chai Ling gave her emotional speech. He failed to get through to her then or find her afterward. But Li Lu recovered from his downbeat mood quickly. His enthusiasm came back. He told Chai Ling that, after all, this was the first time in Chinese history that a mass movement was crossing the boundary between life and death. "Let's see how it will end." He reasoned, "If Zhao Ziyang really wanted to resolve it peacefully, he would still have his chances."

Chai Ling agreed.[125]

WANG Chaohua learned the news that the government was ready to meet the Dialogue Delegation when she was at the makeshift office of Beijing Students Autonomous Federation at Peking University writing her resignation letter. She was exhausted. She had not been back home to see her little boy since she joined the organization. With the movement escalating into a hunger strike, her family was pressuring her to stay away from this very dangerous direction. She was also disheartened by the defections of many Federation personnel to the hunger strike camp where the action was going to be from now on.

Instinctively, she knew that the sudden change in the government's stance had to be a consequence of the hunger strike. She immediately changed her mind. The least she could do, she decided, was to stand by and provide support to the hunger strikers.

Meanwhile, Xiang Xiaoji and Shen Tong could not get their dialogue with the government on the right footing. Their Dialogue Delegation had distanced themselves from the movement so much that students at large had no idea who they were and what they represented.* Students in many campuses demanded to send their own delegates in-

---

*So much so that Wang Dan admitted that he did not know the existence of the Dialogue Delegation until after the hunger strike.[126] This also showed how out of touch Wang Dan himself had become.

141

stead. The Dialogue Delegation, on the other hand, was also wary of falling into a trap for another staged session and losing their credibility. In a quibble over pre-conditions, the very first sanctioned contact between the government and a renegade student organization died out before they even met face-to-face.[127]

But all was not lost. Contact materialized again almost immediately. Rather curiously, this time it came from the United Front Department within the apparatus of the Communist Party. Between its staunch allies and perceived enemies, the Chinese Communist Party viewed a wide stretch of the middle as comprising potential allies as well as trouble makers. It was the job of the United Front Department to keep a close eye on them, dishing out favors and punishments as the situation required. Its portfolio included the minor political parties allowed to exist by the Communist Party, the independent intellectuals, officials and dignitaries of the former Nationalist government, ethnic minorities, compatriots from Hong Kong and Taiwan, and so on. College students, the future of the Party and the nation, were not the jurisdiction of this Department.

Except that the Department was headed by Yan Mingfu, a fifty-eight year old bureaucrat who had sensed the arrival of his own moment in history. Like the Premier Li Peng, Yan Mingfu was a second generation official. His father was a successful spy during the war era who worked undercover in the Nationalist government. In his own career, Yan Mingfu had experienced many ups and downs, from serving as Mao Zedong's personal Russian interpreter to being imprisoned as a Soviet spy during the Cultural Revolution. At the United Front Department in more recent years, he nurtured a reputation for being friendly and open-minded. He made many personal friends in the intellectual circle and was regarded as a reliable lieutenant in Zhao Ziyang's "reform wing" within the Party.[128]

On May 14, *The New York Times* reported that "an unannounced Politburo meeting has endorsed the moderate line of the Communist Party leader, Zhao Ziyang, toward student demonstrators, including more discussions with the students and limited steps toward greater democracy." It went on to say that, after the "tense meeting," the leadership position of Zhao Ziyang's faction had been strengthened. The paper also hinted that even Deng Xiaoping had fallen in line behind Zhao Ziyang. The April 26 *People's Daily* editorial, the stubborn road-block to the movement written based on Deng Xiaoping's own words, might not be sacred after all:[129]

> Mr. Deng did not attend the Politburo meeting, but he did send a statement in which he seemed to support the moderate approach. He also indicated that his earlier warning on April 25, calling for a crackdown on student demonstrators, was based on misleading information apparently supplied by the Beijing City Communist Party authorities, a party official said.

Yan Mingfu felt more than a sense of urgency. In the morning of May 13, he was chairing two meetings in his office compound simultaneously. In one, Hu Qili was conducting another dialogue session with journalists. In another, Yan Mingfu was soliciting opinions from a group of intellectuals on the current situation. Shuffling between the two, Yan Mingfu was most interested in finding an avenue for direct contact with student leaders to halt the coming confrontation. The scenario of Mr. Gorbachev coming to a Tiananmen Square occupied by hunger striking students horrified him. He had not much time to spare. Barely recovered from a bad cold, Yan Mingfu repeatedly stressed the importance of this task. While he refused to acknowledge that there were two separate factions in the top leadership, he did warn his audience that "some comrades had strong opinions" regarding the student movement. In particular, he said that the Beijing city government might resort to drastic actions should students continue. Then, "we would all be gone." It was clear who he meant by "we."[130]

It was then that Yan Mingfu was advised reaching out to people like Chen Ziming and Wang Juntao, who were thought to possess closer connections to students. Yan Mingfu was aware of these names. With their histories from the April Fifth Movement in 1976 to the Democracy Wall in 1978 and then the election campaign in 1980, these marked characters did not even belong to the category of "potential friends of the Party" for his United Front Department. But these were drastic times. Yan Mingfu felt that he had no choice. He needed to do whatever was necessary.

Standoff At Tiananmen

For much of early May, Chen Ziming and Wang Juntao had been arguing about how much, if at all, they should get involved in the movement. The students' initial success had caught them by surprise. But they also had other things to worry about. For many frustrated years, Chen Ziming had worked diligently to get his think tank accepted by the government. He had finally seen the appearance of a crack. A reform proposal prepared by his Institute was receiving rave reviews. They had been cordially received by ministry-level officials and an audience with Zhao Ziyang himself was in the plan.[131] It was not a good time for them to take unnecessary risks.

In this afternoon of May 13, Chen Ziming was chairing his board meeting when it was rudely interrupted by an intruder who busted open the door and burst out, "Hurry up! Yan Mingfu needs to see you, you, and you." He was pointing his finger at Wang Juntao, Chen Xiaoping, and a few others, sparing no time to make eye contact with anybody else in the room. Chen Ziming did not appreciate the drama. After hearing that Yan Mingfu needed help to contact students, he was still not convinced. They had important work to do as it was.

Wang Juntao, on the other hand, was more than willing. There was no time for debate. A big van was waiting outside with its engine humming. Chen Ziming had no choice but to send out those named by the visitor and continue on with his meeting.[132]

T HE hunger strikers took their time to assemble at Beijing Normal University. Tapes of Chai Ling's speech had reached other campuses and inspired more participants there. Pu Zhiqiang led his group from University of Political Science and Law into the campus, accompanied by his teacher Wu Renhua. Wu Renhua had bought another bottle of hard liquor to send the students off before he decided to join in as well.

When they finally departed from Beijing Normal University in late afternoon, Wuer Kaixi was leading the way. He and his classmates marched on foot. Wearing matching headbands and stretching their right arms forward with clutched fists, they walked slowly. In front of numerous cameras, they acted as if they were ancient warriors heading into a battlefield.

They arrived at Tiananmen Square just before sunset. There were only a few foreign journalists waiting. Wang Dan and Wuer Kaixi opened a brief press conference on the stairs of the Museum of Chinese History. Wang Chaohua was also there to provide support as the representative of Beijing Students Autonomous Federation. Chai Ling declined to attend. She was more comfortable staying with her hunger strike troop. So, it was Wang Dan who read a statement to reporters. He vowed that they would never give up until their demands were met.

The hunger strikers settled down in the middle of the Square just north of the Monument to People's Heroes. With all the colleges combined, there were almost eight hundred of them. Most came from four major campuses: Peking University, Beijing Normal University, People's University, and the University of Political Science and Law. About a quarter were female, a group that was usually not as involved in such political activities.[133] There were no camps to be made. They just sat down on the concrete in small circles. Many brought novels and magazines to read. Some had English vocabulary and grammar books to prepare for TOEFL and GRE exams. Others chatted quietly. The hundreds of volunteers set up a perimeter by sitting down in a tight formation. They would not allow any unauthorized person to come in contact with the hunger strikers.

The sun was setting. The students made up only a small cluster in the vastness of the Square. Commuters on the busy Chang'an Avenue did not notice them. As the wind howled and the temperature plunged, they became aware how unprepared they were for the night. Urgent messages were dispatched back to campuses for winter coats and quilts. In the Square, they huddled closer to each other and shivered. They had had their "last meal" at noon. The sense of hunger was just starting to bite into their consciousness. Not a single complaint was heard. Of course, nobody was thinking about how many nights they would be staying out there either.

Just then, a runner rushed over and called for leaders. They were requested for a dialogue with the government. Surprised and anxious, Wang Dan, Wuer Kaixi, Ma Shaofang, and Chai Ling all took off immediately.

T HE big van that had fetched Wang Juntao and Chen Xiaoping zigzagged through the city to pick up various people along the way. They briefly passed Tiananmen Square but did not stop. Wang Juntao looked out of the window and saw the small crowd of students. He knew the tough task he had just taken upon himself.

They headed to the University of Political Science and Law and found the Dialogue Delegation having a meeting in a classroom. Soon, Xiang Xiaoji and Shen Tong were in the van. After many similar stops, the van was almost full. Many of its passengers did not know each other and had absolutely no idea of what was going on. So they kept quiet. The van eventually pulled into the compound of the United Front Department across a small street from Zhongnanhai. The passengers were guided into a large conference room already packed with even more people. In fact, probably too many people.

Yan Mingfu was sitting at the top of a long conference table. Amidst the crowd, he appeared to be strangely alone but confident. Along one side of the table was Wang Dan, Wuer Kaixi, Ma Shaofang, and Chai Ling, in that order. They all wore the hunger strike headbands, providing a hint of drama to the scene. Having arrived late, Xiang Xiaoji, Shen Tong, and the rest of the Dialogue Delegation had to stand behind them. Wang Chaohua was also there to represent Beijing Students Autonomous Federation. She completed the triumvirate of the student leadership currently in play. Wang Juntao, Chen Xiaoping, and other intellectuals took the seats at the other side of the table. They were not sure of their roles but presumed to have been invited as mediators.[134]

There was no time to waste. Yan Mingfu opened the meeting by stating that a dialogue was not his top priority at the moment. He had to get the hunger strikers out of Tiananmen Square first. Zhao Ziyang, Li Peng, and other top leaders had been busy holding dialogues with workers and intellectuals. They should be ready to do the same with students in a week or so. But students must exit the Square right now so that the welcoming ceremony could be held there for Mr. Gorbachev. But at least, Yan Mingfu was willing to listen to what the students had to say.

Wang Dan and Shen Tong, in their respective responses, intentionally played down the urgency of Mr. Gorbachev's visit. They insisted that students, while remaining in the Square, would be on their best behavior and cooperative for the ceremony. They would never embarrass the country with an international scene. But they both insisted that, for students to leave the Square, there had to be something in return. The least the government could do, they said, was to accept their demand for a formal and equal dialogue and proclaim the student movement as patriotic and democratic, not turmoil. In essence, they were condensing the long list of demands they drew up in April into two core focus points: "Not Turmoil, Equal Dialogue." It would become a widely adopted battle cry.

Seeing an impasse, the older Wang Chaohua tried to lighten the air. She pointed out that both sides had already made compromises. The students had shrunk their demands and put the moderate Dialogue Delegation in charge. The government, on the other hand, had shown its own flexibility by inviting everyone here, a de-facto recognition of them as legitimate student leaders. Yet even Yan Mingfu was not ready to have his agenda hijacked in such a manner. He promptly interrupted Wang Chaohua to clarify the matter. He did not know any of the students in the room, Yan Mingfu claimed, they were here only as guests of the intellectuals who were helping him to persuade students to withdraw from the Square. It was clear that he did not, and could not afford to, have this meeting seen as any form of a recognition of student leaders. All he could offer in that regard, he said, was that he would pass along students' issues to his superiors. He promised that.

In what might have been a slip of tone, however, Yan Mingfu did not rule out the possibility of rescinding the April 26 *People's Daily* editorial, which would have satisfied one of the two demands. He cautioned that decisions like that could not happen overnight. It had to take a lot of time. And right now, first things first, he needed students to vacate the Square.

The intellectuals, who were just informed that the true purpose of their presence was to play surrogate hosts, did not offer much in the way of mediation either. In speech after speech, they lauded lofty principles but offered no concrete proposals. Wang Juntao felt that Yan Mingfu was naive in thinking he could accomplish his goal by persuading the student leaders. He issued a warning regarding the delicate positions of student leaders: "They may promise you while they are here. But as soon as they go back, they will be regarded as traitors by the rest of the students." He praised Yan Mingfu for his frankness. "Your sincerity might have moved God and all of us teachers," Wang Juntao said, "But it was the students who had behaved more maturely than the government today. The students had lowered their demands to a minimum. If they retreated any further, they would no longer be able to be student representatives." It was the government's turn to offer something substantial. Otherwise, he warned blatantly, "We may not be able to get over this obstacle on May 15. And that would not be a good thing."

Yan Mingfu was visibly frustrated. He was reaching the end of his wit. All he could do was to keep repeating the importance of the Sino-Soviet summit. Perhaps in a fit of desperation, he let out: "You students think that there are two factions in the government. That is not true. But if you believe that, then you are hurting the reformers by your very action right now!" He went on to explain that there were things he was not at liberty to disclose. But clearly, he was giving the impression that Zhao Ziyang himself would be in danger should the students hold to their stubborn ways. "If you students do not leave the Square by May 15, the consequences will be hard to predict. None of us wants to see anything bad happen."

A chill swept through the room. Student leaders were clearly rattled. Chai Ling, who were quiet all evening, had already left and was on her way back to Tiananmen Square. She was worried about the students on their first night of the hunger strike. The rest of them could not help but feel the pressure of history. Wang Juntao then played his mediator role and prodded the students to call off the hunger strike. After talking it over, they tentatively agreed to withdraw from the Square before May 15. However, they knew that nothing could be achieved without Chai Ling's consent.[135]

THE rising sun gradually warmed up the hunger strikers in Tiananmen Square on the morning of May 14. They woke up with an unmistakable feeling of starvation. These youngsters belonged to the first generation of Chinese who had grown up without war, famine, or the severe rationing during the Cultural Revolution. Most of them had never had to skip a single meal. Their spirits sagged. The Square was as empty as ever. The busy morning commute was underway in the distance but nobody took a second look at them. Their actions had failed to generate any interest, not to mention drama, as they had expected.[136] Just then, Feng Congde showed up.

Feng Congde's personal departure from the movement was short-lived. Before he could get back to his thesis work, his wife Chai Ling was already emerging as a new leader. But even Chai Ling was not able to convince her husband, who had strong reservations about the tactic, into joining the hunter strike. Yet he could no longer sit on the sideline either. As the hunger strikers marched into the Square the day before, Feng Congde took a different route. He delivered a petition to the Soviet embassy with three thousand signatures from students in his school to invite Mr. Gorbachev to visit Peking University. Beating them to the punch, however, Wuer Kaixi had gotten there earlier and delivered a similar petition but with twice the signatures from Beijing Normal University.

Feng Congde then rode his bicycle toward Tiananmen Square. He stopped at Chang'an Avenue and observed the hunger strikers from a distance. Under a heavy overcast and in the vast emptiness of the Square, the cluster of over a thousand students looked tiny and in-significant. Looking at the tall flag poles around the Square, he real-ized what they needed: a banner to advertise their presence and pur-pose. It had to be big enough for everyone to see from outside of the Square.

He spun into action right away. On his way back to Peking Univer-sity, he purchased a large piece of black cloth and a few cans of yellow paint. In his dormitory room, he spent a good part of the night sewing the cloth into a banner. It ended up measuring thirteen feet wide and ten feet tall. He used up all the paint to write two gigantic characters, "Hunger Strike," on the banner.[137] Besides its size, the banner was unique and eye-catching with its black background. It took quite an effort that morning to secure it to flag poles. From Chang'an Avenue, it looked like a pirate's flag. But the two bright yellow characters were sending out an alarm of a different kind.

As the morning progressed, hunger strikers milled around, making their temporary settlement more comfortable. They were also putting up makeshift banners of their own in a way of decoration. One of them stood out. It said, quite simply, "Mom, I am Hungry."

It was an echo from the sentiment in Chai Ling's original speech. The hunger strikers identified themselves much less as fighters for democracy than "we the children" who were suffering to gain sympathy from the grownups. The *Hunger Strike Manifesto* had cried out desperately:

> But we are still kids, we are still kids! Mother China, please take a good look at your sons and daughters. Hunger is ruthlessly destroying their youth. As death is approaching, would you be able to stand by untouched?

The flags and banners lifted the spirits of the hunger strikers. Now they no longer looked like a bunch of stragglers but had manifested a presence in the Square. Feng Congde's job was not finished yet. He had also brought audio tapes of Chai Ling reading the *Hunger Strike Manifesto* to distribute. With a meager fund from donations, Feng Congde took off again to purchase equipment and batteries for a new broadcasting system.

5.14

IN that same morning Yan Mingfu learned that a decision had already been made to move the welcoming ceremony for Mr. Gorbachev out of Tiananmen Square. He was stunned. The summit was not only a diplomatic milestone for China, it had also attracted a huge crowd of international media. It would be worse than a slap in the face for the government. Visibly angry, he was nonetheless still clinging to hope. Encouraged by the previous meeting, he thought he might still have time. But he had to act even more boldly and quickly.

Yan Mingfu found Wang Dan, Wuer Kaixi, and Wang Chaohua still in the compound of his United Front Department. He gathered them in a small conference room. Calmly but officially, Yan Mingfu told them that the government was now ready for a formal dialogue. Students were free to select their own representatives. Yan Mingfu, and several other minister-level officials would represent the government side.

The students could not believe what they were hearing. It was a major concession to the demands of the students, something Yan Mingfu

150

Major concession !!!

was not ready to do even the night before. Essentially, he was holding this dialogue completely on the students' terms: not only had he recognized them as legitimate student leaders, he also framed them as an equal party. Only a week earlier, the State Council Spokesman Yuan Mu had sworn to the world that this would never happen. In a state of shock, Wang Dan and Wuer Kaixi murmured that the representation on the government side might not be high enough. They would prefer either General Secretary Zhao Ziyang or Premier Li Peng. Yan Mingfu would have none of that. He cut them off and vigorously defended his own rank. Wisely, the students did not insist.

But they did have another request. The dialogue had to be broadcast live. Because of censorship rules, very few events were broadcast live in China. Everything, from government proceedings to the popular gala for Chinese New Year, was taped and edited before it could be shown to a general audience. The student leaders had no choice however. Rumors of contact with Yan Mingfu had been circulating in Tiananmen Square. The hunger strikers were worried that they might be sold out behind their backs. Without a live broadcast, they told Yan Mingfu, they might never be able to keep the confidence of their own people.

It was Yan Mingfu's turn to be reasonable. He was open to the idea but not sure if it would be technically feasible. Most equipment had been allocated to the summit. They might not be able to set up a live broadcast in time. He proposed an alternative that the dialogue would be videotaped. As soon as each tape was completed, it would be sealed and transported to *CCTV** under students' monitoring. So, even though it was not live, it would be a faithful delayed feed to be shown in its entirety. In the mean time, students could also make audio tapes on their own and send them to Tiananmen Square for replaying.

While the student leaders were still pondering the idea, Yan Mingfu dropped the bomb: the Gorbachev welcoming ceremony might not be held at Tiananmen Square whether if they withdrew from it or not. That sealed the deal.[138]

The very possibility that the government might call their bluff on

---

*Chinese Central Television, the national television broadcaster in China.

such a grand scale weighted heavily on Wang Dan, Wuer Kaixi, and Wang Chaohua. They had never intended to interfere with the nation's diplomatic work and never thought that it could even be possible. Not only would they bear the responsibility of embarrassing the nation, they would also lose the biggest bargaining chip in their hand. Without it, how could all this come to an end?

Wang Chaohua volunteered to find some prominent intellectuals to help persuade students to leave. Yan Mingfu was ready to help. He dispatched an office vehicle for Wang Chaohua to use. Another van was sent out shortly after to the University of Political Science and Law. Its mission was to fetch the Dialogue Delegation.

Wang Chaohua was familiar with the intellectual circle in the capital from her family background. She was particularly fond of Dai Qing, a famous journalist at the intellectual-oriented newspaper *Guangming Daily*. Ten years younger than Yan Mingfu, Dai Qing was also a child prodigy. After her father was martyred in the early years of revolution, Dai Qing was raised by Ye Jianying, one of the ten marshals of the People's Liberation Army who was instrumental in the coup that deposed the "Gang of Four". Yet Dai Qing had acquired a strong sense of independence. Taking advantage of the protection from her background, she published many daring essays echoing the views of dissidents such as Fang Lizhi. She also made a name for herself with a staunch, Quixotic opposition to the plan of building the Three Gorges Dam on environmental grounds. Wang Chaohua had known Dai Qing since her childhood. The two also worked on the same floor when Wang Chaohua interned at *Guangming Daily*.

On the night when the hunger strike decision was made, Wang Chaohua had visited Dai Qing and did nothing but cry in her tiny living room. She was hoping Dai Qing, with her name recognition, could provide needed guidance to the much younger students.[139]

But Dai Qing had her own agenda in mind. This had been a couple of very good weeks for journalists. With Zhao Ziyang's blessing, the decades-old censorship policy melted away over night. With much personal nagging, Dai Qing had managed to get Hu Qili's approval for *Guangming Daily* to publish a full page of opinions by prominent but controversial intellectuals, an opportunity that was unthinkable just

Media open-up

weeks earlier. She was busy assembling them into a symposium. Her invitees included many big names, such as Yan Jiaqi, a political scientist who had written a book on the history of the Cultural Revolution, and Bao Zunxin, who had spearheaded a series of enlightening books introducing ideas from the west. A month earlier, a similar but unauthorized symposium with many of the same attendees had convened to commemorate Hu Yaobang's death. The proceedings were published in the Shanghai-based *World Economic Herald* and resulted in its shutdown. Now, Dai Qing had the approval from a Politburo standing committee member to do the very same thing.[140]

Wang Chaohua arrived at *Guangming Daily* just as Dai Qing was greeting her distinguished guests in a conference room. Dai Qing was in an exhilarated mood. She could see the paper, carrying the words of these people, causing a storm in its readership. She was not, however, prepared to see Wang Chaohua.

With one look at Wang Chaohua's tired and sad face, Dai Qing knew why she was here. Although sympathetic, Dai Qing was not about to have her little symposium hijacked by the student movement. Nonetheless, she invited Wang Chaohua into the room and introduced her as a student leader from the Square. But before Wang Chaohua could say anything or even shed a tear, Dai Qing laid out the purpose and importance of their symposium. With great excitement, she announced the deal she had struck with Hu Qili. A full page on *Guangming Daily*! Her enthusiasm was shared. To her audience, this was a tremendous breakthrough.

One by one, the intellectuals in their fifties and sixties read through their prepared speeches. There was little discussion or interruption. Wang Chaohua felt excruciating pain with the slow and dull pace of their lofty words with no substance. But she had to bite her tongue. She was raised with the greatest respect and deference for learned scholars. Hours were ticking away.[141]

Finally, all of them finished what they had planned to say. As a courtesy, they asked Wang Chaohua for a few words. That was when she choked up. Tears streamed down her cheeks before she could utter a single word. In a rambling, bumbling voice, she told the meeting that the situation at Tiananmen Square was not the glorious and historical event the intellectuals had been fantasizing in their talks. Rather, it was extremely dire. As she went on, she was getting more and more upset because she knew her words were incoherent. She felt panic because she was failing to express what she needed to say. But through her teary eyes, she sensed that many in the room were also crying. As she begged the intellectuals that they must go to the Square and persuade students to withdraw, everyone echoed, "Yes, we have to go. We can't just sit and watch."

As Wang Chaohua was regaining her composure, the intellectuals set out to do what they did best. In a matter of minutes, they came up with a draft statement. Addressing the students in a parental manner, it expressed that the authors were "very understanding, very sad, and very worried" after hearing the news of the hunger strike. Since democracy could not be achieved in one day, and for the sake of long-term interests of China's reform and the Sino-Soviet summit, it appealed to students "to carry on the spirit of rationality and temporarily withdraw from Tiananmen Square."

It was not clear what the term "temporarily" meant. But it would not matter anyway, as the statement changed its tone right after that and spelled out its own demands of the government. It asked top leaders to make a public speech praising the student movement as patriotic and democratic and promise not to punish student leaders after the dust settled. It also demanded that the government recognize the autonomous organizations and pledge never to use force against students engaged in hunger strikes or sit-ins. If the government could not fulfill these demands, the statement said, its authors pledged to "fight to the end along with the students."

Perhaps the ending statement was just an empty slogan thrown in to appease students or to satisfy the authors' own egos. But it appeared that these intellectuals were ready to join the movement, thereby negating the appeal for students to withdraw. Their demands actually went beyond of those of the students, who had already consolidated theirs into two core items: "Not Turmoil, Equal Dialogue."

Wang Chaohua knew something was not right with this statement. But with her state of mind she could not quite put her finger on the flaw. It started to dawn on her that her hopes with these intellectuals might have been misplaced. They were hopelessly out of touch with reality. Reluctantly, she expressed her worry that a statement like this would not be able to persuade students to withdraw. Her voice was weak. She knew that she was not convincing anyone. Yan Jiaqi was already frustrated with the statement as it was. He smashed his palm on the table and declared that they were barking up the wrong tree. It was the government, not the students, he shouted angrily, that they should appeal to.

Wang Chaohua held a last bit of hope. Maybe she could get these intellectuals in a room with the hunger strike leaders. If they could persuade Chai Ling privately, the mission could become more hopeful. Dai Qing called the United Front Department, a natural place for such a meeting. She only heard a frantic voice on the other end claiming that nothing was available. After a few more phone calls, Dai Qing secured a small place for the meeting. Wang Chaohua took off in her designated car toward the United Front Department. She thought she would find Chai Ling there at the dialogue with Yan Mingfu.[142]

But she was not prepared for what she would encounter.

Real Dialogue 5.14

It was finally the time for the Dialogue Delegation to shine. They were founded for this very purpose and had been preparing for several weeks. They had assigned designated speakers, each with a supporting team, to address specific issues. They had practiced and rehearsed. They felt confident and even comfortable to sit across a table with government officials to voice their issues reasonably and rationally.

In order for that to happen, though, Xiang Xiaoji and Shen Tong understood that they had to control the crowd on their own side, especially the hunger strikers. Yet they did not have much leverage. It was the hunger strike that had finally brought Yan Mingfu to the table. It would be impossible to exclude the hunger strikers, who distrusted the Dialogue Delegation, at this point.

The hunger strikers, on the other hand, had their own ideas. The prospect of a national broadcast, even with tape delay, had gotten them excited. What a great opportunity to get their voices heard! Chai Ling hurriedly collected banners from Tiananmen Square, including the one saying "Mom, I am Hungry" and rushed to the United Front Department. She placed them in the conference room as a backdrop on the students' side. She also brought a tape of her reading the *Hunger Strike Manifesto*. If they got to play the tape during the session, it would be broadcast nationwide and recorded permanently in history.[143]

The large conference room on the second-floor was now set up like a diplomatic meeting with a long oval table. Yan Mingfu was not at the head of the table this time. Rather, he sat in the middle on the government side, flanked by the State Education Commissioner Li Tieying and ten other minister-level officials. Across the table, Shen Tong sat down directly facing Yan Mingfu. Xiang Xiaoji sat opposite Li Tieying. They were flanked by the assigned speakers from the Dialogue Delegation. Xiang Xiaoji had made sure that the arrangement demonstrated the equality of the two sides in the dialogue.

Wang Juntao was sitting in another room in the same compound. He and other young intellectuals were not invited to this formal dialogue. Perhaps in Yan Mingfu's mind, they had already served his purpose.

In the conference room, the formal, diplomatic atmosphere was broken by a group of hunger strikers standing right behind the Dialogue Delegation. They wore signatory headbands and solemn expressions. Xiang Xiaoji had made a compromise to allow a limited number of them in the room, presumably only to listen in. Many tape recorders were scattered about on the conference table. They were already running. In one corner of the room was a video camera with a *CCTV* logo. Shen Tong made sure that he saw a little red light blinking on the camera as he opened the meeting.

Initially, the dialogue was cordial and gracious. Speakers from the Dialogue Delegation presented their prepared cases. Yan Mingfu and Li Tieying listened intently and answered most questions with sincerity. But pretty soon Xiang Xiaoji and Shen Tong were flooded with little paper notes passed in from the hunger strikers behind them, who were getting impatient and wanted to raise their own concerns instead. It did not take long for the session to deviate from a focused theme. Both sides at the table tried to be patient but the discussion was getting more and more scattered.

Soon the hunger strikers were dissatisfied with simply passing the notes. Someone spoke up and suggested that the meeting hear them directly. Wuer Kaixi volunteered that he had a letter from a hunger striker with him. Without asking for permission, Cheng Zhen, a female student from Beijing Normal University and one of the initiators of the hunger strike, read the letter aloud.

Chai Ling had been quiet as usual. But she was upset about Wuer Kaixi's unilateral move. The letter was moving but lacked substance. She thought that Wuer Kaixi had wasted a golden opportunity. As the session moved on, Chai Ling could not wait any longer. Jumping on an opening, she asked Yan Mingfu pointedly: "What do you really think of the student movement?" Being put on the spot, Yan Mingfu struggled with being honest but not crossing the party line: "Personally, I would very much like to say that you are patriotic. But I can't say that."[144]

Some more heated arguments erupted. A finger finally pressed down the play button on a tape recorder. All of sudden, Chai Ling's emotional voice, reading the *Hunger Strike Manifesto*, filled up the room:

> We would like to ask all upright citizens of this country, ask every worker, peasant, soldier, resident, intellectual, celebrity, official, police, and those who made up the labels for us, place your hand over your heart and ask your conscience: what crimes had we commit? Did we cause turmoil? We boycott classes. We march and protest. We go on hunger strike. We give our lives. For what? But our emotions have been repeatedly played by others. We suffer through hunger to pursue the truth but only get beaten by soldiers and police. Our representatives knelt down to appeal for democracy but were ignored. Our requests for an equal dialogue are being delayed again and again. Our student leaders are facing grave danger.

As if another button had also been pushed, the rowdy room fell silent. For ten mesmerizing minutes, nobody made any sound or move. Everyone in the room, including Yan Mingfu himself, was in tears. At the table, Xiang Xiaoji and Shen Tong held hands.

> We do not want to die. We want to live nicely because we are at the most beautiful age of our lifetime. We do not want to die. We want to study hard because our motherland is still so

157

poor and we can't just die like this and leave her behind. Death
is definitely not our desire. But if the death of one or a few
could make the lives of many better, make the motherland rich
and prosper, then we have no right to live shamelessly.

As soon as the recording was finished, a voice came from the hunger
strikers: "The only thing we ask for is that the government stop calling
us instigators of turmoil."[145]

IT had been more than an hour into the dialogue session. Students at
Tiananmen Square were becoming restless. They had been told of the
compromise that they would hear the proceedings with an hour delay.
But there was no sign of any broadcast.

Feng Congde had completed a new broadcasting station in the Square
with their own loudspeakers rigged up on flag poles. With others at
the dialogue session, he became the de facto leader there. Anxious,
he dispatched runner after runner to the United Front Department for
updates. None of them had come back.*

Another hour passed. It was now seven o'clock, time for the regular evening news broadcast on *CCTV*. There was no mention of the
dialogue in the news. That was the last straw. Spontaneously, all
hunger strikers in the Square gathered up and marched toward the
United Front Department, which was only two to three miles away.
They chanted "Stop the dialogue," "Direct Broadcast!" along the way.

Wang Chaohua arrived at the United Front Department and immediately found her car blocked by the raging hunger strikers on the street.
She ran inside and saw Xiang Xiaoji stepping out of the conference
room. They were separated by a throng of hunger strikers, some of
whom were runners dispatched by Feng Congde. More and more of
them were pouring in. It was at the verge of a disaster. Xiang Xiaoji
was doing everything he could to dissuade the crowd from storming
the conference room. He was obviously fighting a losing battle. In
desperation, he proposed to have Wang Chaohua, who he had known
as a mature and rational leader, into the room as a representative for

---

*Audio tapes of the dialogue, made by students themselves, might have indeed
reached the Square. But in the confusion, they were not delivered to Feng Congde.[146]

everyone outside. The crowd did not really know or trust Wang Chaohua either. They demanded to have two of their own to accompany her.

Xiang Xiaoji was not aware that Wang Chaohua was already in a daze herself. After an exhausting day, she could no longer comprehend what was going on. In a rush, the three of them burst through the door and startled everyone inside. Without missing a beat, Wang Chaohua declared, "Stop the dialogue! There is no Broadcast!" We students must stay together as a whole, she explained, the dialogue could not go on without the approval of the hunger strikers.

It was the second time the room fell into a dead silence. Shen Tong lost his cool. He stood up, slammed his palm on the table, and pointed his finger directly to Yan Mingfu's face: "Why aren't you broadcasting this? You knew full well that we can't continue if there is no broadcast!"

Yan Mingfu's face turned ashy pale. He appeared to be genuinely puzzled. Surveying the ministers on his side, he got no answers. After a painful while, he muttered: "If we can't continue, then we can't."

He stood up and slowly walked out of the room.[147]

Disaster ......

The highest principle of peace is sacrifice.

Chai Ling

9

The Confrontation

5.14 BEFORE she crashed into the conference room to put an end to the dialogue, Wang Chaohua had the presence of mind to delegate her original task to someone else nearby. She gave instructions to get the leaders of the hunger strike to meet the intellectuals gathered by Dai Qing. But in the ensuing chaos, Chai Ling was nowhere to be found. The intellectuals ended up meeting a small group of hunger strikers who were polite and in awe of the famous names. They spent much time obtaining autographs.

When the band of intellectuals headed to Tiananmen Square, it was already dark. On this second day of hunger strike, the area in front of the Monument to People's Heroes had already been transformed. Feng Congde's banner and broadcasting drew thousands. While the crowd was diligently kept outside the circle of hunger strikers by student marshals, the place was slowly turning into a carnival. Word of an upcoming visit by prominent intellectuals had been spreading for hours. Students packed the area eager for a rare glimpse of the famous figures they had previously only read about in newspapers and books.

160

The Confrontation

Student marshals struggled to clear a passage. The intellectuals had to be escorted hand-in-hand like kindergartners on a field trip to. Dai Qing was not among them.

There was magic in the night air. Facing the thousands of excited students, these intellectuals instantly transformed themselves into little pupils. One by one, they rose to praise the students. They claimed that the students, through their courageous actions, were the real teachers and they were the ones who had come to learn. They pledged to stand by the students. They denounced the government as impotent and corrupt for refusing to dialogue. One after another, they were saying everything they thought the students would like to hear. In return, they won loud applause and cheers and appeared to be enjoying every minute of it.

Sitting behind them, Wang Chaohua was devastated. This was exactly the opposite of what she had hoped for. Over the roar of the crowd, she screamed into the ears of the intellectuals to change their tone. But everyone was overtaken by the atmosphere. It was then that Dai Qing finally showed up.

Dai Qing had stopped by at the United Front Department and caught a moment alone with a distraught Yan Mingfu. She made an attempt to talk about the demands that the intellectuals had drawn up. But Yan Mingfu was certainly in no mood to hear any more demands. Eager to make something happen, Dai Qing abandoned the demands altogether and proposed to Yan Mingfu: what if Zhao Ziyang or Li Peng could come out in person to meet and greet the students? All they had to do was to make a gesture. Yan Mingfu told her that it could be possible but she should not expect anything more than that.[148]

Still basking in her own glory of getting Hu Qili's permission to publish a full page of intellectuals' speeches in *Guangming Daily*, Dai Qing felt that she had a resolution of the crisis in her hands. It was also a surreal scene she was facing. There were thousands of students all around her and they were all quiet as she was introduced. They knew her name and her unique background. Already warmed up by the other intellectuals, they were eager for some inside information.

Dai Qing told the students about her *Guangming Daily* story and hailed it as a huge achievement of the movement. There was only

Students: way too radical & emotional & dramatic

silence. Her audience did not understand what she was talking about. Undaunted, she went on to sell her deal with Yan Mingfu.

"So, if Zhao Ziyang or Li Peng came out to see everyone here, we would all go back to our schools, OK?"

There were confused murmurs in the crowd. One loud voice spoke out:

"What would they say when they come here?"

Dai Qing was taken aback by the question. After a brief pause, she said,

"How about they come and say 'students, how are you'? We just return to our schools. OK?"

Just then, she received a thunderous response:

"No Way! No Way!"

Dai Qing was shocked. She was not the only one either. The other intellectuals looked at each other very confused. These were not the conditions they had agreed upon. It was as if Dai Qing had poured a bucket of icy water onto their feverish heads. Sensing the mood turning against them, they left the Square slowly with their heads down. Nobody greeted them on their way out.[149]

It took almost an hour for Wang Chaohua to recover from this disaster. Upon being informed that all the intellectuals were crying after they got back to the United Front Department, she felt that it was she who had let the intellectuals down. At the broadcasting station, students were still debating the merits of withdrawing. Wang Chaohua grabbed the microphone and tried to explain to students the sincerity of the intellectuals. After all this was over, she said, they were the ones who would be accused as the "black hands" behind the movement. We students had to take our own responsibility, she mumbled on, mostly incoherent. All she wanted to say was a simple sentence, "Please, let us all withdraw." But in the charged atmosphere, she could not bring herself to actually say it aloud either. Instead, she repeated the mantra that they should all unite and persevere. When Feng Congde finally had enough and disconnected her microphone, she dumped all her emotion on him and screamed: "You will have to bear the responsibility of history!"[150]

Dai Qing's condescending manner left a big scar. She was there-

162

after regarded as a government agent and lost all her credibility. Wuer Kaixi would later remember this whole fiasco vividly:[151]

> The problem with these intellectuals was that they were playing the wrong role. They were acting as mediators between the students and the government. We made the government agree to face-to-face negotiations. This was unprecedented in the last forty years and this was accomplished by us, the students, acting as an independent political force. And then when we invited the intellectuals to join us, they came to the Square and addressed us as "children."

The next day, the proceedings of Dai Qing's symposium were published in *Guangming Daily*. Hardly anyone paid attention.

T HE collapse of the dialogue with Yan Mingfu hit everybody very hard. Wang Juntao stayed at the United Front Department and huddled with student leaders. He advised them to keep in touch with Yan Mingfu and seek every possibility to resume the dialogue. It was still their best and maybe last hope. Shen Tong, on the other hand, led most of his Dialogue Delegation members to Tiananmen Square. It was their first time to see the hunger strikers on site. Their hearts sank. Shen Tong felt a deep sense of guilt for having let his fellow students down. He broke down after attempting to apologize to the students in the Square.[152]

Wuer Kaixi also rushed back to the Square. The fasting and the drama of the dialogue had driven him into near hysteria. He could not believe that the welcoming ceremony for Mr. Gorbachev would not be held in the Square. He was surveying the quiet and peaceful scene at the early hour of four o'clock. Most hunger strikers were asleep. A few student nurses were lightly walking around and checking on them. All of a sudden, Wuer Kaixi broke the silence with a scream over the loudspeakers. He urged everyone to wake up and move. As students, we had to make our own sacrifices for our national interests and image, he said. He instructed everyone to move over to the east side of the Monument to People's Heroes. There, they would still be in the Square but not directly visible from the Great Hall of People where welcoming ceremonies were traditionally held. This would be a good-will gesture to the government, he went on to explain, an action to demonstrate that we were indeed as patriotic as we claimed to be. He did not mention that the decision not to have the ceremony in the Square had already been made. He probably still hoped that their action could prompt someone to reverse that decision. Someone like Yan Mingfu, who he had grown to trust and admire.

The hunger strikers neither appreciated being woken up at this hour nor agreed with his decision. But they were too weak to argue. Slowly, they stood up, gathered what few things they had, and walked over to the new location. Disgusted once again, Feng Congde left the scene. There were other dissents. Hunger strikers from People's University stood their ground and refused to move. They stayed put until early morning, when, after much arguing, they rejoined the main group.

Although Wuer Kaixi had emphasized that he was acting on his own, most took his action as another bad move by the Beijing Students Autonomous Federation, which formally expelled him for his erratic behavior. But the damage was already done. Very few people were aware of the expulsion anyway. Wuer Kaixi continued to appear as the public face of the Federation.

LI Lu was out that night procuring salt water for the hunger strikers from a hospital. By the time he came back in the morning, he could not believe his eyes. In fact, he could not even find the student camp. The new area they occupied was not only invisible from the Great Hall of People, it could hardly be seen from Chang'an Avenue. Morning commuters were passing by. They looked over and saw an empty Square. With the forthcoming arrival of Mr. Gorbachev, they must have concluded that the students had ended their strike.

This was a total disaster! Li Lu yelled at Chai Ling, who was equally distressed. Li Lu told Chai Ling that they could not afford having people like Wuer Kaixi running the show any longer. It was time for them to take charge and prepare for the long haul. They had to bear the responsibility for the health and lives of these thousands of hunger strikers. Chai Ling agreed readily.

But Li Lu did not appear to be his usual cool and collected self either. He went on and on. Since the government might simply ignore them until the hunger strikers started to die, he reasoned that they needed to up the ante and force the issue. The leaders must be willing to die before the masses. The only qualification for leaders, he stressed, should be a willingness to commit self-immolation when the time came.

Chai Ling's tears came down as soon as she heard the word self-immolation. The images of her parents and her husband flashed before her eyes. But in the noble spirit of self-sacrifice, she agreed with the idea. Her admiration and affection for Li Lu also grew. The movement needed a strong leader, she told him, and he was the one. Li Lu declined. He was aware of the fact that he was an outsider without any platform to lead. It was Chai Ling to whom everybody listened and looked for leadership.[153]

Around eight o'clock, just as the morning sun warmed up the Square again, the two walked to the broadcasting station. Chai Ling took up the microphone. They were surrounded by hunger strikers who were clearly under duress. They, the hundreds of them, were alone. There were no longer many students or residents around them. Even the student marshals had disappeared. In an instant, Chai Ling regained her confidence. With a shy and disarming smile, she introduced herself softly, "I am Chai Ling, I am the one who wrote the *Hunger Strike Manifesto*." She was greeted with applause. Suddenly, without warning, she raised the pitch and volume of her voice and boldly proclaimed, "I declare, we will fight to the end with our lives. I will accept death if necessary, but I will not take defeat lying down." Applause and cheers, albeit still weak, echoed.

After acknowledging their bleak situation, she continued, "Doctors said that three days [of hunger strike] is the limit. I cannot just wait for so many young lives to disappear. If we are doomed to death, I will be the first one to walk to death. If my life can save all of us here, I will not hesitate to set fire to myself in order to save the rest of us."

Gloom once again set in and many cried. But the undaunted Chai Ling proposed the founding of a Hunger Strike Headquarters "to coordinate our efforts and protect ourselves." She offered herself as the first commander-in-chief. "My qualification is my pledge to achieve our goals and protect you with my life."

Standoff At Tiananmen

There were more tears and applause. Spirits were gradually lifting. A dozen or so hunger strikers stood up to volunteer their services. Without explanation, Chai Ling introduced Li Lu as her deputy in charge of daily operations. There was neither an election nor any apparent dissent.

Then, the new Commander-in-Chief led the hunger strikers in reciting their pledge. Chai Ling's voice was now calm and strong: "For the democratization of our motherland, for the prosperity of our country, I am willing to take part in the hunger strike. I will not stop the hunger strike until our goals are achieved."

Li Lu was more than ready. Within minutes of taking over the microphone, he put a series of actions into motion. A census was carried out. In that morning of May 15, there were 1,030 hunger strikers on site, about two hundred more than when they had started. Already, there were eighty of them who had fainted and been taken to hospitals. The hunger strikers came from more than forty colleges. Li Lu instructed each school to elect two representatives of their own. They would form a parliament and make all necessary decisions for the Headquarters. Not only would it provide some checks and balances, he explained, they could also learn and practice democracy themselves.[154]

A new life began in the Square. Students from medical colleges set up emergency tents marked with Red Cross signs on the northeast corner. Ambulances from nearby hospitals were parked nearby and ready for action. As the day went on, people started to pour into the Square again. The deteriorating state of the hunger strikers heading into their third day of fast drew many tears from well-wishers.

After the exhausting previous day, nobody seemed to notice the news of Yan Mingfu that morning. At half past eight, the tireless bureaucrat was already commencing another dialogue with students. This time he went back to those from the official, now essentially defunct, student unions. There was no drama with this crowd. But he appeared to extend his hands further out and publicly suggested a re-evaluation of the April 26 *People's Daily* editorial: "The massive demonstrations by the students on April 27 and May 4 should be positively assessed, except for the fact that the demonstrators failed to

166

apply for approval with the relevant departments."[155]

Mikhail Gorbachev's plane touched down at the Capital Airport on the outskirts of the city at noon. As a twenty-one gun salute roared over the runway, President Yang Shangkun, the nominal head of China, welcomed Mr. Gorbachev in an abbreviated ceremony at the terminal. The majority of the foreign press who had come to cover this historical summit was absent. They were either stuck at Tiananmen Square or in the traffic jam trying to figure out how the presidents could negotiate their planned itinerary while avoiding the messy Tiananmen Square.

It was a huge embarrassment to the Chinese government. When the news of the ceremony at the airport reached the Square, students' heads dropped and their hearts sank. Their good-will gesture had been ignored. The stakes had been raised. The government had indeed called their bluff.

4.15 afternoon march

THINGS started to look better for the hunger strikers later in that afternoon. Having been snubbed by students the day before, intellectuals decided to take a stand on their own. Under a banner of "Chinese Intellectuals," forty thousand people marched along Chang'an Avenue and arrived at Tiananmen Square at four o'clock. Yan Jiaqi, Bao Zunxin, and many other famous names marched and waved at crowds. To enhance publicity, they wore banners across their bodies proudly displaying their names and titles of their significant works. At the front of the procession, several of them held up a large white bedspread with a calligraphed statement with their respective signatures. Dai Qing was not among them. She had come to join the march but was spurned by angry organizers who accused her of being a mole.[156]

Also missing were Chen Ziming, Wang Juntao and their band of intellectuals on the fringe of this community. Chen Ziming was still trying to maintain his distance from the movement and keeping his people focused on their research work. As the march progressed down Chang'an Avenue, Chen Ziming and Wang Juntao were participating in a symposium organized by the official labor union, in which they expressed hope that workers would not get involved in the ongoing movement.[157]

This rather unusual march drew thousands of curious spectators.

Standoff At Tiananmen

They followed along and entertained themselves by matching faces to their names. As they circled Tiananmen Square, the place came back to life.

The march of intellectuals was the handiwork of Zheng Yi, the author who had helped seed the idea of a hunger strike with students. As soon as the hunger strike was announced, he was busy on the phone getting his friends together. Many of these middle-aged intellectuals had personally experienced the Cultural Revolution. Some remembered it, at least its early years, not as turmoil but a popular uprising. With the new generation launching a hunger strike in Tiananmen Square, the heart and soul of the country, they were experiencing a kind of excitement that they had not felt in decades. Zheng Yi and Yan Jiaqi had worked all night on their statement. They were too excited to be exhausted. For the first time in decades, they felt, the intellectuals in China were going to have a voice of their own.

Even Zheng Yi was surprised by the turnout as they started to assemble at the west end of Chang'an Avenue. They were only expecting dozens when they saw an endless inflow of people. Unlike the younger students, Chinese intellectuals had traditionally never been a force for mass protests. They tended to strive for personal gratification and survival. The hunger strike was changing many people's mentality.[158]

At the Square, they read their statement through the students' loudspeakers. Yan Jiaqi and Bao Zunxin showered superlatives on the students. They expressed their unconditional solidarity. There was no more talk about withdrawal. As the crowd finally dissipated, Zheng Yi and his wife decided to stay at the Square. The students needed their help. His friend Zhang Boli had also made his way there, bringing friends from his "authors class" and the community. Together, they formed an informal advisory board and secretariat for the much younger student leaders. In between drafting speeches and statements for them, they also developed the makeshift broadcasting station in the Square into another full-fledged media center.

T HE shortened welcoming ceremony at the airport was just the beginning of a bumpy first day for Mr. Gorbachev in Beijing. Entering the city, his motorcade was reduced to dodging traffic in back streets

168

and alleys as intellectuals marched on Chang'an Avenue. In his limousine, Mr. Gorbachev smiled and waved gamely, enjoying this unique experience in this ancient capital. Eventually, they sneaked into the Great Hall of People through a back door. There, a state banquet in his honor was being hosted by Yang Shangkun.

Just as the toasts were being given, a situation developed outside of the main entrance of the Great Hall of People. In the twilight, a noisy crowd gathered on the flights of stairs threatening to break through. They were shouting for national leaders to come out and talk with the students. It was a familiar scene. Thirteen years earlier, during the April Fifth Movement, thousands also tried to storm the Great Hall. While they did not succeed, it had led to arson and violence in the Square.

At the new Hunger Strike Headquarters, Li Lu had a much harder time bringing his new parliament together than creating orders for their camp. The newly minted representatives were all starved and temperamental. They spent much of the time arguing with each other. Displaying his organizational prowess, Li Lu laid down rules and pushed his agenda along. Slowly, a process was put in place. The parliament voted against an immediate withdrawal. They also voted down a few radical proposals, such as refusing water, lying down on Chang'an Avenue to block traffic, as well as self-immolation, originally proposed by Li Lu as a qualification for their leaders.

The situation on the steps of the Great Hall of People, however, demanded their immediate attention. These students were too young to make the connection with the April Fifth Movement. But they knew by instinct that the government was looking for any excuse to validate their accusation that this movement was inciting turmoil. An angry mob of non-students starting a violent act and ruining their movement was exactly the nightmare they had feared from the very beginning. They had to step up and stop this madness. Chai Ling called on the hunger strikers, whoever had enough energy to stand up, to go and help defend the Great Hall.

All very weak and many hardly able to talk, they rose up one by one and walked across the Square in a line, hand-in-hand. It took a tremendous effort for them to sneak through the crowd onto the top level of the stairs. There, they inserted themselves between the crowd and the soldiers guarding the entrance. In front of them there was already an angry mob of thousands, shouting and pushing. At their back, however, was merely a thin line of soldiers, who did not appear at all concerned about an imminent storming.

Li Lu had a funny feeling about the scene. He looked up and saw the National Emblem on top of the building and thought that it looked like an ugly wolf. He commented to Chai Ling that they were indeed standing at a juncture in history, only that they appeared to be on the wrong side as they were defending the Bastille from a raging mob. Chai Ling did not have time to appreciate the irony. She fainted. Li Lu called for help but the soldiers showed no interest. When she regained consciousness, Chai Ling screamed through a bullhorn: "We are the hunger strike students. Please understand and do not storm the Great Hall. If you want to do that, you will have to step over our bodies."[159]

The crowd was still pushing up. The hunger strikers stood their ground. Wuer Kaixi arrived with reinforcements and led them into a throbbing chant "Get Down! Get Down!" Gradually, the chant grew stronger and stronger as the crowd joined in. The tide had turned. Thousands of people slowly retreated from the stairs and dissipated.[160]

No sooner had the exhausted hunger strikers made their way back to the camp, however, than another crisis was brewing. This time, it came within their own ranks.

ONE of the rules Li Lu had implemented to maintain the order of their camp was simple and straightforward. Everyone must have a valid student identification card before gaining entry to an inner zone guarded by student marshals. It did not take long for some people to find out that Li Lu did not possess any identification card himself. In fact, nobody knew him before he mysteriously appeared in late April. When confronted, Li Lu could not produce any solid evidence to back up his claim of being a student from Nanjing University. Suspicion grew that he might be a spy.[161]

Chai Ling would hear none of it. She had come to admire, trust, and indeed, totally depend on Li Lu for the work at the new Headquarters. She felt upset that Li Lu had to face such unfair accusations. In what would develop into a pattern on critical issues, Chai Ling let her tears do the reasoning. If anyone trusted her, she cried in anger, they would have to trust Li Lu as well.

So, in the evening of May 15, only hours after the Hunger Strike Headquarters was founded, Chai Ling and Li Lu were confronted by three hunger strikers just as they got back from the steps of Great Hall of People. Ma Shaofang, Cheng Zhen, and a couple other participants of the restaurant meeting that launched the hunger strike with Wang Dan and Wuer Kaixi were upset with the way the Headquarters was created and with Chai Ling stealing the show and playing dictator. They told Chai Ling that the unelected Headquarters was illegitimate. They must hold an election. They also produced a slate of candidates. Li Lu was not in it.

Li Lu had almost had enough of it. He informed Chai Ling that he was ready to quit and return to Nanjing. Dejected, he sat at the base of the Monument to People's Heroes, alone, for the entire night. The starry and peaceful spread of the open square cleared his mind. He decided to stay.[162]

The morning could not have come quickly enough for these troubled hunger strikers. An election was quickly held in the student parliament, and Chai Ling and Li Lu were reaffirmed as their leaders. The Hunger Strike Headquarters gained a symbolic legitimacy. They were too busy to notice, or too young to be aware that this day, May 16, was yet another, albeit unrecognized, anniversary date in China's busy political calendar. On this day in 1966, a terse directive from the Communist Party Central Committee lifted the curtain of the decade-long Cultural Revolution. To this new generation, however, this was just the day they would be entering their fourth day of hunger strike.

THE Soviet Union and China, the two biggest communist countries, famously broke off in the early 1960's amid verbal sparring on ideology accompanied by sporadic armed conflicts along their shared border. As China descended into the chaos of the Cultural Revolution domestically, the country became hopelessly isolated from the rest of the world, defying both the "American Capitalist Imperialism" and the "Soviet Revisionist Hegemony" superpowers at the same time. It was not until the early 1970's when a dying Mao Zedong showed a rare instance of flexibility and steered the nation onto a path of reconciliation with the United States. His motivation was much less an ideological alignment with the Americans than the pragmatic need to counter the more imminent threat from the Soviet Union.

The Sino-Soviet relationship finally showed signs of recovering a decade later. Mr. Gorbachev's glasnost and perestroika in the Soviet Union had echoed Deng Xiaoping's reform in China. With both countries shifting their attention away from ideology and world revolutionary leadership, they needed a peaceful border in order to both reduce military budgets and promote trade. A gradual thaw culminated in this summit, the first since 1959, which would mark the official normalization of their estranged relationship.

Students at Tiananmen Square were also excited about Mr. Gorbachev's visit for a different reason. The reform in the Soviet Union was seen to have surpassed that in China, particularly in the touchy areas of political reform. While Deng Xiaoping had stubbornly restricted his reform within the confines of his Four Cardinal Principles, Mr. Gorbachev had welcomed free press and open challenges to the Communist Party, exactly what the students were striving for with their demonstrations and hunger strike. Among the many new banners erected by students this day, one pointedly stated: "Welcome Mr. Gorbachev, the True Reformer."*

Their sincere welcome aside, Mr. Gorbachev's visit continued to be hampered by the movement. His plan of laying a wreath at the Monument to People's Heroes had to be canceled this morning. His motorcade continued to enter and exit the Great Hall of People by side doors. His official agenda, though, started without a hitch. The first meeting was with Deng Xiaoping himself. Being semi-retired, Deng Xiaoping was officially neither the head of the Party nor the state. Yet Deng Xiaoping had no problem proclaiming his meeting as *the* summit. With great fanfare, he and Mr. Gorbachev happily marked the occasion as the formal rehabilitation of the relationship between two Parties and two nations.

---

*Mr. Gorbachev, on the other hand, was less than impressed. During a press conference, he famously commented on the students: "We have our hotheads, too."

The Confrontation

In the afternoon, the General Secretary, Zhao Ziyang, who was the actual leader of the Chinese Communist Party, sat down with Mr. Gorbachev.

Just outside of the Great Hall of People, hundreds of thousands of spectators had returned to the Square with concerns for the hunger strikers as the strike prolonged. The spectacle attracted most of foreign reporters who had come to cover the historical summit. Western television crews jostled with each other to place their news anchors at the best angles. With ingenuity and persistence, *CNN*'s Mike Chinoy broadcast the very first live shot from within Tiananmen Square itself.[163] It was from this vantage point that *CNN*'s anchor Bernard Shaw later delivered in his trademark low and booming voice: "I came to cover a summit. I walked into a revolution. The situation in Tiananmen Square is that it is a standoff." It was a sentiment echoed by *CBS*' anchor Dan Rather, who was also at the scene.

The standoff was escalating to a dramatic stage on this very day. Approaching the seventy-two hour deadline speculated by Zheng Yi, more and more students were fainting. The sirens of ambulance vehicles carrying collapsed hunger strikers to hospitals became disturbingly frequent.* Li Lu had ordered student marshals to open up a "life line" for the ambulances. These marshals linked up their arms in two rows to keep open a passage from their camp to Chang'an Avenue. They were under strict orders to keep the passage clear day and night. Standing either in the hot sun during the day or the chill of night sometimes for hours without food or water, numerous volunteers manned the "life line" religiously. Many of them fainted during their services. They were immediately replaced by others stepping in from the crowd.

Along with the "life line," other security measures were put in place. Student marshals were deployed to make secured perimeters

---

*The first time a siren of an ambulance was heard in the Square, it was not for a hunger striker or even a student. Among the spectators in the Square in the evening of May 14 was poet Luo Yihe. He became uncontrollably excited by the scene and then collapsed suddenly. An ambulance took him to a hospital immediately and he was diagnosed as having suffered a cerebral hemorrhage. He died in the hospital a few days later. His illness and death were kept a secret so that it would not stir up the ongoing crisis. To this day, Luo Yihe remains the only known death during the hunger strike period.

in concentric circles with the headquarters at the center. Various forms of passes and passwords were issued. Only trusted personnel with the right credentials could gain access to the nerve center of the movement. Others were kept safely at bay. Tiananmen Square was slowly turning into a "People's Republic" of its own, complete with a government no less bureaucratic than the one that students despised.

In the Great Hall of People, Zhao Ziyang did not waste time to put his own talk with Mr. Gorbachev into context. For this occasion, Zhao Ziyang was wearing a dark gray stripped western suit and a light purple tie. He smiled warmly to the cameras despite the chaos outside. Your meeting with Deng Xiaoping earlier was the real summit between our two Parties, he told Mr. Gorbachev. Ever since Deng Xiaoping chose to "retire" two years ago, the Chinese Communist Party Politburo had made a formal resolution that any decisions of significance must be made in consultation with Comrade Deng Xiaoping. So, despite his title, or the lack thereof, Deng Xiaoping's supreme leadership was indispensable to the Party. The resolution was never made public, Zhao Ziyang said, but I wanted to let you know today.* Mr. Gorbachev responded politely that he appreciated the level of confidence they had achieved. They then proceeded into a philosophical discussion of reforms. Zhao Ziyang referred to the ongoing movement as a temporary difficulty caused by miscommunication and mistrust between the generations. However, to Mr. Gorbachev's puzzlement, Zhao Ziyang also raised the question whether true freedom of speech could be possible in a one-party system. Mr. Gorbachev, the "true reformer," had no answers.[164]

Mr. Gorbachev met with Premier Li Peng next. Long regarded as the figurehead of the conservative force, Li Peng on this day impressed Mr. Gorbachev and the foreign press in stressing the need for reforms in China. "People in socialist countries should also enjoy freedom,

---

*Bao Tong, the long-time political secretary for Zhao Ziyang, later explained that he was the one who inserted the message of Deng Xiaoping's leadership role into briefings for Zhao Ziyang after learning details of Deng Xiaoping's own meeting with Mr. Gorbachev. He argued that the resolution was not really a secret and Zhao Ziyang had said similar things to other visiting dignitaries in the past. The latter account could not be verified.

grand theme of the century: |Reform|

democracy, and human rights. China is prepared to improve these aspects of its political reform," he said in what believed to be the first positive mention of the term "human rights" by a Chinese leader.[165]

5/16.

ABOUT the same time as Zhao Ziyang sat down with Mr. Gorbachev, Yan Mingfu walked out of his office at the United Front Department and found quite a few of his guests still in his compound. Wang Dan, Wuer Kaixi, Xiang Xiaoji, and Wang Juntao, among others, had lingered on the premises in hopes of finding an opening to revive the dialogue. Wuer Kaixi, in particular, had found a home for himself there. His unpopular decision to move the hunger strikers to the edge of the Square had completely ruined his standing in the movement. Isolated and unwanted, he took refuge in the United Front Department whose mission included working with the many ethnic minorities in China. As a Uyghur, he was enjoying extra attention in this office. Cadres in the department developed personal relationships with this charming youngster. Yan Mingfu had also personally encouraged him to consider a career in the department after his graduation.[166]

But right now, Yan Mingfu had more urgent matters on his mind. Quietly, he told the students, "I am willing to be your hostage in the Square if you agree to stop the hunger strike. I will stay as your hostage until the government agrees to have a formal dialogue with the students."

Stunned, Wang Dan and Wuer Kaixi did not know what to make of this absurd offer. But they had both come to respect and trust the man. In these short and turbulent days, the steady and sincere Yan Mingfu had become a much needed father figure. They were quite moved that Yan Mingfu was putting the health of hunger strikers above his own agenda and career. So, they urged Yan Mingfu to go to Tiananmen Square and make his appeal directly to the students there. With great reluctance, Yan Mingfu agreed.

It was not a long journey, but streets near the Square were packed with people. The identity of this little entourage was soon discovered. A spontaneous and angry mob surrounded them and hurled insults at Yan Mingfu. They threatened to beat up the "corrupt government official." Visibly shaken, Yan Mingfu and his body guards sought refuge

Yan Ming fu's last offer as a hostage

in an ambulance van as Wuer Kaixi and Wang Dan tried to control the situation. Finally, a band of student marshals came to their rescue. They pushed and shoved to reach the student broadcasting station at the center of the Square. It was the first time an officer of Yan Mingfu's stature had appeared among the masses. The crowd went totally out of control. Even the student "life line" collapsed under the pressure.

Over loudspeakers, Wang Dan made the introduction by vouching for Yan Mingfu's integrity: "I guarantee with my own personal character that Yan Mingfu is a true communist, an upright communist, and a very good person. Please listen to him."[167]

Facing the surreal scene, Yan Mingfu might have had a flashback to the days of the Cultural Revolution when he was dragged in front of angry mobs of thousands denouncing his "crimes." With streaming tears and a slight tremble in his body, Yan Mingfu screamed into the microphone with his personal appeal. He told the hunger strikers that they had no right to destroy their own health and life because the future was going to be theirs and the reform needed them. In an even more obvious hint of the split within the government, he told students that the "reform faction" needed time and the students must give them the time to resolve this crisis. In vague terms, he promised students that a "day of justice" would come soon.

Amid the chaos, it was not clear how many people got a close look at Yan Mingfu or heard his speech. Some students chanted their demands, "Not Turmoil, Equal Dialog!" "Not Turmoil, Equal Dialog!" as he talked. Yan Mingfu still could not address these demands directly. He personally guaranteed that students would be safe after it was over.

Then, he made the offer of himself as a hostage.

Those who did hear the speech were shocked. Wang Dan and Wuer Kaixi each spoke up again to endorse Yan Mingfu's character and appeal to the crowd to stop the hunger strike. Just as a raucous debate broke out, Wuer Kaixi fainted. Crowds scrambled to reestablish the "life line" and get Wuer Kaixi into an ambulance. The dreadful siren once again permeated the Square. After the ambulance took off amid the chaos, Yan Mingfu was nowhere to be found. Curiously, having just made his offer to be a hostage, Yan Mingfu chose not to remain in the Square. He had departed with Wuer Kaixi.[168]

Debate raged on. Beijing Students Autonomous Federation and the Dialogue Delegation, two organizations not directly involved in the hunger strike, resolved to heed Yan Mingfu's advice and withdraw. The hunger strikers took a survey of their troops. Out of 2,753 hunger strikers present at the time, only 54 agreed to withdraw. So they decided to stay the course. Beijing Students Autonomous Federation and the Dialogue Delegation had no choice. They changed their stance right away for solidarity.[169]

D ESPITE the determination of the hunger strikers, however, their conditions continued to deteriorate and their fate grew more dire with each passing hour. They had been reduced to slumping down on the ground with no energy to stand or walk. The wailing sirens of ambulances had replaced singing and chanting as the dominant sound in the Square. In the afternoon of May 16, the seventy-two hour mark sneaked by.

Dissent also flared up among their ranks. The hunger strike was facing a severe challenge to its own credibility. Some of the original hunger strikers had been taken to hospitals or back to campuses where they silently dropped out. Some of them returned after having consumed food. Many, if not most, of the current strikers had joined in late and had not fasted as many hours. Within their camp, empty milk bottles, chocolate bar wrappers, and the remains of nutritious fluids were frequently found, hinting that at least some of them were violating their own rules of fasting.*

*While wide-spread cheating did exist during the later stages of the hunger strike, the issue of whether its leaders had violated their own rules was more complicated. Shen Tong had once walked in on Wuer Kaixi eating a box lunch.[170] Yet Wuer Kaixi later revealed that he had already stopped fasting on the fifth day after being diagnosed with a heart problem.[171] Shen Tong also investigated the rumor about Wang Dan and concluded that there was no evidence of Wang Dan cheating. To this day, Wang Dan has maintained that he had never taken food during the entire hunger strike period.

On the other hand, other student leaders such as Feng Congde faced the opposite problem. They were never part of the hunger strike. But they had to eat discreetly away from the public eye so that they were not mistaken as cheating.

Standoff At Tiananmen

An angry group of hunger strikers from the University of Political Science and Law broke off from the main camp. They walked the block down Chang'an Avenue and settled in front of Xinhuamen where they vowed to have a purer version of hunger strike. In fact, they would up the ante and refuse water as well. Wu Renhua, a teacher from the school who had joined the hunger strike from the beginning, rushed over with several of his fellow young teachers. They persuaded the students to conduct their thirst strike only in the form of a relay. When one was taken to hospital for treatment, another started to refuse water. In the meantime, while maintaining their hunger strike, everyone should continue to take in water, especially the salty water their bodies badly needed.

These were not the only ones who tried to force the issue. Four students from the Academy of Performing Arts showed up at the northwest corner of Tiananmen Square between Xinhuamen and the Monument to People's Heroes that afternoon. True to their artistic characters, they wrapped themselves like mummies and laid in a line side-by-side. A big sign declared their action: "Hunger Strike, Thirst Strike!" A large group of people surrounded them. Student nurses knelt down and tearfully begged them to drink fluids.

In the middle of Tiananmen Square, Li Lu ran into a group of students who had sealed their mouths with tape. With great compassion, Li Lu managed to talk them into removing the tape and accepting water before he fainted for the first time.[172]

In the pre-dawn hours of May 17, Zhao Ziyang and Li Peng paid a visit to hunger strikers receiving treatments in a hospital. Other than pleasantries and sympathies, they had little to offer. The students, who were bedridden with intravenous needles attached to their arms, begged the leaders to go to Tiananmen Square.[173]

To Chinese at large, the fact that Deng Xiaoping still had the final say on decisions was hardly shocking at all. If anything, it was taken as a matter of course. As the news of the summit, including Zhao Ziyang's mention of the secret resolution, was reported in the official press, few paid close attention. Except for some of Zhao Ziyang's closest advisers.

178

Zhao's "hint" to break ranks w/ Deng?

The Confrontation

The political scientist Yan Jiaqi was the first to react. He took Zhao Ziyang's disclosure as a signal to break ranks with Deng Xiaoping and immediately produced a statement. At high noon, in the middle of Tiananmen Square, an ambitious and triumphant looking Yan Jiaqi exclaimed:*

> The Qing Dynasty has been dead for seventy-six years. However, there is still an emperor without title in China, an old and fatuous dictator. Yesterday afternoon, General Secretary Zhao Ziyang publicly announced that all important decisions in China must go through this old and decrepit dictator. Without the words of this dictator, the April 26 *People's Daily* editorial could not be recalled. After almost a hundred hours of hunger strike, we now have no other choice. The Chinese people can not wait for the dictator to admit his mistake. Now, we have to rely on students themselves, rely on people ourselves. Today, we announce to the whole nation, and the whole world, that the hundred hour hunger strike has achieved a great victory. Students have proved through their own actions that this movement is not turmoil, but a great patriotic and democratic movement that will finally bury the emperorship and dictatorship in China!

March 5.16

Adding to the effect, Yan Jiaqi ended his speech by leading thunderous chants that included "Down with the Dictator!", "Dictators Must Go!", "Government by Old Men Must End!"

Yan Jiaqi had a great audience that day. From the early morning, it appeared that the entire city of Beijing was coming out to the streets and to Tiananmen Square. Workers, peasants, intellectuals, and even Buddhist monks in their orange uniforms, marched along Chang'an Avenue and circled Tiananmen Square with flags and banners. With no fear of repercussions, they proudly displayed the names of their work units, which included numerous government bureaus and agencies. The contingent from the *People's Daily* office was especially

---

*The statement referred to the history of the Qing Dynasty during which the Empress Dowager Cixi became the de facto ruler of China despite the fact that she had no official title. She ruled behind a curtain while her young son, the Emperor Guangxu, nominally held the court.

eye-catching. Young reporters and editors disowned its April 26 editorial to the wildest cheers. Indeed, the same paper would publish an emotional report written in poetic language the next day with a glowing headline *History will Remember this Day!*

The hunger strikers had long hoped that their display of extreme suffering would wake up the consciousness of the general populace. On this day, they appeared to have achieved that goal, and then some.

MEANWHILE, however, the hunger strikers discovered that they had yet another crisis looming on the horizon, literally.

In the evening of May 17, Li Lu was informed that a big thunderstorm was in the forecast. It would surely be welcoming news as they had suffered days of dry heat. But the hunger strikers still had no real shelters. They were especially vulnerable to the elements as their bodies could no longer provide any meaningful defense. To make matters worse, Tiananmen Square, the holiest place in the country, had become a filthy garbage dump. Sanitary operations in the area had been suspended. Millions of spectators who visited every day left tons of trash behind them. A substantial rainfall mixed with garbage, Li Lu was warned, could ignite an epidemic fatal to his hunger strikers.

This time, though, it was the city that came to the rescue. At five o'clock in the morning, more than seventy buses arrived. One by one, they were parked in a tight formation along the north side of the Square. With greatest efforts, Zhang Boli and Feng Congde led the hunger strikers, some of whom had to be carried along, onto the buses. At last, they had shelters. Alert for possible sabotage, students released the air in the tires so that they could not be driven off when they were asleep.

The strenuous move took hours. As the morning progressed, Li Lu and Feng Congde were interrupted by Cheng Zhen who came with an urgent message: there would be another dialogue. This time, she explained as she struggled to catch her breath, it would be with someone higher ranking than Yan Mingfu. It could be either Zhao Ziyang or Li Peng! Busy at their work, Li Lu and Feng Congde did not think it was worth their attention. Neither did Chai Ling, who, like Li Lu, was already on the verge of another collapse.

Wang Chaohua knew that they had to find the Dialogue Delegation. She and Cheng Zhen rushed to the United Front Department. But neither Xiang Xiaoji nor Shen Tong was there. Shen Tong was running a bad fever that morning and had gone home to rest. The rest of the Dialogue Delegation had also retreated to the University of Political Science and Law to regroup.[174] The one person who was there and very happy to see them was Wuer Kaixi, who had just came back from the hospital, still wearing a hospital gown. As Wang Chaohua and Cheng Zhen were administered intravenous fluids, they saw Wuer Kaixi and Wang Dan enter a small conference room with Yan Mingfu. After a short while, they came out and Wuer Kaixi announced that Yan Mingfu had decided that the two of them would be the lead for the students in the dialogue. Others should remain silent as much as possible. With that, they and a few other students were loaded into a van and driven into the Great Hall of People through a side door.[175]

MR. Gorbachev concluded his much disrupted stay in Beijing before the approaching storm. He headed south for Shanghai from where he would tour some of the southern cities. As he was departing, a joint communiqué between the two nations formally normalized their relations. But it hardly made the news. Almost all the foreign press who had come to shadow Mr. Gorbachev's visit stayed in Beijing. The standoff was now a global affair.

The reporters were richly rewarded. Everyday millions marched on Chang'an Avenue and around Tiananmen Square. Domestically, Zhao Ziyang's bold experiment with free press was in full swing. In the absence of official censorship, however, objective reporting did not quite materialize. Rather, newspapers were filled with sensational stories of hunger strikers and their supporters. The movement was portrayed as a holy occurrence.* It was as if the movement had been endorsed by the authorities. People from all walks of life crowded streets in a festive carnival atmosphere. Famous television personalities mingled

---

*The chaos at Tiananmen Square, along with the infighting and questionable behavior of some students, were never reported. Neither was Yan Mingfu's efforts to bring an end to the crisis. Young journalists decided not to cover that story because they were disappointed in the students' performance.[176]

with young residents. Factory workers in their uniforms rode in trucks decorated with their factory flags. Office dwellers proudly displayed the names of their working units from Party bureaus to offices in the State Council. Even companies of soldiers and policemen were seen marching through, flashing V-for-victory signs and shouting slogans. Among the masses, some carried giant portraits of the late Chairman Mao Zedong, adding an unsettling hint of a Cultural Revolution revival.

None of them, however, could match the appeal of one young man. Cui Jian showed up unannounced to the wildest cheers of young students in the Square. With long hair and a baby face, the twenty-eight year old looked like a smaller version of a young Paul McCartney. That comparison was not far off as Cui Jian was the undisputed king of rock 'n' roll in China.

Cui Jian got his first exposure to rock music in the early 1980's through smuggled tapes when he was an unknown trumpet player in an orchestra. He formed a band and had trouble finding an audience for this new brand of music. So, he frequently performed free concerts in the smelly dining halls of university campuses, where the new generation of educated youth embraced his rowdy music first. One song, in particular, struck a chord. It was titled *Nothing to my Name*:

> *I used to ask again and again,*
> *When would you come along with me?*
> *But you always laugh at me that*
> *I have nothing to my name.*

As Deng Xiaoping's reform was opening up China, the young generation got their first peek outside. It was a world they had not imagined. Businessmen and relatives were flooding in from Taiwan and Hong Kong and showing off their abundant wealth. The youth in China suddenly faced the reality of their poverty. It was not just a material thing either. The lofty ideals of communism were fading away fast and they were at a total loss for spiritual guidance and purpose in life, as Cui Jian went on desperately:

> *I want to give you my heart's desire,*
> *And my freedom.*
> *But you always laugh at me that*

The Confrontation

I have nothing to my name.

From that humble beginning, Cui Jian went on to perform in the largest stadiums all over the country. He wrote a series of songs expressing the frustrations of the youth and mocking the holy grail of the nation's revolutionary heritage. So, on this day, Cui Jian came to Tiananmen Square himself perhaps to be with the people who had been with him years earlier. The biggest star in the country was at complete ease. He walked between the buses shaking hands and signing autographs. He did not mince many words. But the song he had sung so many times suddenly acquired a new meaning with the hunger strike in Tiananmen Square:

I am telling you I have waited too long.
I am telling you this is my final request.
I want to take your hands,
So you will come along with me right now.

Cui Jian jammed on his guitar and belted the lyrics with his trademark incomprehensible mumble, sending spectators into a crazed frenzy. They shouted and screamed along and enjoyed the unexpected open air concert. His intended audience was however much less than amused. The hunger strikers squeezed deeper into their bus seats and tried desperately to block out the sound. The pounding drumbeat and piercing guitar were all too much for their weakened hearts. Unable to voice any protest, they cursed in silence.

As music played in a triumphant Tiananmen Square, the presidents of a dozen major universities in Beijing published an open letter calling for the government to talk to students. In an unprecedented gesture, the official workers' union donated 100,000 RMB (26,600 USD) to the hunger strikers.[177]

5.18

WUER Kaixi was still dressed in a hospital gown and attached to an oxygen bag as his group was ushered into a large conference room inside the Great Hall of People. The room had high ceilings and vast space like a royal palace. A ring of comfortable sofas was placed in the middle of the room surrounded by circles of chairs. End tables with elegant flowers and tea cups stood between the sofas. There were also

disastrous "meeting" w/ Li Peng

microphones on each table to facilitate conversation. Strangely, Wuer Kaixi felt somewhat at home. This was the Xinjiang Hall, named after the northwest Uyghur region where he had spent three years of his adolescence. The room was decorated with giant murals depicting the natural beauty of the region and artifacts of the Uyghur heritage. Typically, this room was used by government officials having audiences with selected visitors from the provinces. Today, it was a group of scratchy and starved students with wide eyes. They were entering a scene they had never dreamed of. Awkwardly, they sat down in the sofas on one side of the circle and waited. They did not know what they were waiting for.

After five minutes or so, Premier Li Peng appeared at the entry, along with an entourage of high level officials including Yan Mingfu and Li Tieying. Li Peng was wearing a gray "Mao Suit" and a solemn expression. He walked over to shake hands with each student and tried to make small talk. He was curious about Wang Dan's thick jacket, to which Wang Dan responded that it was cold in the Square at night. Wuer Kaixi's hospital gown also caught his attention. But the premier looked gloomy and uneasy. The only time he managed a half smile was when a student claimed to share the same hometown with him. Finally, he settled into his seat on the other side facing Wuer Kaixi and Wang Dan. He started the meeting by apologizing for being late, explaining that they had been held up by a traffic jam outside. Then he stated that there should be only one item on the agenda for this meeting. That was to stop the hunger strike immediately based on humanitarian principles.

It did not take long for Wuer Kaixi to get impatient. He was upset about Li Peng's apology which implied that the student movement was creating chaos in the streets. As Li Peng went on with a patronizing lecture, Wuer Kaixi cut him off: "Premier Li Peng, I am sorry that I have to interrupt you. Perhaps you thought you were only five minutes late. But I have to say, you are a month late!"*

Wuer Kaixi was referring to the time when he led students chanting "Li Peng, Come Out!" outside of Xinhuamen on the evening of April

---

*In a later interview, Wuer Kaixi defended his interruption as a consequence of treating the premier as a citizen equal to the students.[178]

19. He stated that it was pressure from students that had led Li Peng to this meeting. Therefore, it should be the students who dictated the agenda. He did have a legitimate point. But his emotion was also starting to creep into his delivery.

Wang Dan, who maintained a calmer posture, interjected that the only way to persuade students to stop the hunger strike was to address the two conditions put forward by the student movement, "Not Turmoil, Equal Dialogue."

The rude interruption not withstanding, Wuer Kaixi and Wang Dan apparently started this meeting on a good footing by emphasizing their strengths and issues upfront. Patiently and intently, the premier was listening.

Just then, however, Wuer Kaixi was getting carried away. Without giving the other side a chance to respond, he burst out even more:

"You are much older than we are so I think it is appropriate for me to refer you as Teacher Li. So, Teacher Li, the problem at hand right now is not to convince us who sit here. We also want the students to leave the Square. But the situation at the Square is not one of a minority following the majority, but of 99.9% of the people following 0.01%. That is, if there is one hunger striker who chose not to leave, thousands of others will not leave either."

This was an absurd statement. Not only that he showed disrespect to the premier personally, but he was also misrepresenting his own side. The students at the Square had worked very hard to establish rudimentary democratic procedures. The student parliament led by Li Lu had almost nightly votes on ending the hunger strike, in which ninety percent or so consistently voted for continuing the strike. Wuer Kaixi had not spent enough time at the Square himself to appreciate or perhaps even be aware of these facts. He was painting himself into a corner by representing students as desperate and out of control.

Wang Dan tried to soften the blow. He calmly explained: "After Yan Mingfu's visit to the Square, we had conducted a poll of whether to leave the Square. More than ninety percent of hunger strikers voted not to leave." Sensing that the agenda was going astray, he quickly reaffirmed the two main student demands, "Not Turmoil, Equal Dialogue." If these two conditions were met, he said, they would be able

Dialogues: Always raising stakes to the points that no compromise was possible

to go to the Square and persuade all of the students to leave.

As other students were invited to express their opinions, Wuer Kaixi urged them to make their points quickly and concretely. But most of them repeated the same sentiments. One student did manage to raise the stakes. With an unusual clarity, Xiong Yan, a student from Peking University who was a member of the Dialogue Delegation, told the officials that it was not entirely up to the government anyway: "No matter whether the government recognizes our movement as patriotic and democratic or not, we believe history will. So, why do we insist on the government recognizing it? That is because it represents the will of the people. The people want to see if the government is still the people's government." Sitting on the other side, the party leader of Peking University could not help but speak up on his students' behalf as well.

Since being interrupted at the start, Premier Li Peng had been sitting quietly with a stone face. It was as if he were waiting for the students to self-destruct, which they did come agonizingly close to doing. After he made sure that all students had had a chance to speak, Li Peng pointedly started with a request that he would not be interrupted.

Perhaps inadvertently, he was immediately interrupted by a student. Li Peng swallowed hard but did not express his displeasure. Instead, he asked his ministers to give the government's response. Li Tieying, Yan Mingfu, and others took their turns with lengthy speeches that toed the party line. Finally, Li Peng spoke again. He emphasized that the only issue he was interested in was getting the hunger strikers off the Square to save their health and lives. Explaining the April 26 *People's Daily* editorial, he repeated the familiar platitude that they had never blamed the "vast majority" of students as instigating turmoil, which implicitly left the door open for "a small clique."

Then, in a confused attempt to directly address students' two demands, he raised his voice and offered a memorable passage: "We understand your two issues. As the premier and as a Communist Party member, I never hide my own opinions. But I can't express them today. I will find a more appropriate opportunity to express them later. But anyhow I think I have pretty much expressed my opinions anyway."

With that, he appeared to be closing the doors to further discussion.

What?

LP diary P.194

For the last time, he asked the students to stop the hunger strike. Wuer Kaixi, who had been clinging to his oxygen bag and becoming visibly weaker, confronted the premier again. Putting a brave face forward, Wang Dan stressed that, if Premier Li Peng's prospect of turmoil did materialize, it would be the government, not the students, who should be held responsible.

It was Yan Mingfu's job to put the meeting to bed. He told the audience that there was a note from the Square asking for the immediate return of Wang Dan and Wuer Kaixi. As soon as he said "This dialogue is now concluded," one of the students rose to protest: "This is not a dialogue. This is just a meeting." Students wanted to set the record straight that their demand for a dialogue had not yet been satisfied. Disinterested in semantics, Yan Mingfu concurred, "Yes, this was only a meeting."

The meeting, not a dialogue, lasted about an hour.

Avoiding eye contact, Li Peng shook hands with each student once again. He appeared impatient and annoyed. Wuer Kaixi had already slumped into his chair and was being attended to by several student nurses. He was suffering from an asthma attack.[179] As everyone was filing out of the room, Wang Chaohua was still holding onto a slim hope. She shouted across the room to Yan Mingfu: "Please give me another hour, we might still be able to persuade the students to withdraw." Yan Mingfu walked away without acknowledging her. It was too little, too late.[180]

The students walked out of the Great Hall of People on their own and informed other leaders that their talk had broken up because of Li Peng's stubbornness. Nobody was surprised. But now everyone was extremely depressed. There appeared to be no more possibility of a peaceful resolution.

Most of students and the general public learned about this meeting in the evening when the nightly news broadcast extensive footage. A transcript was published in *People's Daily* the next morning. The reports were remarkably faithful, with only a few direct confrontational episodes left out. The government did not have to edit much anyway. The students, most significantly Wuer Kaixi, had come through as rude, arrogant, and disrespectful.

Standoff At Tiananmen

Wang Chaohua could not help wondering. What would have it been, if this meeting was led by Xiang Xiaoji and Zhao Ziyang, instead of Wuer Kaixi and Li Peng, respectively?

It pains my heart to think about this question.

I am old. I don't care any more.

Zhao Ziyang

10

Martial Law

5.18

L<small>I</small> Lu woke up in a hospital bed to the sound of pouring rain that evening. He had finally collapsed. After five bottles of intravenous drip and eight hours of sleep, he felt a lot better, especially after he was told that his hunger strikers were all safe and sound in the buses long before the arrival of the storm.

It was his first look inside of a hospital. It was full of hunger strikers with intravenous tubes strapped to them. There were bowls of porridge, buns, and fruits available but hardly anyone looked at the food. Li Lu was deeply touched. Speaking as the deputy commander, he appealed to the patients to take in food. He set an example himself by eating the porridge. Reluctantly, most followed.*

---

*It was likely that most hunger strikers consumed food in hospitals. On May 19, 1989, *The New York Times* profiled a student by the name of Xie Wanjun who was persuaded to end his hunger strike while in a hospital after fasting eighty-four hours. In this instance, however, Li Lu did not consider it the end of his, or others', hunger strike because they ate in the hospital. Li Lu also met Chai Ling in the same hospital but did not mention whether Chai Ling had any food there.[181]

Standoff At Tiananmen

To his pleasant surprise, Li Lu found the Square tidy and clean on his return. A huge cleanup effort by student volunteers had removed most of garbage before the storm. The rain washed away the rest along with the scorching heat. In the middle of the bus formation he found one marked with a banner: "Hunger Strike Headquarters." Loudspeakers were rigged on top of that bus, ready to broadcast in all directions. It was a lovely sight.

THAT evening, the student parliament debated and resolved once again to continue their hunger strike despite the fact that it would be entering its seventh day and dangerous territory. Most hunger strikers, although bravely displaying their persistence, seemed to be resigned to their fate. They fell into sleep that night not knowing what the next day, May 19, would bring.

At the early hour of five o'clock, a disturbance developed in the darkness in the northwest corner of the Square, as students there were seen shouting and running. Before long, runners came into the Hunger Strike Headquarters bus to report that Zhao Ziyang and Li Peng were spotted there. Caught by surprise, Li Lu hurriedly dispatched a band of student marshals over to bring them into the headquarters and then rushed in that direction.

But they were too late. The entourage stopped at the edge of the Square and made no attempt to go into the Square. Zhao Ziyang was accompanied by a glum faced Li Peng and aides that included Yan Mingfu.* A team of reporters followed, illuminating the area with lighting for television cameras. Zhao Ziyang's face appeared pale and exhausted. Unlike the smiling and glowing General Secretary when he last appeared in public while meeting Mr. Gorbachev, he now looked like a beaten old man. This time, he was wearing a gray "Mao Suit" buttoned tightly at the collar. His hair was still neatly combed backward with more white on the top than usual. With students converging around him, he was at a loss of what to do.[182]

Students guided him onto a bus nearby while Li Peng boarded a dif-

*Wen Jiabao, then the Chief of Staff of the Communist Party Central Committee, also accompanied Zhao Ziyang. Wen Jiabao survived in the political aftermath and eventually became the premier in 2003.

ferent one. In the cramped space, Zhao Ziyang struggled to maintain his balance while students moved around and rocked the bus. There were many shouts for students to sit down and be quiet but more students were still trying to get in. Facing a television camera, Zhao Ziyang took a small megaphone from a student and spoke with a heavy accent. His lips were dry and his voice hoarse. It was not the normal prepared speech of Chinese leaders. Zhao Ziyang appeared to speak directly from his heart. He apologized to the students for coming too late and admitted that he deserved the criticism. He had not come to ask for forgiveness however, he explained. He came only to ask students to stop the hunger strike, though he appeared unsure how many days it had already lasted. But he rambled on for six minutes, alternately appealing for students' health and promising that the government would keep the channel of dialogues open. But he had nothing substantial to offer. In a grandfatherly tone, he begged the students to value their youth, "I am old. I don't care any more. But you are still young..." There was no response of any kind from the students on the bus. They shoved notebooks, hats, and scarves into Zhao Ziyang's face for autographs. Zhao Ziyang patiently obliged. Then, before any student leaders could arrive from the headquarters, the entire entourage was whisked away, disappearing into the darkness as fast and mysteriously as they had appeared. Zhao Ziyang would never be seen in public again.

ONE week earlier, just as the hunger strikers were settling into Tiananmen Square, Liu Gang made a phone call to Chen Ziming. By that time, Liu Gang was not only seeing his influence disappearing from Beijing Students Autonomous Federation, he had also become painfully aware that the organization itself was going to be sidelined. They all had opposed the tactics of hunger strike and preferred a more conservative direction in institutionalizing democracy within campuses. But the hunger strikers were marching to a different drummer and they would all be left behind.

Foreseeing a train wreck, Liu Gang urged Chen Ziming to step forward. The movement needed a stronger leader. Only Chen Ziming and Wang Juntao, with their independent Institute, had the personnel, organization, and resources to handle this tremendous but delicate task. With the hunger strikers occupying the Square, he argued, the movement would be entering a new phase. It would no longer be a student movement but one involving teachers, intellectuals, workers, and residents alike, who would be rushing onto streets to support the hunger strikers. Therefore, he urged Chen Ziming to organize new leadership in the mode of his Beijing Students Autonomous Federation but with a much expanded constituency.

Chen Ziming was not convinced. He was still not sure that this movement was going to be a real significant force. There were more important things for him and his Institute to work on. He had spent years building up this infrastructure. He was not going to risk it on something that might threaten its very existence.[183]

Liu Gang's prediction became reality in just a matter of days as millions of people poured into the streets. Chen Ziming finally realized that they needed to get involved. He asked Wang Juntao to use his personal connections and invite as many young intellectuals as he could for a brain-storming conference.

Jimen Hotel was a new and moderate place at the northwest corner of the Third Ring Road of the city near the University of Political Science and Law and conveniently located on the way between Tiananmen Square and the college district. Wang Juntao and their Institute had already occupied an entire floor there for research work. The informal conference started in the hotel on May 17 and was attended by many notable young and middle-aged intellectuals. Wang Juntao chaired the first day's meeting without much of an agenda. Yan Jiaqi and Bao Zunxin arrived to solicit signatures for their statement denouncing Deng Xiaoping as the last emperor. Wang Juntao refused to sign. He thought it was not the time for such aggressive charges. Although most at the conference sided with Wang Juntao, the statement nevertheless set an aggressive tone for their meeting.

Chen Ziming chose to stay away. He hoped to maintain a buffering distance between the movement and his precious Institute. He was upset when he learned that a proposal calling for an end to the hunger strike was not even discussed. Wang Juntao could only manage a bitter smile. It was simply impossible with the charged atmosphere, he told his friend.

For the next few days, Jimen Hotel became a hot spot of activities second only to Tiananmen Square itself. Wuer Kaixi and Wang Dan, when they were not hanging around at the United Front Department, spent most of their time there. More people came and went, stopping by in their shuffle between the Square and campuses. They all appeared to be busy and important as if they were generals returning to headquarters from front lines. Yet it was hard to tell what their purposes were, if they had any at all. The conference was stuck in a permanent session. There were endless debates but no decision was ever made.

It took the crisis of a coming thunderstorm for them to find something they could all agree on. Swiftly, they made a decision to help the cleaning efforts at Tiananmen Square. Platoons were dispatched over for the task. At the Square, they also managed to persuade the group of students from the Academy of Performing Arts to stop their thirst strike.[184]

T HE Hunger Strike Headquarters had expanded to include Feng Congde and Zhang Boli as deputies.[185] It had also become obvious that the commander-in-chief rarely made any decisions of significance herself. Chai Ling delegated it entirely to her trusted deputy Li Lu. Whenever needed, however, she made passionate and inspiring speeches that kept everybody together. In this morning, an audio tape of Zhao Ziyang's speech during his bizarre visit was broadcast over the loudspeakers on top of their bus. A feeling of desperation slowly sank in. The dark shadow of death or permanent body damage was on the horizon.

Rumors were rampant. At Xinhuamen in the afternoon, Wu Renhua was pulled aside by a middle-aged bureaucrat who called his name. Wu Renhua and his fellow teachers and students from the University of Political Science and Law had camped out there for days since they broke off from the main hunger strike camp, effectively shutting down this main entry to Zhongnanhai. The man revealed his identity in confidence and told Wu Renhua that Zhao Ziyang had already been deposed and martial law was imminent in Beijing. Wu Renhua immediately dispatched a trusted student marshal to the Square with this information.

Meanwhile, Zhang Boli was talking with Li Lu when two intellectuals came in for him with urgent news. They literally dragged him across Chang'an Avenue to the Working People's Cultural Palace, a park bordering Tiananmen on the east. There, they told him that martial law would be declared by midnight and it was imperative for the students to call off the hunger strike. There was still hope, they urged, that if the hunger strike was called off, the martial law troops would lose their justification to enter the city.

Zhang Boli had no quarrel with calling off the hunger strike. But it was not his decision to make. So he rushed back and talked to Li Lu first and then found Chai Ling. To Zhang Boli's greatest surprise, both of them agreed instantly to stop the hunger strike. A general meeting of the student parliament was immediately called and commenced in an empty bus. Student marshals were ordered to establish a tight picket line around it. They were ordered not to allow anyone to interrupt this meeting, especially Wuer Kaixi if he showed up.

Inside the bus, the meeting was uncharacteristically brief and smooth. The rumor of looming martial law was not revealed. Chai Ling and Li Lu proposed a decision to stop the hunger strike entirely on humanitarian grounds. With their endorsement and the life-threatening danger, there was not much resistance among the previously aggressive representatives. With 173 of them voting for stopping the hunger strike, 28 against, and 7 abstaining, the decision was made.

Just then, Wuer Kaixi angrily burst onto the bus, followed by doctors and nurses holding intravenous bottles that were attached to him. He had been fighting the student marshals who at the end were no match for his fame and determination. Wuer Kaixi was not at all pleased at being excluded even though he was neither a member of the Headquarters nor a representative from his school. Wuer Kaixi had his way though. As the supreme leader in his Beijing Normal University, he dismissed the representative from his school on the spot and assumed the role himself, notwithstanding the fact that the meeting had already adjourned with a decision made. The new representative Wuer Kaixi insisted on reopening the session with a claim that he had critical

Wuer Kaixi acted like a dictator

information to present. It was then that Wuer Kaixi finally bothered to inquire what the decision was. Upon being told of the end of hunger strike, he raised his hand and meekly said "I agree."[186]

Wuer Kaixi had felt the urge to see Yan Mingfu one more time that afternoon. He sneaked into the United Front Department in an ambulance with his girlfriend Liu Yan. After much cajoling, Yan Mingfu came out to meet him and give him the news of the impending martial law.[187] Sensing the gravity of this development, Wuer Kaixi dispatched Liu Yan to get as many hunger strike leaders at the United Front Department as possible. They would have to talk it over with Yan Mingfu.

Ma Shaofang and Cheng Zhen showed up first. They were immediately overwhelmed by the news. They cried and swore to give up water or set themselves on fire in protest. Yan Mingfu, being the father-figure he was, managed to calm them down. Eventually, Wang Dan, Xiang Xiaoji, Shen Tong, and a few others arrived.[188] Only the leaders in the Hunger Strike Headquarters were missing. Nevertheless, they had a quick meeting and reached a decision to call off the hunger strike.

Yan Mingfu was greatly relieved. He had his office cafeteria prepare a big pot of noodles for the students. Everyone ate despite the fact that their decision to resume eating was neither official nor made public. It was the best meal of their young lives. A gigantic load had just been lifted off their small shoulders. For that moment, the coming martial law did not feel like a big deal. They talked, laughed, snapped pictures, and playfully signed autographs for each other. Wuer Kaixi clumsily knocked down two thermos bottles, causing explosions that amused everyone. Then, they boarded separate vans to head back to Tiananmen Square, where Wuer Kaixi had to fight through student marshals to bring their decision to the parliament meeting.

Now that Chai Ling, Li Lu, Wuer Kaixi, and the student parliament were all in agreement, it was just a matter of announcing the decision to the thousands of hunger strikers. Zheng Yi already had a statement drafted. In the headquarters bus, Chai Ling read it calmly. It was broadcast through their loudspeakers.

The reaction was immediate and chaotic. Loud and angry shouts of "Traitor!" erupted all around. Many converged on the big bus. They pounded and shook it. As Li Lu was trying to calm down the crowd with his microphone, Feng Congde shot into the bus. He had just returned from a hospital and heard about the parliament meeting. He argued that the meeting was not properly called and that there were not enough representatives present to make such a critical decision. So, he called for a meeting of his own. In his hasty but carefully audited meeting, eighty percent of delegates voted against the ending of the hunger strike. Chai Ling, Li Lu, and Zhang Boli were outraged at his unilateral action. They refused to recognize the meeting and its result. A shouting and pushing match ensued in the headquarters bus and a deeply hurt Feng Congde resigned in protest.[189]

Grudgingly, the breaking of the fast became a matter of fact.* Li Lu carefully arranged student marshals to take the weakest hunger strikers to hospitals or back to their campuses. Others chose to stay. While slowly taking in food, they decided to continue their occupation of the Square as a massive sit-in. Zhang Boli was ushered, or rather, carried by a two people to the entrance of the Museum of Chinese History. There was a telephone waiting for him. He picked up the phone and identified himself. A voice on the other end informed him that they were the State Council and they were ready to record what he had to say. Zhang Boli read the statement into the phone. He then distributed copies to several reporters from *CCTV* and *People's Daily*.[190]

CCTV was unusually efficient this time. At nine o'clock, as the regular news broadcast was in progress, a line of scrolling text appeared at the bottom of the screen: "Students at Tiananmen Square Stop their Hunger Strike."[191]

AN hour later, the giant auditorium in the Great Hall of People was alight. A thousand cadres assembled at this unusually late hour wearing their most serious expressions. The large podium looked excruciatingly empty without the usual grandiose floral decorations. There was only one long table draped with a white tablecloth. Several officials sat behind the table, some of whom appeared to be wearing casual jack-

*It is not clear how many of the hunger strikers at the end belonged to the original group who started the strike about noon on May 13 and had fasted for about 150 hours.

ets. Premier Li Peng and the nominal President Yang Shangkun were at the center, flanked by other Politburo members. Most significantly, however, Zhao Ziyang was absent.

Li Peng was in a dark blue and tightly buttoned "Mao Suit." His hair was neatly combed backward. Wearing a pair of oversize eyeglasses, he stood and read a prepared speech. Even at such an obviously rushed occasion, the speech was typically lengthy. He made the accusation that conspirators had been using the hunger strikers as hostages against the government. He also claimed that student leaders had admitted that they had lost control of the situation, a clear reference to Wuer Kaixi's outbursts during their once and only meeting. There had been anarchy in Beijing and chaos all over the country. "The fate and future of the People's Republic of China, created by many revolutionary martyrs with their blood, are facing a serious threat!" he emphasized with a clenched-fist jab across his body. With that, he declared that martial law would be imposed in Beijing at ten o'clock in the morning.

In his own brief speech, President Yang Shangkun explained that troops of the People's Liberation Army were already in the vicinity of the city. They would be moving in that night "to restore law and order." He emphasized that the troops were not against the students. Finally, Chen Xitong, mayor of Beijing, issued a series of orders specifying the rules of the martial law.

Li Peng's speech and the coming martial law were made public at midnight with broadcasts on television and through loudspeakers all over the city. Immediately, Tiananmen Square became a sea of protests as the rousing *L'Internationale* was played on the students' own broadcasting station over and over. Thousands sang in unison.

In the middle of the chaotic Square, Zhang Boli hosted a press conference. He was crying and shouting incoherently. When asked by a reporter what they would do about the martial law, he screamed that the student leadership had called on the estimated two hundred thousand students remaining at the Square to stage a massive hunger strike in protest. Everyone was stunned. Li Lu poked Zhang Boli, who quickly realized that he had badly misspoken: "I meant a sit-in, not another hunger strike."

Standoff At Tiananmen

HUNDREDS of thousands of students did remain at the Square that night. They had visions of soldiers marching in and taking them away one by one. They had wet towels for tear gas and resolved not to fight back when violence came. Once again, many wrote their wills. They taped their student identification cards onto their bodies just in case. They were ready for bloodshed. They only hoped that they could stand their ground until dawn. The daylight would be their friend. In a tent, Chen Ziming and Wang Juntao discreetly spent the night with student leaders.[192]

Yet when daylight broke, they saw no soldiers. There had been reports throughout the night that residents of the city were blocking the martial law troops in the suburbs. That had sounded too good to be true.

With a thunderous roar, a large gang of motorcycles rushed onto Chang'an Avenue. The bikes were decorated with flags. Their punk-looking riders wore headbands similar to those of the hunger strike students. Some of them had young girls riding on the back seats proudly letting their long hair fly in the wind. They circled the Square several times, shouting out the news: "The troops have been blocked!" "We Beijingese will never let them in!"

A motorcycle was an ultra-luxury item at the time. It had become a status symbol among the young entrepreneurs who had heeded Deng Xiaoping's "let some people get rich first" call and become wealthy. Their rebellious spirit and arrogance, coupled with the unbearable noise of their motorcycles, did not endear them to the general public. Indeed, they were precisely the "wrong people" who were getting rich, as a major complaint went. But today, they came out en masse to support the students, their contemporaries who had had the better fortune to be able to attend colleges.

They called themselves the "Flying Tigers."* From now on, they would be at the service of students and residents as scouts and communication carriers between the city and its suburbs. They promised to keep an active vigil on all roads to spot any martial law troops trying

---

*Flying Tigers is the nickname of a group of American Air Force dare-devil volunteers, led by General Claire Chennault, who had fought during World War II in China.

198

to sneak into the city on back roads.

The martial law troops, mostly foot soldiers sitting in the back of military trucks, had attempted to enter the city through five main roads during the night. As it happened, it was a clear night with a full moon. These convoys were easily identified by residents living along the routes. Spontaneously, truck drivers parked their heavy vehicles in front of the military processions. Old ladies laid down their bodies on the roads. Completely unprepared for such resistance, the military convoys halted. They were then surrounded by gathering residents who let out the air in their tires yet were otherwise friendly to the troops. They brought food and water for the soldiers and talked to them patiently and emotionally. The soldiers, who were the same age as the students, sat idly. They were at a complete loss for how to handle what was happening.[193]

Martial law was supposed to take effect at ten o'clock in the morning of May 20. The only presence of troops at that time was a column of helicopters flying over Tiananmen Square dropping leaflets with orders from the martial law troop headquarters. The same orders were repeated continuously in the loudspeakers along the streets. Under martial law, they exclaimed, no demonstrations of any kind would be allowed.

Yet demonstrations were all the rage underneath these very helicopters. Residents marched through the streets in their trucks and on foot. Students assembled and shouted "Li Peng, step down!" "Li Peng, step down!" in unison. Overnight, Li Peng had become public enemy number one. The feeble attempt to targeting Deng Xiaoping, "the last emperor," a couple of days ago faded away. Instead, posters of Li Peng's likeness, in Nazi uniforms and other distorted forms, were everywhere. Many banners carried his name in upside down characters with black crosses over them, a fashionable style of humiliating opponents during the Cultural Revolution.

Most civil liberties, even previously non-existent ones, were specifically forbidden under martial law. These included any public assembly and demonstrations, class boycotts, general strikes, and unofficial organizations. It also became illegal to be interviewed by the foreign press. With the martial law troops making no real attempt to break-

5.20 demonstration

199

through, however, the only visible enforcement of martial law was seen from outside the country.

Morning in Beijing was prime time on the east coast of the United States. *CNN* was broadcasting its nightly *Prime News* live from a garden in the back of Beijing's Great Wall Sheraton Hotel. Mike Chinoy had managed to convert that little space into a makeshift studio with a direct satellite uplink. Bernard Shaw was supposed to sit behind a small table and narrate the top news of the day. But at this historic moment, the little table looked painfully inadequate. Knowing that they could be cut off at any moment, *CNN* summoned its top guns in Beijing, Tokyo Bureau Chief John Lewis, Moscow Bureau Chief Steve Hurst, and the Beijing Bureau Chief Mike Chinoy to the scene. The three sleep-deprived journalists, together with Bernard Shaw, stood crowding themselves in front of the table and shared their thoughts of the moment with the camera. Yet the live shot almost immediately cut away to a different location.

With martial law declared in Beijing, close to a million American homes tuned in. As the camera switched away from the anchor desk, they saw two Chinese government officials walking into *CNN*'s control room in the hotel to order a shutdown of the broadcasting. *CNN* quickly switched to a split screen, showing both the activities in the control room and at their headquarters in Atlanta where its vice president Jane Maxwell was handling the situation on the phone. *CNN* insisted on having an order in writing. With obvious reluctance and discomfort, one of the Chinese officers took out a legal pad and scribbled an order. With a world-wide audience watching, *CNN* terminated its live coverage from Beijing after a last shot of its anchor desk. Bernard Shaw and each of the three bureau chiefs gave their last words, expressing their shock at the most extraordinary event they were witnessing. Bernard Shaw was so shaken up that he, who was two days shy of his forty-ninth birthday, went back to his hotel room and cried.[194]

CBS was in the middle of the thick plot of the season finale of its popular soap opera *Dallas* when Dan Rather interrupted the show from Beijing. He had just intercepted a group of Chinese officials marching to the *CBS* control room inside the Shangri-La Hotel. Dan Rather attempted to question the visitors on live television. He failed to get

World-wide coverage on Martial Law

any clear answer and was reduced to lament on camera: "For those of you who find this hard to follow, welcome to the club." His audience, however, was not amused. Many called to protest that he had ruined their favorite show.[195]

The networks continued to cover the events unfolding in Beijing. Telephone interviews and still photographs, transmitted through telephone lines, were supplemented by videotapes smuggled out of the country every day.

THE fact that martial law troops had indeed been blocked from entering the city brought jubilation to Tiananmen Square. Emboldened, every organization, from Beijing Students Autonomous Federation and Hunger Strike Headquarters to a newly established Workers Autonomous Federation were busy announcing their new statements. They called on workers and residents to continue blocking the troops and called on the soldiers to mutiny. Confrontations, albeit peaceful ones, were no longer shunned. The standoff was turning into a revolution. Ten intellectuals including Bao Zunxin, Yan Jiaqi, Wang Juntao, and Chen Xiaoping issued a statement in which they pledged to never betray the student movement or submit themselves to the last emperor of China.

Zheng Yi was more than ecstatic. Before his very eyes, the hunger strike had exploded into a drama far surpassing his original imagination. This must be a critical juncture of historical importance. With Zhang Boli, Zheng Yi hurriedly wrote yet another open letter to the people of Beijing. They called Li Peng and Yang Shangkun "a small clique of conspirators" who had staged "a counter-revolutionary military coup" to depose Zhao Ziyang and impose martial law.* In a state of excitement, the irony must have escaped them. They were using precisely the same language that was used in the *People's Daily* editorial they had so despised. But this was not a time for reflections.

---

*The accusation of a military coup is a weak one. As the General Secretary of the Communist Party, Zhao Ziyang had no direct commanding power over the military, which took orders from Deng Xiaoping, the Chairman of the Central Military Commission. The president and the premier, on the other hand, did have the power to impose martial law.

Standoff At Tiananmen

The open letter went on with more language that echoed the Cultural Revolution. It called upon all the people of the capital city to rise up and defend the city and Tiananmen Square.

Then, they started the engine of their headquarters bus. Slowly, the bus negotiated its way onto streets. The banner on the bus still proclaimed it as the "Hunger Strike Headquarters." The loudspeakers on top blared that this was a propaganda bus for the Headquarters and they had come to speak to the people. It drew a large following in an instant. People on bicycles converged and mobbed the bus for leaflets being handed out from its windows. Others walked behind, cheering and shouting as the loudspeakers repeatedly read the open letter. Quite fittingly, the bus stalled from overheating. With rhythmic chants of "Li Peng, Step Down," spectators pushed the bus all the way back to the Square.

Meanwhile, martial law was bringing subtle changes. Running water was cut off in the vicinity of the Square. Subway trains stopped running. Almost all hunger strikers had left, replaced by other students who arrived to defy the martial law. The student parliament vaporized. Having served its purpose, the Hunger Strike Headquarters was also defunct. Tiananmen Square was becoming a messy place once again.

Wang Chaohua suddenly found herself needed. After multiple exoduses of personnel, Beijing Students Autonomous Federation was only a shell of its previous self. Yet after being sidelined for a long time, Wang Chaohua found that students were seeking her out, or rather, seeking any sort of leadership on site. She was inundated with reports on where the martial law troops were stopped and where reinforcements were needed. Playing field general, she dispatched student marshals and volunteers as if sending them out into battles.

SUNDAY, May 21, started just like the day before with no martial law troops in sight. Official newspapers were carrying stories about the city under martial law, describing it as calm and peaceful.* They continued to report demonstrations, forbidden by martial law, in a positive

---

*The tone of the official media's coverage eventually changed after May 25, when martial law troops entered major media outlets. However, stories sympathetic to the students continued to appear until after the massacre.[196]

202

light and refer to students occupying Tiananmen Square as petitioners.

There were perhaps a hundred thousand students staying at the Square every night. The anxiety level had subsided significantly. Most students settled into a routine of coming in the evening and leaving in the morning to catch up with their sleep during the day. The military was not expected to make drastic moves during daylight. Yet as glorious as their defiance was, everybody understood that it would not last. Something would have to give, soon.

Wang Dan was slumping in a tent at a corner of the Monument to People's Heroes when he was awakened by a middle-aged reporter. It was Gao Yu, someone he knew well from the intellectual circle. Gao Yu told Wang Dan that she had come on behalf of Hu Jiwei, an influential member on the Standing Committee of the National People's Congress. With General Secretary Zhao Ziyang disappearing from public view and Premier Li Peng denounced in public, it might be time for the rubber-stamping congress to exercise the power it had on paper.

Hu Jiwei was a well known reformer in the early 1980's when he was the editor-in-chief of the *People's Daily*. Working along with Hu Yaobang, he instituted many reforms in this rigid propaganda machinery including publishing criticisms of government affairs in letters-to-editor pages. After Hu Yaobang's downfall, he retired from the paper and was relegated to the ceremonial position on the Standing Committee of the National People's Congress.

A regular meeting of the committee was scheduled to convene on June 20 with its agenda set to evaluate the ongoing student movement. With martial law, Hu Jiwei felt that they could not wait that long. With help from intellectuals including Gao Yu, Hu Jiwei was circulating a petition to call for an emergency meeting to re-evaluate the martial law and the status of the national leadership. In a rush, they collected thirty-eight signatures from Standing Committee members who were in Beijing at the time. It soon ballooned to fifty-seven, more than required.[197]

With a splitting headache, Wang Dan finally grasped the message Hu Jiwei was trying to convey to students: they should withdraw from the Square first and allow the system to do its work. Gao Yu promised

attempts to peacefully withdraw

203

that the students would be allowed to publish a formal statement in the official press when they withdrew. Wang Dan agreed and asked Gao Yu to draft a statement for him.[198]

Wang Dan, however, would soon learn that his influence at Tiananmen Square was quite limited.

AT the center of the Square, former leaders of the hunger strike were sitting around reminiscing when Chai Ling suddenly felt sentimental. She remembered that it was the eve of her and Feng Congde's first anniversary. With all that had happened, both of them felt lucky just to be alive on this day. In a moment of weakness, Li Lu mused, "I am twenty-three years old. In my short life, I have experienced everything but sex and marriage. I may die at any time. I owe myself this pleasure."

Li Lu's timing, once again, was impeccable. His girlfriend Zhao Ming had just arrived from Nanjing and found him here. She had not heard anything from him since he took off for Beijing weeks ago. Naturally, everyone prodded the couple to get married, right there, right then. Zhang Boli drew up a marriage certificate on a piece of paper and stamped on the "official" seal of the Hunger Strike Headquarters. Chai Ling and Feng Congde were anointed bridesmaid and best man, respectively. They gathered up a convoy of well-wishers and with exaggerated fanfare marched to the Monument to People's Heroes for a ceremony.

The unusual hoopla caught the attention of the entire Square. Everyone responded. For once in a long, long time, they had something joyful to cheer about. As the "new couple" went through a typical wedding ritual, the crowd cheered, laughed, and sang the *Bridal Chorus*.

The soaring Monument to People's Heroes loomed large and heavy as a backdrop. This new generation had learned many glorious legends of past communist martyrs. One of them told of a couple being executed by the Nationalist government. Their last request was to stage their wedding on the execution ground. Under the Monument, Li Lu and Zhao Ming kissed and danced, as if they were a part of that legend. Li Lu gave a rousing speech, ending with a catchy "We have to fight,

Martial Law

but we must marry too!"[199]

There was to be no honeymoon.

Like a summer thunderstorm, the jubilation from the spontaneous wedding was short-lived. The mood of the Square turned gloomy as evening approached. There was a strong belief that this was going to be the night. The martial law troops were not going to sit back forever.

Li Lu forcefully persuaded his new bride to leave for safety and went back to his anxious peers. The hunger strike was already over. The Hunger Strike Headquarters was no more. They did not know what to do next. But they were keenly aware that, as soon as the martial law troops showed up, they would be the first targets. For the first time in their young lives, they feared for their lives.

Without much debate, they made a decision to leave discreetly that night. A few safe houses had already been arranged for them in case of emergency. Chai Ling justified the decision because it would preserve the seeds of the movement for a later time. The leaders were the ones truly in danger, she said, while the student masses could be protected by their anonymity and sheer numbers.

Li Lu volunteered to stay behind. He did not feel like leaving in this manner right after his "wedding." He handed 1,000 RMB (125 USD) to each of his fellow leaders from donated funds. They shook hands with each other. Then one by one, they sneaked into the crowd and disappeared into the darkness. Li Lu sat down alone at the highest level of the base of the Monument to People's Heroes. He could see the thousands of people below in the Square. He could not sleep but kept wondering what it would look like in the morning.[200]

The silence of the night was broken by a sudden scream from the loudspeakers of the student broadcasting station. Once again, it was the unmistakable voice of Wuer Kaixi. Just a few hours earlier, Wuer Kaixi was contacted by someone claiming to be a representative of Deng Pufang, the eldest son of Deng Xiaoping. He was told that everyone must be out of the Square by five o'clock in the morning one way or another. There would be thousands of soldiers suddenly emerging from subway stations and the surrounding buildings. There might even be tanks and machine guns.[201]

If the purpose was to scare students into action, it definitely worked

205

on Wuer Kaixi. Shocked into a panic and thinking thousands of lives were on the line, he rushed to the Square and screamed over the loud-speakers: "I am Wuer Kaixi. We must withdraw from the Square. Right now!"

Awakened from their sleep, everyone was startled and confused. Someone asked where they should move to. Wuer Kaixi barked, "To the embassy district! Immediately!" He was referring to a small district on the northeast where most foreign embassies and consulates were located. With the international exposure, he thought it should be a relatively safe outlet.

As the confused crowd debated whether going to the embassy district was a proper thing to do, Wuer Kaixi urged them to get moving. Then, in what had become a typical Wuer Kaixi moment, he fainted. A voice came over the loudspeakers to call for an ambulance. It conveyed more than a hint of mockery. People laughed. As Wuer Kaixi was carried away, students thought that he must have gone delirious.

Wang Chaohua was concerned about the credibility of her organization. She immediately sprang into a damage control mode. Without knowing the gravity of the situation, she calmly announced that Wuer Kaixi did not represent anyone but himself. There was no decision from Beijing Students Autonomous Federation to withdraw. They should remain at the Square.

T HE morning of May 22 was tense but peaceful just like the two previous mornings under martial law. During the day, Chai Ling, Zhang Boli, and Feng Congde returned discreetly and perhaps a little sheepishly. Only a handful people were aware of their absences.[202]

Tension was gradually easing. Martial law troops had been immobilized for two days and three nights. Soldiers were confined inside their cramped trucks during those endless hours. Students and residents who kept a strict vigil surrounding the troops supplied them with food and water. Yet if any solider needed to come out of his truck, be it to go to bathroom or simply stretch his legs, he had to ask for permission from the crowd first. They were effectively captives. On this day, their commanders apparently came to the conclusion that such a humiliating situation was hopeless and detrimental. The troops were ordered to withdraw and make camps in the far outskirts of the city. Students and residents cheered and gave the departing troops a warm send-off.

In the city, groups of workers organized by city government came out to disassemble roadblocks on streets. Although the students were still suspicious, they were relieved that some normalcy was returning. Yet at Tiananmen Square itself, the situation was far from settled.

Despite Wang Chaohua's efforts, Wuer Kaixi's pre-dawn outburst caused another fatal blow to the reputation of Beijing Students Autonomous Federation, even though he had been previously expelled from the organization. Upset with the chaos, Wang Chaohua kept herself busy planning for a way to end the standoff. She took a survey and found most local students agreed to withdraw from Tiananmen Square. Yet students were also arriving from the provinces on an hourly basis. Many of them had started their journey inspired by the hunger strike but before martial law was announced.[203]

She ran into Zhang Boli whom she had known before the movement through her husband. As a trusted friend, she showed him the survey results and asked him for help in organizing a withdrawal. But Zhang Boli had other ideas. He had already acquired a strong sense of distrust of and disdain for Wang Chaohua as a person and, even more so, Beijing Students Autonomous Federation as an organization. Disinterested, he told Wang Chaohua that it was not a decision for them to make.

In fact, Zhang Boli saw the failure of the martial law troops as the greatest victory of the movement. It was therefore not a time to retreat. This victory could be the platform they had wanted for something bigger and better. Besides, what could they tell the brave Beijing residents who had laid down their bodies for them, if they just walked away themselves? His priority was to strengthen the leadership, so that another Wuer Kaixi episode could not happen again.[204]

In a hasty meeting of student representatives in the evening of May 22, Zhang Boli asked for the microphone and laid out his thoughts. They needed stronger leadership and Beijing Students Autonomous Federation was not ready. He suggested that Wang Chaohua and her Federation people take a leave and reorganize themselves off-site. They probably needed two days, he said. In the meantime, there should be a provisional headquarters to reestablish order. After forty-eight hours, he promised Wang Chaohua that the provisional leadership would hand over all responsibilities back to her Federation which by then should be ready to take over.

It sounded good and reasonable. The plan was overwhelmingly approved. Even Wang Chaohua could not dispute much. She had been too busy trying to keep things together. The Federation was for all purposes her one-woman show. It could use some time to straighten itself out.

Zhang Boli was now having his way. He next proposed to transfer the personnel from the defunct Hunger Strike Headquarters to the new provisional headquarters as a natural continuation. Chai Ling would once again be the commander-in-chief with Li Lu, Feng Congde, and himself as her deputies. The nomination sailed through with a round of applause.

Wang Chaohua became upset when Zhang Boli next demanded that she hand over donated funds. "This is a coup," she angrily accused Zhang Boli. But there was nothing much she could do. Zhang Boli promised again that power would be returned to Beijing Students Autonomous Federation in forty-eight hours. With a heavy heart, Wang Chaohua reluctantly left Tiananmen Square.

funding disputes
power struggle w/in Student leaders.

Standing in Tiananmen Square, I become a free person.

Chen Mingyuan

The Standoff

ZHANG Boli was not alone in becoming alarmed by the power vacuum at Tiananmen Square after the martial law. Wang Juntao had also been surveying the scene with his worried eyes. On that same day, he finally decided to get personally involved in the movement.

Up until now, Wang Juntao had taken his role as a mediator between the government and the students very seriously, even after Yan Mingfu himself had abandoned that effort. He spent most of his time looking for opportunities to bring the two sides back together. That hope was finally crushed by martial law. The game had now changed. In his view, martial law had been unjustly, and perhaps unlawfully, imposed. It had to be opposed with a frontal attack. Yet he was also deeply pessimistic. It would take a miracle to avoid bloodshed.

Wang Juntao and Chen Ziming also had to abandon their unfruitful conference at Jimen Hotel. The place had come under heavy surveillance. With martial law in the city, they decided on a new strategy. Wang Juntao, with his wide personal connections and experience, would seek a leadership role on the front line and try to reorganize

209

the fading student protest into a mature civil movement, one that Liu Gang had envisioned earlier. Chen Ziming, on the other hand, would continue to stay behind the scenes to provide logistical support while actively seeking out any possible communication channels with the government.

On the morning of May 22, Wang Juntao and Liu Gang took a car ride along the outskirts of the city to assess the military situation. When they arrived back at Tiananmen Square, they were greeted by an obviously distraught Wang Dan. Wang Dan had spent too much time away from the students to maintain any personal following or organizational support. Lacking charisma, he now found it difficult to make a difference. He pleaded for Wang Juntao to take over as they were in desperate need for adult leadership. Wang Juntao spent the day at the Square observing the scene. He chatted with Chai Ling and Li Lu without introducing himself to them.[205]

Zhang Lun, the graduate student who had introduced Liu Gang to Wang Juntao, cleared out an area at the base of the Monument to People's Heroes for a meeting. It was already ten o'clock and in the darkness they could not locate any student leaders other than Wang Dan and Ma Shaofang. Unbeknownst to them, a new provisional headquarters had just been created nearby to address the very same leadership issue. Wang Juntao looked over the thirty or so people around him and saw that most were intellectuals who had spent time at Jimen Hotel. He told them they had to get organized and assume strong leadership. But he did not have any ideas yet. So, in his typical cocky manner, Wang Juntao promised that he would come with a plan first thing in the morning.

That night, Wang Juntao replayed the entire landscape of the movement in his mind. All of a sudden he realized that he was already occupying a strategic high point. Everywhere he looked among the numerous organizations that had sprung up within the movement, he saw some of his personal friends in charge. Student leaders from the major campuses in Beijing had been upset with the developments at Tiananmen Square. They deeply resented Chai Ling and Li Lu and stayed away from the student parliament there. Through Wang Dan, Wuer Kaixi, and Liu Gang, they were gravitating toward him. Yan

The Standoff

Jiaqi and Bao Zunxin were leading an independent union of intellectuals. Li Jinjin, the graduate student who had led the early sit-in at the Great Hall of People, had now become the legal council to the new Workers Autonomous Federation.[206] Similarly, he found close friends in leadership positions in the new Teachers Union, Writers Union, Beijing Residents Federation, Journalists Union, etc.* The only leaders he was not familiar with were Chai Ling, Li Lu, and Feng Congde at the Square. But he knew how to make friends fast.

If this new, expanded movement needed a commander-in-chief, he would be the one best positioned for the job.

The only problem was that he himself was not ready. Wang Juntao could not shake off his pessimistic view of the final outcome. Therefore he felt that he would be the wrong person to lead. He could not assume the responsibility of leading the masses into an inevitable failure and bloodshed.†

On this night, Wang Juntao took inspiration from another commander-in-chief he had long admired. He had read the history of the convention that produced the American Constitution. Presiding over a conference of much heated debates among divergent views for the new nation, George Washington was neither opinionated nor a decider. He used his reputation and patient presence to keep the convention from falling apart. He ensured that every faction and opinion had its day in the sun. With a similarly divergent collection of new organizations around Tiananmen Square, Wang Juntao felt that he had a similar situation at hand, albeit on a smaller scale.

As he promised, when he showed up at Tiananmen Square the next morning, Wang Juntao had a plan. In a quick couple of hours, he mobilized all the resources and connections he had to start an all-inclusive convention. A large conference room was secured, with a

---

*Most of these organizations consisted only of a few activists and did not represent any mass following. The best organized one was the Workers Autonomous Federation which relied heavily on student leaders and resources.[207]

†Wang Juntao's ambivalent attitude had irritated many friends such as Liu Gang, who regarded him as too soft to be a leader. Liu Gang urged Chen Ziming to step forward instead. But Chen Ziming did not possess the same relationships as Wang Juntao had, particularly with students.[208]

touch of irony, in the Institute of Marxism, Leninism, and Mao Zedong Thought, a few miles east of Tiananmen Square. Several vans
were in service to ferry people he had gathered to the location. All the
new organizations were invited and they accepted with excitement.

The only exception was the new provisional headquarters at the
Square, whose existence Wang Juntao had just come to know. Li Lu
had heard about the conference at Jimen Hotel and knew these intellectuals were only good at debating theories but useless when it came to
making decisions. He was not entirely interested. His absence would
just be fine with other student leaders who resented his leadership style
and lobbied heavily for his exclusion. They told Wang Juntao that Li
Lu had been acting as a dictator using Chai Ling as his figurehead. If
they hoped to achieve anything, they would have to remove Li Lu from
the leadership. Besides, they suggested, to this day Li Lu still could
not prove his identity, a ready excuse to banish him.

Wang Juntao sensed the appearance of a first crack in his grand
design. Undaunted, he put his personal charm to work. With much
persuasion and cajoling, he managed to pull Li Lu into a van without
upsetting others.

THE conference room was packed and rowdy. Most people did not
know each other. But one way or another they had a connection with
Wang Juntao who chaired the meeting with a charming efficiency.

Chen Ziming had proposed a long and awkward name: "The Joint
Conference of All Circles in the Capital to Patriotically Uphold the
Constitution through Social Consultation." He explained that, first
and foremost, martial law was unconstitutional and that was what they
were up against. And they would be doing it with dialogues and con-
sultations just as Zhao Ziyang had advocated many months ago. The
name was formally adopted but never caught on. Most people called it
simply "Capital Joint Conference."

Wang Juntao spelled out two tasks for its agenda. The first one
was imminent: to establish a clear chain of command to stabilize the
situation at Tiananmen Square. The other would be the soul of the
coming movement: an agreed-upon goal and strategy.

Wang Juntao had intended to anoint Wang Dan as a new commander-in-chief before he learned that a provisional headquarters was already in place. It was a proposal backed by Liu Gang and others who were closer to students. Wang Dan had been involved in leadership roles since the very beginning from the Preparatory Committee at Peking University, to the Beijing Students Autonomous Federation, to the hunger strike. Unlike Chai Ling and Li Lu, Wang Dan displayed willingness to listen and adapt, perhaps to the point of a fault. With Wang Dan at the helm, students at the Square would be more likely to be on the same page with this new Joint Conference. Yet the last thing Wang Juntao could afford was a power struggle on personnel issues as the famous author Zheng Yi ferociously advocated for Chai Ling's leadership. It had also become obvious that Chai Ling had already surpassed Wang Dan and Wuer Kaixi as the most recognized leader. So, against strong objection from Liu Gang, Wang Juntao nominated Chai Ling as the commander-in-chief with her provisional headquarters formally renamed the Headquarters for Defending Tiananmen Square.

Wang Juntao was still reluctant to assume a leadership role himself despite much lobbying effort by his friends. Instead, he asked Bao Zunxin to be the chairman of the Joint Conference.* Wang Dan, meanwhile, was assigned the job to establish a new student parliament to provide support and balance for the new headquarters at the Square. As many as eight departments were established with most of them headed by people from the independent Institute of Chen Ziming and Wang Juntao: Liu Gang as the chief of staff, Zhang Lun heading the security operations, and so on. Of the student leaders, Zhang Boli and Feng Congde, while continuing to serve as deputies in the new headquarters, were put in charge of propaganda and finances, respectively.

With a new team in place and a new beginning in the air, Wang Dan read a prepared statement bearing a grandiose title: *The Final Decisive Struggle between Brightness and Darkness.* Forty-four years earlier and on the eve of a civil war, Mao Zedong had used the same phrase to proclaim that the brightness of communism would displace the darkness of the then Nationalist government. That "final decisive struggle" led to the founding of the People's Republic. Wang Dan was

---

*Bao Zunxin would later recall that he had been used as a figurehead and was confused about his role the whole time.[209]

ambitious / radical

obviously less ambitious. But he was declaring that China's history had entered into a brand new era with the "old China" finally coming to an end. The current struggle for democracy and human rights, he said, had surpassed all previous revolutions and left the legends of the April Fifth and the May Fourth movements in the distant dust of history. He stated that the failure of martial law troops to enter the city was not because of the tolerance of the government but rather the power of the people. While acknowledging that people could still fail, he urged that there was no more ground to retreat. Their backs were already against the wall and the only thing they could do now was to persevere. Through the perseverance of the people, he declared optimistically, the incompetent government would have to fall.

The bravado manifesto, authored by intellectuals who never shied away from such hyperbole, set the tone for the conference. There was no talk of withdrawing from Tiananmen Square. Rather, they formulated plans for sustaining the occupation. Fred Chiu, a scholar who had just arrived from Hong Kong, wondered aloud, "Do you guys have to be this serious all the time?" He suggested to organize parties to have fun and make the Square an open-air youth center.

Chai Ling found herself in a rare good mood. She was particularly relieved that Wang Juntao had chosen to back her headquarters. She had been painfully aware that many individuals and groups were looking to take over her leadership role, not least the Beijing Students Autonomous Federation which at this very moment was biding their time. The backing of Wang Juntao, along with this new Joint Conference, provided a sense of legitimacy she had long coveted. Happily, she followed up on Fred Chiu's idea and asked for help in its implementation. Particularly, she indicated that they would need camping tents, a luxury sporting goods not yet available in mainland China. Fred Chiu assured Chai Ling that donated tents could be transported from Hong Kong in a matter of days.

Li Lu did not share Chai Ling's enthusiasm however. His doubts about the intellectuals ran much deeper. He pulled her aside to caution that their headquarters was, and should remain, a product of Tiananmen Square. Their obligation ought to be with the students there, not the people at this conference. Nonetheless, Li Lu welcomed Fred

214

Ouch ---

Chiu's idea to enliven the Square with educational and recreational activities even though he thought that it did not match the seriousness of their movement.[210] He was, after all, a man who had just staged his own "wedding" there.

Indeed, even Wang Juntao himself was unsure of the roles and responsibilities. Having just "authorized" the Headquarters for Defending Tiananmen Square and its personnel, the Capital Joint Conference immediately declared itself as a body for coordination and logistical support only. Therefore, it would not have any direct leadership role at the Headquarters it had just authorized. Although a contradictory act, it appeared to be the logical thing to do. Nobody could realistically impose themselves as leaders of the students at this stage. On the other hand, Wang Juntao had hopes that Wang Dan would be able to assert influence once he got the new student parliament off the ground. It would be an all-people movement spearheaded by students.[211]

WITH all recognized leaders at the conference, students at Tiananmen Square were left to fend for themselves on this fourth day of martial law. On the northern outskirts of the city, several small-scale skirmishes clashes broke out between soldiers and civilians. Both sides sustained injuries. In one scuffle, a soldier was inadvertently entangled under a military truck and lost his life. Dozens of residents rushed into Tiananmen Square with bloody shirts to call for reinforcements. Luckily, restraint won out and the situation did not escalate further.

It was also an unusually hot day. There was no wind. The temperature on the dry concrete at the Square was rising so fast that by noon it felt like an oven. The rows and rows of city buses were slowly departing in an effort to restore public transportation services. Gradually, buses and subway trains started running again after three days of phantom martial law.

Peace was suddenly disrupted in the early afternoon when three men were seen throwing egg shells filled with paint onto the giant portrait of Chairman Mao Zedong on the wall of Tiananmen. Visible stains were left on the Great Helmsman's face. Alert students sprang to action immediately and detained the perpetrators. The three men identified themselves as teachers from Hunan Province, Mao Zedong's hometown. They had come here to join the protest in their own manner. Students were not sure. They suspected a conspiracy by the government to create trouble for the movement. Thus a quick decision was made to hand over the men to the police. It was a hot potato they were not willing to hold onto.*

The late chairman must not have been pleased. While his portrait was being covered up for repair, a raging sand storm engulfed Tiananmen Square. Makeshift tents were blown apart. Garbage were swirling all over in the air. People scrambled for cover. They buried their faces to escape flying sand and debris. A few moments later, the sky opened up. Heavy rain mixed with hail pelted the area relentlessly. A flash flood washed away trash along with much of the students' shelter. When the sun reappeared shortly after, Tiananmen Square appeared cleaner and the air more pleasant.

W ANG Chaohua did not get an invitation to the Capital Joint Conference. She was at Peking University making tremendous progress in reorganizing Beijing Students Autonomous Federation. With the forty-eight hour deadline looming, she was working around the clock to recruit personnel and setting up procedures and policies. It was only the end of the first day and she was already feeling much better about the prospect. Looking forward, she had never been this confident since she got involved in the movement. It was then a van arrived with Wang Juntao, Liu Gang, Wang Dan and Wuer Kaixi in it. They brought the news of the Capital Joint Conference and its founding of the Headquarters for Defending Tiananmen Square.

Nobody paid attention to the fact that Beijing Students Autonomous Federation was not formally represented at the Capital Joint Conference, which was inclusive to a fault. Many thought that Wang Dan and Wuer Kaixi were still part of that organization. Wang Juntao did not learn about the forty-eight hour deal until after all the personnel decisions had been made. Wang Chaohua was crushed. She refused to join forces with the Capital Joint Conference.

---

*Two months after the massacre, the three teachers were convicted for their crime of "counter-revolutionary propaganda and damaging public property." The sentences ranged from sixteen years, to twenty years, to life, respectively.

The Standoff

AFTER the storm, in the morning of May 24, Tiananmen Square looked much better. A giant red banner was wrapped around the Monument to People's Heroes to spell out new goals of the ongoing sit-in: "Commence the National People's Congress! Enhance Democracy! Impeach Li Peng! Stop Martial Law!" Underneath, the middle tier of the Monument base had been cleared out. A crowd estimated to be a hundred thousand students was waiting for the unveiling of the Headquarters for Defending Tiananmen Square. At ten o'clock, Wang Dan made the formal announcement and read aloud *The Final Decisive Struggle between Brightness and Darkness*. What followed was a scene reminiscent of that at the start of the hunger strike. Chai Ling led her officers and students with a solemn oath:

> I swear: I will protect the republic and Tiananmen Square with my young life. Heads can roll, blood can flow, but the people's Square can never be lost! We are willing to fight until the last person.

The oath, drafted by Wang Juntao, had a familiar tone. A generation ago, the Red Guards had plunged into the Cultural Revolution with a similar oath of their own: "Heads can roll, blood can flow, but Mao Zedong Thought can never be lost!" 头可断, 血可流

Newly appointed officers sprang into action as soon as the ceremony was completed. They unified two dueling student broadcasting stations into a consolidated media center with a regular broadcasting schedule. They also started a newspaper called *News Herald*. A new commanding structure was put in place for student marshals headed by Zhang Lun. A clean-up effort was underway to make room for tents coming from Hong Kong. All of a sudden, Tiananmen Square looked like a location for a mass settlement. It was going to be their home for the long haul.

The new broadcasting station was also devoting much of its time to playing music and hosting karaoke parties. Rock 'n' roll concerts and dancing parties were all the rage. In sharp contrast to the hunger strike days, students were now coming to the Square to have a good time.

The singers and dancers were not alone. Tiananmen Square was also transforming itself into a gigantic "Hyde Park" Liu Gang had dreamed of having in China. Every evening, people came here to

Carnival

make speeches surrounded by hundreds of eager listeners. They debated freely, either over the loudspeakers at the broadcasting station or among themselves with an ad-hoc audience. In a flashback of history, one young man dressed the part of a protesting student during the May Fourth Movement seven decades earlier to deliver a passionate speech. Freedom, unprecedented in this People's Republic, permeated the air. A poet happily declared, "Walking on Beijing's streets in May, I feel freedom." Chen Mingyuan, the intellectual whose speech had inspired students back in April, proclaimed, "Standing in Tiananmen Square, I become a free person."

W ANG Dan did not spend much time enjoying this free atmosphere himself. Rather he hung around at the Capital Joint Conference which was in permanent session. He never got around to implement the student parliament envisioned by Wang Juntao either. At Tiananmen Square, it was Li Lu who resurrected his version of the student parliament during the hunger strike days. He named this new installment the Parliament of All Camps in the Square. In its first meeting, more than four hundred delegates showed up to represent the three hundred institutions present. The large number of schools indicated that the majority of them were from outside of the city of Beijing. Li Lu firmly believed that it should be these students at Tiananmen Square, instead of the superficial Capital Joint Conference, who should provide guidance and supervision for their Headquarters for Defending Tiananmen Square.[212]

There was a strong sense of deja vu. Just after the oath to defend Tiananmen Square with their lives, the most prominent issue debated in this new student parliament was whether to withdraw, an exact replay of their days during the hunger strike.

This time, however, they did not have any bargaining chips like Mr. Gorbachev's visit on hand. The city was under martial law, which meant everything they were doing was strictly illegal and punishable at the sole discretion of martial law troops. Despite the efforts led by Hu Jiwei, there appeared to be no progress in having an emergency meeting of the National People's Congress Standing Committee. All eyes were turning to the chairman of that committee, seventy-three year old Wan Li who had been on a multi-country state visit in North America.

A pragmatic technocrat, one of Wan Li's earlier accomplishments was the reconstruction of the modern Tiananmen Square in the early 1950's. He was also a well-known ally of Zhao Ziyang, a rarity among leaders in his age group. Yet his credentials as an open-minded re-former were not entirely without question either. In 1986, when Pro-fessor Fang Lizhi was in the midst of his speaking tour advocating democracy, Wan Li had personally sought him out and the two en-gaged in a debate in front of hundreds of Party cadres. Wan Li insisted that democracy could only be gradually handed down by the Commu-nist Party, a stance Fang Lizhi vehemently opposed.[213] Nonetheless, rumors spread that Wan Li had cut his trip short in defiance of orders from Beijing. He was now the best or only hope of defeating martial law. Students dispatched a delegation to Capital Airport to welcome him with an open petition.

They waited in vain. Wan Li never made his way back to Beijing but stopped, or was stopped, at Shanghai "for health reasons." The hope that he could call for an emergency meeting in the students' favor vaporized. There was only the scheduled regular meeting on June 20 left. It was almost a month away. Could they sustain their occupation of Tiananmen Square, under martial law, for that long?

L IU Gang was not at all thrilled with the "Hyde Park" scene at Tiananmen Square. In fact, he was getting angrier each time he visited. The freedom people enjoyed there, he observed, was not accompanied by any responsibilities. Trash continued to pile up everywhere. At the base of the Monument to People's Heroes, he saw a man in his seventies who had come with his granddaughter who was seven or eight. They offered free porridge and tea eggs, a traditional Chinese breakfast. The old man filled bowls with porridge while the little girl de-shelled the eggs with a bright smile. Yet students who took the food did not show any gratitude or manners. They took it for granted and even smashed the bowls on the ground after they were done. The old man did not complain. He quietly deposited the fragments in a trash bag. But Liu Gang saw tears in his eyes.

A "republican" that was autocrat & corrupted
just like the one they wanted to overthrow.

Standoff At Tiananmen

Tiananmen Square had become a campground for thousands and thousands of students arriving from the provinces who were entirely dependent on the headquarters to supply food and shelter. Without anyone noticing it, it had become a society with a population of some hundreds of thousands. Indeed, it was the "People's Republic of Tiananmen Square," a self-governing entity with its own news media, student government, as well as its own police force. The latter was made up of the hundreds and hundreds of student marshals who established layers upon layers of picket lines to keep "unauthorized" people out of the center of the Square, namely the Monument to People's Heroes. Nobody could even get close to student leaders without multiple passes issued by different people who happened to be in charge of security on any given day. Student leaders themselves, when they did venture out occasionally, were accompanied by an entourage of bodyguards and assistants not at all different from government officials.

Along with the flourishing of bureaucracy, something else was also rearing its ugly head. The "Hyde Park" also seemed to be flush with loose money. Liu Gang was seeing donation boxes everywhere. Any person could put out a box or a bag at any street corner with a banner or flag. There was no accountability. The movement, which had started as an anti-corruption force, had been corrupted by its own power.

Money and corruption was also the new focus of Feng Congde, who volunteered to look after the finances after observing the same dreadful scenes. Feng Congde set out to install formal financial controls. He posted daily reports on donations and expenditures. To his astonishment, he found that they were not awash in cash as it appeared. With a crude auditing, he estimated that the daily tab in Tiananmen Square was running at 50,000 RMB (roughly more than 6,000 USD) just for feeding and caring for all the students. Donations were indeed coming in, but only at the rate of 20,000 to 30,000 RMB each day. They were running a huge deficit with much of it covered by the goodwill of their suppliers who handed out bread and water for unofficial debt slips issued with only a signature by a student leader. Beijing Students Autonomous Federation appeared to have taken with them a sizable amount of donated cash when they were forced to leave. Now the headquarters had only 9,000 RMB worth of loose change. The situation was obviously not sustainable.[214]

In the evening of May 25, Li Lu had a particularly hard time maintaining order in his parliament meeting. There were as many as three hundred student representatives, most of them from out-of-town universities. With more and more students arriving from the provinces and taking up aggressive stands in the movement, local students, who were suffering from fatigue, chose to stay away. Other than Chai Ling, Feng Congde, and Zhang Boli, there were no known student leaders from Beijing in either the headquarters or the parliament. The major schools that had led the movement so far, such as Peking University, University of Political Science and Law, and Beijing Normal University, were all conspicuously missing in action.

The main item on the agenda was once again whether to withdraw. It took almost five hours before Li Lu was able to consolidate the discussions into four options and put them up for a vote. They ranged from the most radical (staying put and maintaining a direct confrontation with the government) to the most sublime (withdrawing immediately). Out of 288 ballots, 162 had voted for the most radical option. Another 82 voted for staying at the Square but seeking a new dialogue with the government. Only 8 votes were for an immediate withdrawal. This result was totally different from what Wang Chaohua got in her informal survey a couple of days earlier. With the majority consistently voting against a withdrawal, Li Lu felt that he had his mandate.[215]

It was now one week into martial law but the measure itself seemed to have been forgotten. Things were returning to a strange normalcy after a few days of siege. Some bus lines were still not running but most were. There had been repeated calls for a general strike but none materialized. People went to work as usual but took detours in their commutes to pass by Tiananmen Square. The continued presence of students there gave them a feeling of assurance that they could not quite comprehend.

There was almost no presence of police forces on the streets. At any busy intersection, traffic flew slowly by the clumsy arm signals of a student. Typically, it was a teenage-looking boy. His face and body were covered by a layer of dirt. He looked tired and downtrodden. But he stood in the center island firm and serious. A red or white headband was the source of his authority. He might have a little red flag or two in his hands. He probably had stood there for hours already without food or water. But he persevered to stretch his arms in, out, and around to direct the complicated traffic patterns. Most likely his signals were confusing or wrong. But it hardly mattered. Buses, vans, trucks, motorcycles, bicycles, tricycles, and even pedestrians came and went slowly and carefully. There were no complaints.

Even the notorious noise of blaring horns had disappeared. Traffic went smoother and the number of accidents plunged. People stopped arguing with each other in public. They talked gently and occasionally smiled to strangers.

Common thieves and petty criminals also went into hibernation. A Big Poster at Tiananmen Square proudly announced that all thieves in the city had started their own strike. They wanted to help students preserve the social order of the city. The poster was almost certainly a humorous prank. But everyone agreed that this ancient city, under the phantom martial law and without official law enforcement, had become a kinder and gentler place.

Yet the shadow of martial law persisted. The city also behaved as if it were in the middle of a war or popular uprising. Traffic was often snarled by frequent demonstration marches. Students did not need buses to get around. Alongside any street, they could flag down passing cars or trucks for a free ride to their destinations. Drivers happily hauled them around, asking for autographs along the way.

The peace was often disrupted by the roaring engines of the Flying Tigers, who continued to keep a vigilant watch over the city. When they reported a slight movement of troops, a squadron of students and residents were quickly organized. They flagged down trucks and rode to the location. Once there, they set up roadblocks and checkpoints and stayed on guard for hours if not days.

B ACK at Peking University, local students were dispirited. More than a month since they started, the Preparatory Committee still clung to that temporary name. Their ranks were seriously depleted. Chai

Ling and Feng Congde were holding the fort permanently at Tiananmen Square. Wang Dan hung around with intellectuals in the city. Even Shen Tong was nowhere to be seen around his own media center by The Triangle. Yang Tao, a close friend of Wang Dan's in the Democracy Salon, and his friends kept it going.

They had been doing quite a significant job behind the scenes. With a commitment to support the hunger strikers, Peking University had become a major supply base for the front line. They set up a station at Tiananmen Square and mobilized students to collect donations and procure and transport needed materials there. This ad-hoc supply chain operated with remarkable efficiency and was one of the reasons that the hunger strike and the subsequent sit-in could be sustained.

In the meantime, they continued to fortify their positions on campus. Their media center had become the news source for the entire northwest suburb. People came in droves everyday just to listen to their broadcasts and receive their daily newsletters. When Wang Chaohua needed personnel for her short-lived reorganization of Beijing Students Autonomous Federation, this was where she found the most resources. They elected Yang Tao as the new head of the organization.

More and more students were returning from Tiananmen Square to report their disillusion with the situation there. It had been taken over by students from provinces who, having just arrived to join the movement, insisted on prolonging the occupation. By their sheer numbers, they were dominating the student parliament and therefore the decision making.

Yang Tao understood that they had to have an exit strategy. From his vantage point on campus, he realized that students really had nothing to do. They were not going to classes or doing anything resembling being a student. They were tired of the scene at Tiananmen Square so they were not heading there as frequently as they did a week earlier. Seeing that many students had left town to go home or travel, Yang Tao came upon the idea of sending all students home and emptying the campuses. By departing from the capital en masse, they would leave the martial law troops without a target. It could be as dramatic an action as the continued occupation of Tiananmen Square.

In the morning of May 26, Yang Tao set foot in Tiananmen Square for the first time since the beginning of the hunger strike. He found Chai Ling and Feng Congde in a parked van and presented his idea of vacating the schools. The couple was very receptive. Feng Congde suggested that they should also plan ahead for further steps. Students who had returned to their home provinces could have scheduled rallies in nearby cities every Sunday morning. It would be as if they were spreading Tiananmen Square all over the country!

Together, they developed it into a proposal for a non-cooperative and social disobedience movement. A single Tiananmen Square could become hundreds or even thousands of "Squares of Democracy" where students could enlighten and educate local people at the grass-roots level. It could be sustained indefinitely so long as the government continued to refuse students' demands.[216]

L IU Gang was also getting impatient. Without any imminent threat, the occupation of Tiananmen Square was deteriorating into its messy and chaotic former self. He was particularly worried about the new arrivals from the provinces, many of whom were taking advantage of the situation. They spent their days sightseeing and only came to the Square for free food and shelter. Invoking his physics background, he found that the movement had entered a phase of Brownian motion ever since the hunger strike. It was a collection of random acts with unpredictable results. Given time, it could evolve into an uncontrollable thermal nuclear reaction. Therefore, he had spent the last few days immersed in the Capital Joint Conference to persuade everybody that they needed to end the occupation. He had won over a few intellectuals including Bao Zunxin, the nominal head of the organization. But many others strongly disagreed. Zheng Yi and Chen Mingyuan argued that Tiananmen Square was truly their last stronghold and victory was already in sight as long as they persevered.

In the morning of May 27, Liu Gang came to Tiananmen Square with a single mission in mind. He had to get the leaders of Headquarters for Defending Tiananmen Square leaders into the conference to discuss a plan for the future. Li Lu had never attended the conference after its first day. He regarded it only as a farce. Occasionally, he sent Chai Ling over so that she could get away and catch some rest during those boring meetings.[217] With his own student parliament backing the headquarters, Li Lu had neither time nor necessity to be involved in the Capital Joint Conference. Liu Gang had come to understand that, for any plan to have a chance, it had to be with the approval of Chai Ling and Li Lu.

But Liu Gang could not persuade Li Lu to attend the meeting this morning. Chai Ling and Feng Congde went with him instead. It happened to be the best attended session in days. There were about a hundred people in a large conference room. Feng Congde, who was a stranger to this scene, recognized many familiar faces. He was surprised to find Wang Dan, absent from Tiananmen Square, playing a central role. But he did not know Wang Juntao, who was there to chair this important proceeding. The agenda was to discuss the second task he had set when he opened the conference four days earlier: a clear and unified goal for the movement.

The meeting opened with Chai Ling briefing on the current situation. To the surprise of many, she gave a depressing account of deterioration. The newcomers from the provinces were out of control. They had started their own organizations to fight with her headquarters for power. Garbage was piling up and the place stank. Chai Ling was exhausted and did not appear at all like a commander-in-chief ready to defend Tiananmen Square. Yang Tao's proposal to vacate the schools was then brought up but received only lukewarm reaction. Wang Dan thought the idea impossible to implement. Wuer Kaixi concurred but added that he would be willing to travel to the provinces himself to drum up popular support for Beijing.

Wang Juntao brought the meeting back to its agenda. A couple of writers in the group had drafted another statement, plainly titled *Our Ten-Point Statement regarding the Current Situation*. It was a laundry list of their collective opinions and demands. To the great dismay and frustration of Feng Congde and Chai Ling, the intellectuals proceeded to argue hours over fine wording choices point by point. At one instance, a prolonged debate erupted regarding whether to use the phrase "purely spontaneous" or "essentially spontaneous" to describe the origin of the movement. Feng Congde noticed that many of the attendees were dozing off. Now he understood what Li Lu had been saying about this conference.

Wang Juntao ordered Kentucky Fried Chicken for lunch. It was a meal of luxury for most people in the room. Like almost everybody else, Chai Ling had a very favorable impression of Wang Juntao. She found him understanding and supportive. A rare person in this crowd whom she could trust. Wang Juntao had been conscientiously playing out the role of his version of George Washington. He went out of his way to make sure that everybody could have a voice in the conference and avoid making any judgment of his own. He smiled and nodded eagerly even when he was listening to something he thought ridiculous or disagreeable. While his approach was winning friends and keeping the conference together, his all-pleasing style was also frustrating his closer friends. "Unprincipled," many scoffed publicly. Liu Gang worried that frequent changes in Wang Juntao's stance could be costing them precious opportunities.

During the lunch break, they learned that Wan Li, the Chairman of the National People's Congress Standing Committee, had issued a written statement from Shanghai in support of martial law. It was yet another major setback.

The meeting continued in the afternoon on their *Ten-Point Statement*. The eighth point spelled out that, if an emergency meeting of the National People's Congress Standing Committee was not called, the occupation of Tiananmen Square would continue at least until June 20, the date for a regular meeting of the same committee. There was no objection to this deadline until Feng Congde rose to speak. As the person in charge of finance, he told the conference that it was not financially possible to sustain the occupation for another three weeks. In fact, he did not think it could last even a couple more days. He proceeded to explain how they were running a large deficit. He demanded that the departed Beijing Students Autonomous Federation return donated funds to the Square.

The audience was shocked. For all their grandiose visions of revolution and victory, they had paid little attention to such details as money and bread supply. Under pressure, a student in charge of finance for the Federation promised to release some of its funds right away. But he also claimed that their fund was not large either. With the burn rate Feng Congde cited, it would not come close to sustaining them till June 20.

Wang Juntao did not think the monetary shortfall was a serious threat. Sizable donations from Hong Kong and Taiwan were already on their way. But Feng Congde's numbers coupled with Chai Ling's briefing had already caused the pendulum to swing to the side of an earlier withdrawal. To the dismay of a few die-hards, the conference quickly settled on a withdrawal date of May 30, chosen to give the headquarters a couple of days to prepare. All eyes were turning to Chai Ling. It would be this diminutive but determined commander-in-chief who would have the final say.

Chai Ling was much more exhausted than determined at this very moment. She spoke up quietly and softly. It had been a grueling time for her since the start of the hunger strike. Despite all efforts, the situation at Tiananmen Square was dreadful. She was ready to have all this over. Yes, she told the conference, as she raised her hand, she agreed with the withdrawal plan. Almost everybody else followed. It was noted as an unanimous decision.[218]

I T was now late afternoon and they finally finished with their statement. But the meeting was not yet over. Liu Xiaobo, a young professor of literature at Beijing Normal University, suggested that they needed a more visible leader for the movement. One who was to be a public hero or a Chinese Lech Walesa, the famous leader of Polish Solidarity. Only with such a figure, he declared, could this movement unite the people and sustain its civil opposition after withdrawing from Tiananmen Square. He already had a candidate and he immediately nominated Wuer Kaixi for the role to be named as the "Spokesman of the People."

The thirty-four year old Liu Xiaobo had been traveling abroad teaching Chinese philosophy and literature in Norway and the United States. He was visiting Columbia University that spring when he felt an irrepressible urge to join the emerging movement. So he hopped on a plane home. As he was transferring at Tokyo, he learned about the publication of April 26 *People's Daily* editorial. In a moment of truth, he hesitated between continuing onto Beijing or flying back to New *fight over who's gonna be the leader ...*

York. Beijing won out.

Back home, he was happy to find students from his school at the center of the storm. Now at the conference, he showered accolades on Wuer Kaixi as a natural leader. Likewise, Wuer Kaixi was ready. He followed up with a speech to claim himself the most charismatic and recognized leader of the movement. He appeared to be well received by the audience.

But Feng Congde was beyond himself. He angrily objected the nomination and accused Wuer Kaixi of being immature, lacking experience, and, worst of all, having a strong tendency to speak for himself in total disregard of rules and regulations. He was referring to the unilateral moves Wuer Kaixi had made at Tiananmen Square that had resulted in his own banishment. To his credit, Wuer Kaixi did not dispute the charges. He defended himself by saying that he could now do a better job with teachers like Liu Xiaobo as his advisers.

That was the last straw. Feng Congde and Chai Ling had no more patience left. They had already spent seven hours in this meeting and it was time to leave. As a parting shot, Chai Ling declared that her Headquarters for Defending Tiananmen Square was no longer on the same page with this conference. As they walked out in disgust, the motion to make Wuer Kaixi the Spokesman of the People was tabled. Wang Juntao rushed out to comfort the angry couple.

Leaving the conference, Feng Congde rushed to Peking University to follow up on funds promised by Beijing Students Autonomous Federation. Chai Ling went back to Tiananmen Square by herself. The images of Liu Xiaobo and Wuer Kaixi lingered in her mind. She had seen too many instances of people trying to wrestle leadership from her. From Beijing Students Autonomous Federation to new arrivals from the provinces, they had always tried to overthrow her headquarters and seize power. Now this Capital Joint Conference, which had backed her just a few days ago, was turning against her as well. As she got closer to Tiananmen Square, Chai Ling started having serious second thoughts about the decision to withdraw in three days.

Tiananmen Square was not her sanctuary on this day either. As she was walking in, the sad realities sank in all at once. It was a dirty and pathetic place. People were tired and angry. A young student marshal came to her in anger and disgust. He told her that he had come from Qingdao, a port city in northeast China. Hundreds of his schoolmates had come together to join the movement. Because of the school uniforms they were wearing, all of them were immediately assigned duties as marshals to work on picket lines protecting the Headquarters for Defending Tiananmen Square. They all worked hard for many days, he told Chai Ling while crying. But what had they witnessed so far? Nothing good, he said. We saw you leaders come and go without doing anything of substance. We saw so much infighting and corruption. We did not see anything good at all! He told Chai Ling that most of his schoolmates had already returned home with profound disappointment. There were only a dozen or so left. Why did he choose to stay? He said, I just did not want to give up. I just wanted to see how bad things could get at the Square and whether our country still had any hope left!

There it was, an echo directly from the *Hunger Strike Manifesto* Chai Ling had written in her own emotional days. It was almost exactly the same language she had used to inspire hundreds and then thousands to Tiananmen Square. But this time, it came back at her. Her own movement was now turning her followers away. She did not have much to say to this teenager. All of a sudden, she thought of her husband Feng Congde. Commenting on the dreadful state of student infighting, he had once quipped, "Now I understand why Li Peng had to impose martial law." It was sad, depressingly sad.[219]

CHAI Ling was happy to see Li Lu, who greeted her at the Monument to People's Heroes. But the nice feeling did not last long. Upon hearing of the withdrawal plan, Li Lu was dumbfounded. "What are you talking about? It has only been two days since three hundred delegates voted to stay in the Square. How can that decision be overturned so quickly? It's against democratic procedures."[220] Chai Ling tried to defend the decision but she was not particularly convincing. Li Lu was getting angrier and angrier by the minute. If they withdrew now, he screamed, it would be impossible to get students together again. The military would have total control. The National People's Congress Standing Committee meeting on June 20, if held at all, would be conducted under bayonets!221

By the time Liu Gang and some of the Capital Joint Conference
people arrived at Tiananmen Square, he found Chai Ling already had
changed her mind. Chai Ling told him that it was Li Lu's call. Liu
Gang immediately sought out Li Lu and briefed him on the plan. He
emphasized that it was not going to be a total withdrawal, but a strategic diversion to campuses. Li Lu listened politely but showed no emotion. Liu Gang stared at Li Lu's dark sunglasses but could not see his
eyes. He knew he had trouble on his hands.222

Feng Congde had scheduled a press conference ahead of time and it
became a rare occasion of the movement. For once, almost all prominent student leaders were present. At the base of the Monument, Wuer
Kaixi, Wang Dan, and Chai Ling were standing in the middle. Li
Lu, Zhang Boli, Liu Gang, Wang Juntao, and a group of intellectuals
from the Capital Joint Conference sat behind them. There were rows
of cameras facing the leaders, ready to record history in the making.
Thousands of students and residents gathered behind the reporters.
The occasion felt more like a mass assembly than a press conference.

Wuer Kaixi gave a speech first. He had not been seen in public
for days and now appeared to have recovered from his illness. There
were no more oxygen bags or nurses in tow. Liu Gang had intended to
have him as a lead-in to summarize the achievements of the movement.
Wuer Kaixi, however, took it as an opportunity for his own comeback.
Happy and at ease, he casually launched into a sincere apology for his
"bone-headed" move in screaming for withdrawal in the early morning
of May 21, which he said might have cost the movement a golden
opportunity to unite. His natural charisma won over the crowd. For
once, he did not faint.

It was a tough act to follow. When Wang Dan came up next, he
appeared to be the opposite of the charming Wuer Kaixi. Stiff and flat,
with a pair of oversize glasses blocking almost half of his face, Wang
Dan was holding the microphone in his right hand and several sheets
of loose paper in his left. He struggled to read as the papers flapped
in the wind. It was the long and drawn-out *Ten-Point Statement*. The
crowd, warmed up by Wuer Kaixi, sat back in a subdued mood.

It was not until he reached the eighth point that he was able to

Withdraw by 5.30 plan
Opposed by C.L

catch the attention of his audience. After pausing for a moment, he slowly and softly read on, "It is suggested that the students evacuate Tiananmen Square on May 30."[223] As Wang Dan continued with the statement, students in the crowd were exchanging confused looks and opinions.

Liu Gang got very worried. He spent the time during Wang Dan's speech to write down a detailed withdrawal plan on a piece of paper, mapping out how students would march out of Tiananmen Square. Knowing that most students were from out of town, he instructed them to go to specific local campuses based on the geographic regions where they came from. He handed the plan to Chai Ling who would be speaking next.

As Chai Ling stood up, she had Liu Gang's notes in one hand and took the microphone in the other. She did not bother to take a peek at the notes. Calmly, she stuffed the notes into a side pocket of her jeans and said, "The decision to withdraw on May 30 was not made by our Headquarters for Defending Tiananmen Square. It was not the will of the students at the Square either." Raising her voice, she turned and pointed her finger at Liu Gang, "It was them! It was only the opinion of these so-called elite intellectuals!"

The press conference ended in a confused state. Liu Gang and his fellow "elites" took refuge in a tent and could not contain their anger toward Chai Ling.[224] When the *Ten-Point Statement* was printed and released publicly the next day, it had already reverted to its original language: "Unless an emergency meeting of the National People's Congress Standing Committee is convened in the next few days, the occupation of the Square will continue at least until June 20."*

T HE Sunday of May 28 was designated as a day of global demonstration. In major cities all over the world Chinese students and nationals marched to support their compatriots at home. But it was a relatively dismal day in Beijing itself. Students here demonstrated on bicycles. In order to reach more residents, they spread their routes away from the city center. It ended up as a far cry from the atmosphere they

---

*Two different versions of the same statement, bearing the withdrawal date of May 30 and June 20, respectively, existed in print.

had gotten used to in the previous weeks. Most alarmingly, there was an obvious drop in support by residents, who now appeared indifferent to the endless marches. The flow of residents coming to Tiananmen Square with food and cash donations had also declined. More students were still arriving from the provinces, however, making up for those who were leaving.

Chai Ling was feeling more depressed than ever. Having demolished the withdrawal plan, she was now haunted by the movement's uncertain future. As she looked around, she actually saw a much improved place. Large quantities of brand new tents had arrived from Hong Kong. Students were busy setting them up and arranging them into neat color-coded sections. By design, these bright red, blue, yellow tents made up ten divisions with specific functions. The new tent city gave an illusion of order and strength. Chai Ling was impressed. Li Lu, her trusted lieutenant, had been hard at work.

Chai Ling had always had a high regard for Li Lu's resourcefulness and leadership skills. She believed that he was the strong leader this movement required. Li Lu's staunch opposition to the withdrawal plan reinforced her opinion. In contrast, she had seen her own weakness.

It was now the eighth day of martial law. Rumors continued to circulate. On this particular morning, there was a "credible report" which said that a group of assassins had infiltrated the Square, ready to take out all the leaders at minutes' notice. The debacle on withdrawal also had a deep psychological impact. Several people came by to offer their resignations that morning. Bai Meng, who had polished Chai Ling's *Hunger Striker Manifesto*, quit in frustration. Zhang Boli informed Chai Ling that he had to take a leave as well. He wanted to write a book about the movement. Author Zheng Yi and his wife were also packing. They too had become disillusioned. Citing that they had run out of spare clothing, the couple decided that it was time for them to head back home to the remote Shaanxi Province.[225]

So, in a matter of hours, the Headquarters for Defending Tiananmen Square dwindled. It was now just Li Lu, Feng Congde, and Chai Ling with a small group of volunteers who were looking for directions. Chai Ling made up her mind. It was time for her to walk away as well. Before taking off, however, Chai Ling thought she had to take care of a couple of things first. She would like to leave a few words so that her thoughts would not disappear when she did. She also wanted to see her husband one more time and maybe persuade him to go with her.

Alone, Chai Ling crossed Chang'an Avenue to the Beijing Hotel. She found Philip Cunningham, an American graduate student who was studying Chinese history at Beijing Normal University. As events in Beijing escalated, many foreign students had either volunteered or been recruited into freelance reporting work for news agencies. Philip Cunningham was no exception. He was working for *BBC News*, through which he had gotten to know Chai Ling.

Philip Cunningham immediately sensed that the "flustered, frightened, and crying" visitor was facing some kind of threat and was ready to flee. He was asked for help in recording a few "last words" before she could run away.[226] On the way out of the hotel, they met up with a female reporter from Hong Kong by the name of Liang Shuying, who invited herself to the occasion.

They got into a taxi and drove aimlessly for a while before Philip Cunningham decided to head to an apartment of a friend of his. In the car, Chai Ling wrote a note authorizing Philip Cunningham to speak on her behalf, presumably after her arrest or death. The young American was both shocked and frightened by her seriousness. In a tiny bedroom, he had Chai Ling sit down on a bed facing a video camera while holding a tape recorder in her hands. Chai Ling started talking right away.

She began calmly but depressingly: "I think these are going to be my last words, as the situation is getting more and more cruel. I am Chai Ling. I am twenty-three year old." She recalled the moment when she joined the movement at Hu Yaobang's funeral on April 22. When the three students knelt down for their petition on the stairs of the Great Hall of People, she saw the tears of students in the Square. She saw her husband Feng Congde biting his finger to write words with his blood on a handkerchief. She remembered the launch of hunger strike, the dialogue with Yan Mingfu, and Li Lu's proposal of self-immolation. She sprinkled her retelling of the movement with many negative observations of other student leaders who had opposed the hunger strike and continued trying to compromise with the government. She was distraught. Her voice was hoarse, pausing, and sometimes incomprehensible. Eventually, she broke down and started to sob uncontrollably. She could not face the fact that her beloved movement was disintegrating and losing its purity. As the government side started to unite and toughen up, she cried out desperately, students were moving in the opposite direction. Without giving specifics, she claimed that there were traitors, embezzlers, and special agents working for the government among the student leadership.

Philip Cunningham felt that he had to interject. He asked gently, "When was the darkest moment of the movement?" Chai Ling was ready with an answer: the darkest days had yet to come. She pointed her fingers at "all the people" who had advised students to withdraw and unequivocally declared that Tiananmen Square was the last and only ground for the students to hold. They just could not retreat.*

Chai Ling appeared to be particularly upset with people trying to seize power from her. She explained that she had to cling to the post of the commander-in-chief because she needed this power to fight against the forces of withdrawal. The other leaders, including Beijing Students Autonomous Federation, the Capital Joint Conference, and all the other self-proclaimed organizations, she accused, were working to undermine her. Especially Liu Xiaobo and Wuer Kaixi, whom she singled out by name and with anger. All they cared about was seeking leadership position even though Wuer Kaixi had already caused great harm to the movement at least twice. The older intellectuals, on the other hand, only cared about making themselves look good.

Then, as if a pendulum were swinging back, Chai Ling recalled the early days of the hunger strike with fondness and deep longing. That was the best period of the movement when everyone was united as one and the movement was pure. The residents were supportive because the students had wakened their sense of sympathy. The movement reached its glorious peak, she said, when Beijing residents laid down their bodies to stop martial law troops from entering the city. But the happy thought did not last for more than a couple of minutes as the

---

*This sentiment of Chai Ling's was of course shared by most attendees of the Capital Joint Conference during its first day of meeting, the very people who she thought had reversed position and pushed the students to withdraw.

uncertain future crept into her mind immediately. With that, she spoke the words that would forever associate with her in controversy:

> The students always ask me. What should we do next? What could we achieve? I feel deeply sad in my heart. I can not tell them that what we are really waiting for is bloodshed. It's when the government reaches the end of its cruelty and uses butcher knives on its own citizens. I think, when and only when blood is flowing like a river in Tiananmen Square, all the people in China could then see clearly and finally unite. But how could I tell students such things?!

Taken at face value, these words carried a sense of conspiracy of their own: that she was willing to steer the movement into bloodshed for the intention of waking up the populace while keeping that goal only to herself. But at the moment, Chai Ling was more worried about other people's conspiracies. She became more and more emotional and incoherent. She talked about her husband, about their original plan to go abroad, about her parents, and about the debt she owed to her family.

Philip Cunningham cut in again. He asked Chai Ling to describe her own plans for going forward. Chai Ling spoke more words that would come back to haunt her later:

> For the next step, I think I myself will try to survive. The students at Tiananmen Square, however, will have to stay and persist to the very end, waiting for the government's last resort in washing the Square clean with blood. But I also believe that the next revolution will be right around the corner after that. When that happens, I will stand up again. For as long as I am alive, my goal will be to overthrow this inhuman government and build a new government for people's freedom. Let the Chinese people stand up at last. Let a real people's republic be born.

Carefully, Liang Shuying inquired about the plan to withdraw on May 30. In no uncertain terms, Chai Ling said that that proposal had caused tremendous damage to the movement. She regretted that she had not opposed it from the beginning. Once again, she labeled the plan as a conspiracy. If they did withdraw, China as a country would go backwards.

"Will you continue to stay in Tiananmen Square yourself?" Liang Shuying poked on pointedly.

"No, I won't."

"Why?"

"Because I am not the same as everybody else. I am a person who is already marked as 'Most Wanted.' I will not be content to be murdered by such a government. I want to live. That's what I am thinking right now. I don't know if people will think that I am selfish. But I believe that the work I am doing now needs someone to carry on. Because such a democracy movement needs more than one person. Could you not disclose these words, please?"

The last question seemed to indicate that Chai Ling had finally realized that her words were not appropriate for public consumption.* With her "last words" taped, all Chai Ling had to do was to say farewell with her husband before she took off.

ALTHOUGH both of them had been practically living at Tiananmen Square since the hunger strike, Feng Congde had not spent much time with his wife Chai Ling. He had been busy with his logistical and financial work and often crashed in any random tent to get rest, leaving the headquarters bus mainly to Chai Ling, Li Lu, and the other leaders. In fact, he could not recall a single moment that they had spent together alone. When being told of the taping of her "last words," Feng Congde did not take it seriously. It had been a fashionable thing for students to leave their wills. He did not sense the desperate anguish in his wife. He only thought that she must be exhausted and, like everyone else, needed a good rest.

That evening, Chai Ling announced her resignation to the representatives of the student parliament at Tiananmen Square. She did not

---

*However, when Philip Cunningham advised against publishing the tape, Chai Ling refused adamantly. They then tried but were unsuccessful to have the tape broadcast through foreign media.[227] The tape was eventually made public only after the massacre. The footage was extensively used later in a documentary film[228] and caused a lasting controversy on Chai Ling's personal integrity.

elaborate on her future plans but apologized that she was too exhausted to continue. She pleaded for them to elect someone stronger and more capable to the position, clearly referring to Li Lu. As a parting shot, she also criticized the new arrivals from the provinces for their lack of dedication. The infighting and coup attempts had to stop. As usual, her teary speech was well received. Many in the audience begged her to stay and volunteered their service.

Li Lu once again chose not to step forward. But Yang Tao did. He had stayed at the Square to push for his proposal of vacating the schools. In this instance, his pitch was immediately shouted down. The representatives saw it as yet another ploy to get them to withdraw. Strangely enough, however, Yang Tao immediately abandoned his own proposal and pledged that he would never leave Tiananmen Square. He had succumbed to what would be known as the "Square fever," by which a calm and rational person would adopt a radical attitude once he or she was exposed to the crazed atmosphere in the Square. At half past two o'clock in the morning, the parliament passed yet another resolution to reaffirm the decision of occupying Tiananmen Square until at least June 20. In a nice piece of irony, they also voted Yang Tao as the acting commander-in-chief.

Yang Tao was far from alone in catching the "Square fever." Many others, including teachers, intellectuals, and students had come with the intent of rational persuasion. But they ended up being overcome by the zealous atmosphere and became part of the "radical" crowd before they realized it. Tiananmen Square in those days was not only a "Hyde Park," someone quipped, it had also become a psychiatric ward.[229]

T HE tent city was taking shape as new tents continued to arrive from Hong Kong. Some of them could hold fifty people, perfect for hosting the endless meetings of the student leadership. Medium sized tents could also hold twenty people. Then there was a large number of small ones, designed for a four-people outdoor trip. In the middle of the formation, a large scaffold was being erected. Students from the Central Academy of Fine Arts, the same ones who had painted a giant portrait of Hu Yaobang and placed it on the Monument to People's Heroes in April, had been readying a new statue. The Goddess of Democracy would arrive later that day to become a symbol of the movement. Music and dance parties resumed. Concerts were planned with live telephone hookup to supporting students in Hong Kong and Taipei.

It turned out that Feng Congde was right about his wife. All Chai Ling needed was one night off. After a good rest and a much needed shower in a nearby hotel, her mood changed drastically. She came back to Tiananmen Square with a big grin and told Li Lu that she was ready to resume her duty as commander-in-chief. Her timing was perfect. Yang Tao did not last for more than a few hours as the acting commander. His sudden adrenaline rush was no match for the chaotic reality. He found himself ill-equipped and already had to resign.[230]

Zhang Boli also made a comeback of his own. He was inspired by the idea of opening a University of Democracy at Tiananmen Square, proposed by Fred Chiu from Hong Kong. He threw himself into the planning work and assumed the position of the school's founding president.

Late that afternoon, Zhang Boli gathered all the student leaders he could find, including Chai Ling, Feng Congde, Guo Haifeng, and Yang Tao, into a big bus for a meeting. Seeing that all of them were from Peking University, he told the driver to head to that campus as they talked en route. The bus took them all the way to the Unnamed Lake.

It was near sunset, the best time to enjoy this famous lake. The early summer air was calm and pleasant. All around the lake, long willow branches genteelly dipped into the water, creating invisible ripples. The sun was moving behind the trees and office buildings on the west, casting a flood of glorious orange on the Boya Pagoda on the hill on the opposite side.

There were many people by the lake. Lovers walked slowly hand in hand. Old professors strutted along, oblivious to their surroundings. Students on their bikes quietly circled the lake at a relaxed pace. Many gave in to dismounting and walking their bikes instead. Occasionally, kids charged up and down the surrounding hills, breaking the silence with their innocent laughter.

Peace.

This was a familiar scene for everyone associated with Peking University. They had admired, walked in, or sat down with it practically every day. Yet it looked so remote and surreal. They had not been back for weeks. Their lives had been so distorted by the excitement and chaos at Tiananmen Square that they had forgotten what it was like back home.

For a long and slow hour, they lingered by the lake. Nobody said anything. Deep down, they knew that this could be their farewell. For the rest of their lives, they might never see this scene again. With eyes full of tears, they slowly got on the bus, one by one.

As the bus departed, a song echoed*

> *Perhaps I say goodbye, and will never return again,*
> *Would you understand? Would you comprehend?*
> *Perhaps I fall down, and will never get up again,*
> *Would you still wait forever?*
> *If it should be so, don't you feel sad,*
> *On the flag of the republic is the glory colored by our blood.*

A dejected Wang Chaohua wandered around a busy Tiananmen Square. She was now a total outsider. Zhang Boli had profusely apologized for his broken promise but it meant nothing. She was not alone. At the base of Monument to People's Heroes, she spotted the equally depressed Shen Tong. Shen Tong had found himself excluded from the movement ever since the Dialogue Delegation's mission evaporated. Xiang Xiaoji had left Beijing several days earlier.[231] Shen Tong was feeling as lonely and helpless as ever. He had already been accepted by a college in the United States. But he had been putting off the task of going to the American consulate for a visa. He was not sure if he should head down that road in the midst of the movement. Grasping a last hope, Shen Tong asked Wang Chaohua to pass a kind word to Chai Ling and see if Chai Ling could find some use for him at the new Headquarters. An ever reluctant Wang Chaohua agreed. However, she soon came back with terse advice: you had better go get your visa.[232]

Toward the end of May, the Beijing Railway Station became a busy

---

Blood Colored Glory was a patriotic song dedicated to the martyrs of the 1979 Sino-Vietnam border war. It had been adopted by the students as their own anthem for the movement.

place. As the flow of students from the provinces slowed, there were larger crowds leaving the capital every day. Local students had largely turned away from the continued occupation of Tiananmen Square. They were packing up for home. It was also a good time to travel: students were allowed to ride the trains for free just like the Red Guards during the Cultural Revolution. At Tiananmen Square itself, railway workers were handing out free tickets to anyone with a student identification.

Sections of the Goddess of Democracy arrived on the backs of four flatbed tricycles in the evening, guarded by student marshals. The art students spent a whole night assembling it in a strong wind. In the early morning of May 30, the statue was formally unveiled. It bore a striking resemblance to the Statue of Liberty in New York City. Curiously, this goddess possessed distinct Caucasian facial features, even with a large nose. But her simple and straight hairstyle was unmistakably Chinese. She raised a torch above her head with both hands in a somewhat awkward pose.*

It was definitely not a sophisticated statue. It was largely made of plastic and emulsion which was not intended for permanent outdoor use. However, it was designed so that it had to be destroyed before it could be moved.[234] To the huge relief of her creators, the lightweight statue stood up to the strong wind that was gusting through the Square that morning. At about thirty feet in height, it was a significant presence even in the vastness of Tiananmen Square. The statue was positioned on the central axis of the Square and the city. Across the wide Chang'an Avenue, the Goddess stared directly at the giant portrait of Chairman Mao Zedong.

Tiananmen Square, the holiest site in China, possessed symbols of historical importance. Along its central axis, the Mausoleum of Chairman Mao Zedong, the Monument to People's Heroes, the giant National Flag Pole, and Tiananmen itself, were all structures of national passion. Now, a new statue made her small foothold without any official permission, but rather in full defiance of it. It was a symbol of this new generation.

---

*Part of the awkwardness came from the fact that the art students had made the statue out of an existing model of a man holding a pole in an off-balance pose.[233]

Please remember June the Third, 1989. The most tragic event happened in the Chinese Capital, Beijing.

Radio Beijing English Service

12

The Massacre

FEW people noticed that the roar of the "Flying Tigers" had disappeared for several days. It was not until May 30 when the government announced that a dozen leaders of that motorcycle gang had been arrested for "inciting violence and public disturbance." There was hardly any reaction. Most people still regarded the gang as punks.

The Workers Autonomous Federation sprang to action when they learned that some of their leaders were seen being dragged into vehicles and hauled away. They asked students for help. Students and workers marched together to the office building of the Ministry of Public Security. After a day of sit-in, they successfully forced the release of the abducted workers. Still, nobody bothered to inquire about the "Flying Tigers".

Just like Liu Gang before him, Wang Juntao was now seeing his influence dissipating. His grand vision of a George Washington style leadership crashed and burned with the failure of withdrawing from Tiananmen Square. The Capital Joint Conference had moved to the university campus area and had rapidly become a mere shell of its previous self. Most prominent intellectuals had disappeared. They left the capital for the provinces or went into hiding. Wang Juntao shared the pessimistic sentiment. He told Chen Ziming that it should be time for them to plan for the aftermath as bloodshed was now inevitable.

Wang Juntao instructed personnel at their Institute to produce fake identification papers for leaders of the movement. He arranged safe houses in the outskirts of the city and concocted a rough plan of evacuation in stages. He even went so far as to pull out Liu Gang and Zhang Lun, two of the non-students from his Institute who were involved the deepest, and send them out into the suburbs. Chen Ziming was not as convinced of the imminent danger. He believed that the movement had reached such a scale that the possibility of an outright crackdown had diminished.[235]

International Children's Day arrived on June 1. Students occupying Tiananmen Square tried their hands at being good big brothers and sisters. They cleaned up the place and prepared small gifts for young visitors who came with their parents for the newest tourist attraction in town: the Goddess of Democracy. But the day did not start well. Li Lu was awoken by the disturbing news that Feng Congde and Chai Ling had been kidnapped. He rushed over and found the couple tied up and gagged in a tent. Li Lu assessed the situation and realized that it was not a government operation but the action of a renegade group within their own ranks. It was yet another coup attempt to overthrow their leadership. Calmly, Li Lu summoned student marshals and resolved the conflict. However, the escalation of their infighting had clearly reached an alarming level.[236]

PROFESSOR Liu Xiaobo was very upset. After the brief excitement at the Capital Joint Conference, he was seeing his fellow intellectuals reverting back to their usual ways. They were running away in droves at the first sign of danger. Some went into hiding. Others were helplessly resigned to the fact that they had no control of the situation dominated by radical students at Tiananmen Square. Nobody, in his mind, was taking any responsibility. It was a deep-rooted tradition of Chinese intellectuals, a community that had been rightfully regarded as pathetic and hopeless by numerous generations.

As someone who had returned to Beijing in the face of the April 26 *People's Daily* editorial, Liu Xiaobo believed that it was time to take a stand. He realized that he had to commit himself to the movement personally before he could hope to have any real influence. To achieve that, he had to make a grand gesture of his own: a hunger strike.

Wang Juntao did not agree with the idea at first but was convinced by Liu Xiaobo's reasoning. To avoid escalating hoopla this time, they decided to launch it as a relay of symbolic strikes only, conducted by teams of prominent intellectuals. When one team finished their strike, another continued on. In this manner, they could parade famous names and faces in Tiananmen Square to sustain the occupation to that precious date of June 20.

The trouble was that there were no longer many prominent intellectuals left within their ranks. Liu Xiaobo was only able to recruit Zhou Dou, a middle-aged scholar who had been active behind the scenes, and Gao Xin, a young school newspaper editor in Liu Xiaobo's Beijing Normal University. Neither of them had any name recognition. But they eventually got the prominent name they needed in the form of a rock star Hou Dejian.

Hou Dejian made his fame with his folksy little songs in the college campuses of Taiwan during the 1970's. In 1978, when the United States abandoned Taiwan for a formal relationship with mainland China, the young Hou Dejian wrote *Children of the Dragon* to express the sorrow and determination of his people. Despite its origin, the song became an overnight sensation when it was introduced on the mainland two years later. The phrase "children of dragon" became a synonym for the Chinese identity.

But Hou Dejian did not see much future in Taiwan for himself. In an act considered traitorous on his home island, he permanently settled in Beijing and cultivated his fame with a much larger audience. Little did he know that his little personal adventure would lead him right into a standoff at Tiananmen Square. Hou Dejian had just come back from a concert in Hong Kong to rally support for students in Beijing. He had already committed to another concert. Therefore, he could only fast for forty eight hours while his comrades pledged a seventy-two hour hunger strike.

Standoff At Tiananmen

"四君子"绝食

In the late afternoon of June 2, the four of them, referred to as the Four Gentlemen, walked into Tiananmen Square. They read a manifesto of their own, with a stab at the Chinese intellectual community:

> We start our hunger strike. We protest. We call upon people. We repent. We are not looking for death, we are looking for the true life. Under the irrational militant violence by the Li Peng regime, Chinese intellectuals must end their all-words-but-no-action tradition of osteomalacia. We must protest the military rule with our actions. We must give birth to a brand new political culture with our own actions.

The lengthy manifesto went on to criticize the government and "radical students" for escalating the crisis with their irrationality. It proudly claimed that they, the new hunger strikers, would "not allow hatred to poison our wisdom, for we have no enemies."

Nobody paid any attention to the manifesto. Thousands and thousands of people rushed into Tiananmen Square with only one thing on their minds: Hou Dejian. People in Beijing found a new reason to come: "Go see the Goddess first and then the 'monkey'!"* Yet even the Goddess of Democracy could not compete with the power of a live rock star. Sitting on the pedestal of the Monument to People's Heroes, Hou Dejian, a shy and skinny figure, was forced to sing his songs repeatedly. Again and again, he led the entire Square in renditions of *Children of Dragon*. When he had to take a break, Liu Xiaobo tried to make his speeches. While hatred did not poison his wisdom, the "Square fever" did. Facing thousands of cheering fans, the rational thoughts contained in the well-written manifesto were blown away. He praised the students with extreme enthusiasm and vowed to carry on their struggle to the very end.[237] He did not get to say much anyway, as the impatient audience broke out into loud chants. "Hou Dejian," "Hou Dejian!"

Just like that, the Four Gentlemen's hunger strike evolved into a freaky circus show.

LATE that night, a military vehicle was seen speeding on Chang'an

---

*In Chinese, "hou" is a homophone for the word "monkey."

The Massacre

Avenue and losing control near Muxidi, three miles west of Tiananmen Square. It smashed into a few pedestrians, killing three at the scene. Thousands of students and residents rushed to the scene as they were told that it was a deliberate act by the martial law troops. As the crowd ran along Chang'an Avenue, they were surprised to spot many buses and trucks packed with sacks of military supplies. With *CNN*'s camera recording, students climbed on top of a bus to display their spoils: helmets, rifles, and bayonets. They were cheered on by the on looking crowd.[238] The troops were on the move! Alarms were broadcast in Tiananmen Square and students were mobilized from their campuses.

This seem too easy

By the early morning of June 3, vehicles carrying military supplies were surrounded in several major streets in the city. Also discovered were regiments of soldiers who were marching on foot without any weapons. The soldiers were not wearing their uniform jackets. But their standard-issue white shirts and green pants easily gave them away. In a role reversal, the troops, singing *L'Internationale* and army songs, tried to push through human barriers like the students did weeks ago against them. But the people were not on their side. They were once again hopelessly outnumbered and pushed into street corners and sidewalks. Dispirited, the soldiers sat with their heads down.*

At Liubukou, a small intersection just west of Xinhuamen, a nondescript van was discovered carrying weapons including machine guns and automatic assault rifles. Students seized the vehicle and displayed the guns on its roof. Its proximity to Zhongnanhai, the site of the central government, was unsettling. At high noon, just as the crowd was taking over the intersection, hundreds of helmeted soldiers burst out of Xinhuamen. They launched a barrage of tear gas canisters into the crowd and took the vehicle with its weapons into Zhongnanhai.

It was the first taste of tear gas for everyone at the scene. Caught by surprise, they scattered quickly, coughing and crying. Many were injured in the chaos. The white and orange smoke lingered on for hours. Wu Renhua and his fellow teachers and students from the University of Political Science and Law, who had occupied the Xinhuamen entrance

---

*It would eventually become clear that the soldiers who were discovered by civilians were only a tiny part of a much larger infiltration effort carried out in those couple of days.[239]

for more than two weeks, finally lost their ground.

WU Renhua retreated back to Peking University and found the Capital Joint Conference, or what was left of it, was meeting there. He noticed that Fred Chiu, the professor from Hong Kong, was diligently writing down personal information of the attendees in anticipation that the data would be critical when a rescue mission was needed after a crackdown.

Although exhausted and sick, Wu Renhua volunteered when he heard enforcement was needed at Tiananmen Square to protect the hunger striking Four Gentlemen. He took off immediately for his University of Political Science and Law. There, he handpicked forty strong male students who had answered his call for volunteers. He handed each of them a piece of red cloth as identification, flagged down a couple of passing trucks and off they went.

They arrived at close to four o'clock in the afternoon. There was a surprisingly small crowd around the Monument to People's Heroes. Wu Renhua found Li Lu and Chai Ling almost alone without any presence of student marshals or picket lines. The Four Gentlemen were sitting in a tent having a quiet time. After the alarms of the previous night, many students had left the place to rest. Others were drawn to scenes where soldiers were surrounded. Wu Renhua arranged his forces to spread out on all four sides of the Monument. He then sat down and hoped for the best.

Reports of troop movements continued to flood into Tiananmen Square. It became evident that an organized attempt by the troops to sneak into the Square was once again foiled by the people. The soldiers were trying to reach the vicinity on foot, with their weapons transported separately in disguised vehicles. There were also emotional tales of fighting. Li Lu refused to broadcast these exciting happenings. He sat quietly holding onto the microphone himself and desperately wanted to keep calm.[240]

At six o'clock, a plainclothes man was sent to the Headquarters by an angry mob. He had a military identification card with him and was accused of scouting for the troops. The poor man had not been treated kindly by his captors and was visibly distraught. Wu Renhua took charge and arranged for a doctor to take care of him and then sent him away in an ambulance.[241]

It was half past six o'clock when the official loudspeakers around Tiananmen Square and along Chang'an Avenue came alive. A lengthy announcement by the city government and the headquarters of martial law troops claimed that "a small clique of people" had incited many into illegal actions such as blocking troops, looting weapons, and hurting soldiers. It went on to say:

> We solemnly declare: Nobody can use any excuse to illegally block military convoys, block or attack the People's Liberation Army, or perform any acts impeding the actions of martial law troops... If anyone does not adhere to this advice and chooses to challenge the law, the martial law troops, police force, and the People's Armed Police have the right to use any means necessary and resolve the matter with force. The organizers and executors [of such activities] must bear all consequences. We hope the general residents of Beijing follow the rules of martial law and support the troops in stopping the turmoil and restoring the peace.

Inside Tiananmen Square, annoyed students scaled light poles to cut off the wires to the loudspeakers belonging to the official broadcasting system. They could do nothing to those mounted on top of government buildings however. Those high-powered loudspeakers continued to repeat the announcement although their penetration into the Square was compromised. Students' own broadcasting station was still outmatched. Their defiant voices were confined to the immediate vicinity of the Monument to People's Heroes, where the student leaders held a press conference of their own. Several victims of violence during the day gave testimony and displayed bloody shirts and injuries. Chai Ling, Li Lu, and Feng Congde each advocated calm. Wuer Kaixi encouraged reporters to stay with them and witness history. As homage to Hou Dejian, he sang a song newly composed by the musician. On this critical night, Wuer Kaixi had unexpectedly reappeared and volunteered his service, preferably as a deputy to the commander-in-chief. That request was denied. Wang Dan, on the other hand, was not at the scene.

Standoff At Tiananmen

By eight o'clock, a contingent of students marched into Tiananmen Square and onto the base of the Monument. There were a few hundred of them, all wearing the same white T-shirt with the big "Peking University" logo. They had heard the call for help and came by to assume marshal duties. Beijing Students Autonomous Federation was mobilizing students from each campus to reinforce Tiananmen Square. Seeing the strong posture and determined faces of these new arrivals, Wu Renhua felt much better. He concentrated members of his original marshals on the north side of the Monument and had the new troops guarding the three remaining sides.

The Monument to People's Heroes was a solemn and majestic obelisk at the center of Tiananmen Square. More than a hundred feet tall, it was erected in the 1950's when the young People's Republic reconstructed the Square. On the front of the monument, facing north, was Mao Zedong's own calligraphic inscription reading "Eternal Glory to People's Heroes!" On the back was a longer inscription, drafted by Mao Zedong but hand-written by the late Premier Zhou Enlai. It traced the "people's heroes" from the most recent communist revolution back to the martyrs who had resisted foreign imperialist invasions since 1840.

The Monument had a wide square base. Eight gigantic sculptures were carved into white marble tablets at the base level, each depicting a significant historical event from 1840 forward, one of which was for the glorious May Fourth Movement. A wide platform around the sculptures provided ample space for people to mingle and enjoy the artwork. On each side, a flight of stairs led down to a second level platform, from which another flight of stairs led down to the Square itself.

It was a sacred monument. Flower wreaths were laid here on many occasions by Young Pioneers or visiting foreign dignitaries. It was also the natural place for spontaneous memorials after the death of a beloved leader such as the late Premier Zhou Enlai during the April Fifth Movement and Hu Yaobang during the recent spring that had ignited the current movement.

As darkness fell, Wu Renhua stood on the highest point at the base of the Monument. From his vintage point, he could survey the entire

Square. Rows and rows of tents laid still under dim lights, surrounded by garbage and wandering students. Despite, or because of, the official announcement, more and more people were arriving. They started to fill up the edges of the Square in anxious anticipation. The Goddess of Democracy stood tall in the far distance. Beyond the statue was Chang'an Avenue where people were in a frenzy of setting up roadblocks. Everything from traffic fences to disabled buses was piled up in the middle of this majestic thoroughfare, the Avenue of Eternal Peace. Occasionally, a stream of students ran toward the Monument carrying someone soaked in blood. They came to the student headquarters to tell of the most recent brutality committed by the military.

Such reports were getting more and more frequent and coming from more and more directions. Yet people at Tiananmen Square had not seen any troops themselves yet. They looked out in the distance and imagined what kinds of battles were being engaged there and were surely coming toward them. The sky remained dark, with occasional flares of orange glow, probably due to fires set by resisting residents.

Minutes before ten o'clock, a more stern warning from the martial law troops was broadcast all over the city. This one was significantly shorter and more threatening:

> The situation in Beijing right now is very grim. An extreme minority of hooligans are spreading rumors, inciting the masses, openly insulting, attacking, beating, and tying up soldiers of the People's Liberation Army, looting weapons and ammunition, blocking Zhongnanhai, and storming the Great Hall of People. They are trying to link up with all [ill] forces and could create a serious and violent rebellion at any moment. For the sake of the capital's social order and protecting the people, the Beijing city government and the headquarters of the martial law troops can not stand by. Therefore, all Beijing people must stay alert. From now on, please do not go on the streets, do not go to Tiananmen Square, so that you could avoid unnecessary harm.

As the official announcements were broadcast in the campus area in the northwest suburb, student broadcasting stations there also came alive, screaming their own urgent appeals for students to go to the streets and Tiananmen Square. Thousands of bicycles rushed into the darkness, most of them heading south toward the Muxidi intersection on Chang'an Avenue. They could either stop the martial law troops right there, or turn east on Chang'an Avenue and head to Tiananmen Square.

There was no panic inside the Square itself. People had gotten used to the frequent alarms, all of which had eventually turned out to be false. Underneath the Goddess of Democracy, Zhang Boli decided to hold the opening ceremony for the University of Democracy as scheduled. Around him, people were still pouring in to see the Goddess and the "monkey." They massed around the Monument with enthusiastic chants of "Hou Dejian, come out! Hou Dejian, come out!" The danger was still remote.

Exactly fifteen days earlier, the army had suffered its most humiliating defeat under the full moon of a clear night when it attempted to enter the city. On this night of June 3, the new moon had yet to appear. It was the darkest night of the month.[242] Far beyond the visible horizon, hundreds of thousands of field infantry were advancing to the center of this ancient capital from three directions: east, south, and west. This time, they came with columns and columns of tanks and armored personnel carriers. Soldiers were now dressed in battle fatigue. Carrying automatic assault rifles and clubs, they marched silently alongside the heavy vehicles. It was a formation for combat and they were ready to destroy whatever was in their way.

T HE inner city of this ancient capital used to be protected by a ring of city walls, in which various gates, or "men," were opened for controlled traffic. The city wall was now the Second Ring Road with clover-style overpass intersections replacing the gates. Chang'an Avenue, the main east-west thoroughfare passing through Tiananmen Square, ended before the intersection of Fuxingmen, the Gate of Renewal, in the west. But the road continued by the name of Fuxingmen Street. A block west of Fuxingmen was the Muxidi bridge where a traffic accident had ignited a frenzy the night before.

Muxidi was where most students from their campuses up north turned the corner on their way to Tiananmen Square. At the immediate northwest of the intersection was the Military Museum, the pride of the

People's Liberation Army. Along the Fuxingmen Street was a mixture of high rise apartment buildings and traditional courtyards. Most of the courtyards were residences for military apparatuses. At this particular hour, mobilized students were arriving by the thousands. They were joined by many times more residents coming out of nearby apartments. They pushed buses and trucks onto the bridge as barricades and stood many layers deep behind them in defiance.

The civilians had no idea that they were facing the 38th Army, a legendary unit that had made its name during the Korean War.* When martial law was imposed, its commander Lieutenant General Xu Qinxian had refused orders and was stripped of his duty. Now led by an acting commander, this army had something to prove for itself. The civilians did not know either that this army had already opened fire and killed residents as they approached the city from the outskirts.[243]

Warning shots were fired immediately as the troops approached. Bullets sailed over the heads of the crowd. Nobody budged. Despite desperate pleas for non-violence, the crowd hurled bricks, bottles, and anything they could get their hands on at the soldiers. Another barrage of gunfire came. Machine guns mounted on the tanks also opened fire. This time, they were not warning shots. Bodies fell down in the streets. People were telling each other about rubber bullets until their attention was transfixed by the sight of blood. In a panic, they ran for cover.

Soldiers paused their shooting periodically. Brave residents rushed in and carried away bodies both dead and wounded. They used flatbed tricycles and everything else to carry the bodies to nearby hospitals.

Jiang Jielian, a seventeen-year old high school student, was forbidden to leave home by his mother that night. But he managed to escape from a bathroom window. The proud teenager told his mother that, on a night like this, "the important thing is not action, but participation." At Muxidi. he and a friend abandoned their bicycles on a grass lawn as gunshots broke out. Scared, they crouched down behind a flower bed. Amid the terrifying noise, Jiang Jielian's friend heard him saying softly, "I think I have been hit." He saw Jiang Jielian stand up slowly, stumble forward a couple of steps and collapse. His shirt was imme-

---

*In the immediate aftermath, various media had mistakenly identified this troop as the 27th Army.

diately soaked with blood. He had been hit from behind right in the heart. It would be more than a day later when his body was identified and his parents learned his fate.[244]

Leaving dozens dead and hundreds wounded, the army pushed through Muxidi. They continued eastward on Chang'an Avenue. On each side of the boulevard, students and residents ducked behind bushes but followed the troops. Along the way, they warned new arrivals that the soldiers were not using rubber bullets. They shouted "Fascists" in between rounds of fire. As they approached the inner city, more residents gathered on both sides of the boulevard. Soldiers kept firing to keep them at bay. Occasionally, machine guns sprayed bullets indiscriminately either at the crowd or into high-rise buildings. Several people were shot inside their apartments high above the street.

Shen Tong was at his home near Xidan, a bustling shopping district between Muxidi and Tiananmen Square. He had left the movement for good after being turned down by Chai Ling. At the American consulate, he was told that his student visa would be ready for pickup on June 5. But he also learned that his father had been hospitalized with leukemia. Feeling sad and guilty, Shen Tong promised his mother that he would stay home no matter what happened.

That proved impossible when gunshots could clearly be heard from his courtyard bordering Chang'an Avenue. As he ventured out, he saw bodies of dead and wounded all over the sidewalks. Then he heard a low rumbling noise and felt the ground quaking underneath him. An endless line of headlights approached from the west. Shen Tong saw hundreds of people rushing into the avenue to set up barricades only to be scattered away by the spray of machine-gun fire. He counted forty-six tanks and armored personnel carriers passing by in a hurry. Soldiers, with automatic assault rifles and clubs, marched along with the tanks. They were heading straight to Tiananmen Square. In an outburst of emotion, two men took a bloody shirt off a dead civilian and marched toward the soldiers. Shen Tong and others followed. They got close and questioned the soldiers about what they were doing. As the angry Shen Tong was lecturing, an officer approached and pointed a pistol directly at him. Shen Tong was pulled away just as the pistol fired. A girl who was standing next to him fell to the ground. Shen

252

OMG ·····

Tong remembered seeing her face becoming a bloody hole. The soldiers charged forward as the civilians ran in panic. Back at the sidewalk, Shen Tong saw a young man fallen down by the fence being surrounded by soldiers. As the young man looked up, the soldiers fired in unison, execution style. The young man's skull and brain tissue were splattered along the white fence.[245]

AT the same time when the 38th Army was advancing from the west, other troops met similar resistance in other directions. From east and south, soldiers encountered crowds made up mostly of factory workers. At Jianguomen, where Wang Dan had once proudly surveyed his parade, columns of military vehicles carrying soldiers armed with automatic assault rifles were surrounded. These soldiers did not open fire but sat hopelessly. Elsewhere, however, troops were able to push through toward Tiananmen Square amid bloody confrontations.[246]

It was also about the same time, around ten o'clock, that people at Tiananmen Square were finally convinced of the gravity of this night. The orange glow in the western sky had grown intense, intermixed with tracer bullets shooting through it. A low rumbling sound could be heard getting closer and closer. People were sill pouring into the Square, many bearing news of shooting and dying. Wu Renhua estimated that there were at least a hundred thousand people present at this time.

Despite the dire situation, curious residents were still crowding around the Monument to People's Heroes and demanding to see Hou Dejian. They were kept at a safe distance by the now hundreds of student marshals sitting in a tight formation along the stairs surrounding the Monument. Other students gathered under the statue of the Goddess of Democracy where Zhang Boli opened the University of Democracy with Chai Ling cutting a ceremonial ribbon. As Zhang Boli described his plan for his new school, a third official announcement was broadcast over their heads. It was a lengthy and repetitive one and duly ignored.

Chai Ling gave a rousing speech. Echoing Mao Zedong on the eve of the communist victory forty years earlier, she proclaimed that "The closer to the dawn, the thicker the darkness. But after this darkness a brand new republic will be born!" Yan Jiaqi delivered the keynote speech. With the sound of gunshots now clearly audible, Yan Jiaqi droned on in his heavy accent for forty-five minutes on the concept of freedom and democracy. As soon as he wrapped up his speech, he and other intellectuals were whisked out of the Square.

Reports of death had already flooded the Headquarters for Defending Tiananmen Square. But it was the news of the first student casualty, one of their very own, that hit them hard. All of sudden, it was all too real. The leaders went silent. Chai Ling started to cry. It was midnight when the student broadcasting station announced the name of the student who was from Beijing Normal University and killed near Muxidi. They had not had the foresight to prepare a tape of traditional funeral music. A student took the microphone and sang a moving rendition of Frederic Chopin's *Funeral March*.

Wuer Kaixi's familiar voice followed. He talked about the dead student whom he thought he knew. His voice broke up frequently and finally came to an abrupt halt. Noises came through the loudspeakers indicating that Wuer Kaixi had fainted, …, "again!" The emphasise on the "again" was a knowing barb ridiculing his frequent fainting episodes.[247] Wuer Kaixi was evacuated in an ambulance.

After the initial shock, students did not know how to react to the unfolding massacre. Most sat quietly, feeling numb. Some became hysterical. At the base of the Monument, a group of students and workers surrounded Chai Ling with knives and guns. They yelled at her not even to think about withdrawal. "So many people have already died for you students. If you dared to announce withdrawing, I would kill you first!" They screamed one after another. It took a while for student marshals to push the angry mob away.[248]

Ma Shaofang and Shao Jiang, another student leader from Peking University, rushed into the headquarters with the idea of withdrawal in their minds. They told Chai Ling that students were asking whether it was time to leave. With tears streaming down her face, Chai Ling slumped in the tent looking completely helpless. Li Lu, however, maintained his composure. "What do you guys think?" he asked back. Ma Shaofang and Shao Jiang argued that, since the soldiers had already started killing, what they were up against was no longer anything rational. They should withdraw now. Too many lives were at stake.

Li Lu and Feng Congde were not sure if it was possible to get all the people out of Tiananmen Square at the moment. They figured that they were probably close to being surrounded from all directions, if indeed they were not already surrounded. It might be a safer choice to have everyone together than creating a chaotic mass exodus. Acting as a de facto commander-in-chief, Feng Congde instructed everyone in the Square to stand up, hold hands, and slowly approach the Monument.[249]

Flags rose in the darkness and crowds followed. Slowly but in an orderly fashion, they came upon the base of the Monument and sat on the stairs and the adjacent ground. Wu Renhua surveyed the scene again. There were probably ten thousand students. More than half of them were sitting at the north side facing Tiananmen and Chang'an Avenue. Looking beyond, there were still tens of thousands of people remaining at the outer edges of the Square. They were mostly workers and city residents mixed with some students.[250]

In the middle of Tiananmen Square, tents were still standing in their formations. It looked like a ghost town. Student marshals were going over them to check if anyone was still sleeping inside. Ma Shaofang went to the headquarters of the Workers Autonomous Federation on the northwest edge of the Square. Before he could persuade the workers to withdraw onto the Monument with the students, he saw groups of emotional workers rushing out toward Xinhuamen which the 38th Army had now reached. The workers shouted to him that too many of their buddies had already died for them to sit back.[251]

Those at Tiananmen Square caught their first sight of the military at fifteen minutes past midnight. It came in the form of two charging armored personnel carriers. They roamed through barricades on Chang'an Avenue. Crowd scrambled away from their path but stayed within close range to throw rocks and metal rods at them. Before the vehicles could be trapped, however, they sped away and disappeared into the darkness to the east.*

---

*These two armored personnel carriers made it all the way east to Jianguomen where they crashed into a crowd surrounding the soldiers there, causing deaths and injuries, including three soldiers who were wounded. They eventually turned around

Standoff At Tiananmen

Before the cheers could die off, two other armored personnel carriers roared up from the south, signaling the approaching of the 15th Army from that direction. They sped around the perimeter of the Square, causing another round of havoc. At Chang'an Avenue, one of them came to an abrupt stop and was immediately surrounded by an angry crowd. Improvised Molotov bombs rained down on the metal beast along with cotton quilts soaked with gasoline. It burst into flames to a round of hysterical cheers. Three soldiers crawled out of the vehicle unarmed and frightened. They were promptly met by a barrage of rocks and sticks. People rushed in with their fists and boots. Blood was streaming from the head of one of the soldiers.

Zhang Jian was only eighteen years old. A student at Beijing Sports College, he was an athletic young man specializing in track and field as well as martial arts. Perhaps because of that background, he had been appointed to lead the student marshals after Zhang Lun's departure. Zhang Jian had been busy since midnight when he led a group of student marshals onto Chang'an Avenue in a feeble attempt to stop the advancing army. With many injuries, they fell back and ran into the scene of the burning armored personnel carrier. When they saw the peril of the three soldiers, they inserted themselves into the crowd without any hesitation. Once inside, they linked their arms tightly together to form a protective circle. A few students protected the soldiers with their own bodies. Together, they walked slowly toward a Red Cross station. Angry mobs rushed toward them throwing objects and punches, most of which landed on the students instead.*

Tiananmen Square now resembled a war zone. There was not yet a clear sighting of the invading army but they were tantalizingly close. Group after group of students and residents rushed out under various flags to block the troops. But many more were pouring back in after their failed attempts. Some had followed the soldiers all the way from

---

and returned to Tiananmen Square.

*This scene of students protecting soldiers was observed by many witnesses including foreign reporters. The three soldiers were later awarded medals as "Heroes of the Republic". The official *People's Daily* described the incident in a report on June 28, 1989. It praised the bravery of the soldiers but did not mention their rescuers.

Muxidi and Xidan. They wanted to see what would happen at Tiananmen Square and perhaps make a last stand there for the students.

Just before one o'clock, numerous flares and tracer bullets shot up into the night sky from all directions outside of the Square, briefly illuminating the entire area. The tens of thousands of people at the perimeter looked back and saw thousands of students sitting motionlessly at the Monument to People's Heroes. Some became very angry. They charged in and cursed the students. With death all around them, they no longer accepted the students' principle of "peace, rationality, and non-violence." They accused the students of naivety, arrogance, and cowardice. People are dying for you out there, they shouted, are you just going to sit here and wait to die? The students sat silently in place.

Feng Congde had always had his eyes on logistical details. He had already set up a new broadcasting station on the top tier of the base of the Monument. He had a generator and enough gasoline to last through the night. He chose to place the station in the southeast corner, away from the main thrust of the military force from Chang'an Avenue. Loudspeakers were strung on the Monument itself. The station became the new site for the Headquarters for Defending Tiananmen Square.

Chai Ling had been crying all night. She finally could not take it any more. She jumped up and grabbed the microphone and screamed for any able students to grab any weapons to defend the perimeter of the Square. Li Lu stopped broadcasting immediately and Chai Ling caught herself just in time. When she spoke again, she was calm and collected. She told a fable of ants. When a colony of ants faced the danger of a forest fire, she told her fellow students, the ants would clump together to make a giant ball and roll down the hill. Those ants on the outside shell would be burnt to ashes. But their sacrifice ensured the survival of their colony. Right here and right now, she preached, they were at the outside of the ant ball, facing the raging fire. Her hoarse voice resonated: "Classmates, we are offering a peaceful petition. The highest principle of peace is sacrifice. Classmates, only "counter-revolution" with our sacrifice, can our People's Republic achieve her new birth."[252]

Amid the approaching gunshots, all the students at the Monument

C.L. ready to die ·· or let some students die.

stood up to take their oath once again, led by Chai Ling:

> I swear: I will protect the republic and Tiananmen Square with my young life. Heads can roll, blood can flow, but the people's square can not be lost! We are willing to fight until the last person.

Then, they sang *L'Internationale* together.

THE main thrust of the army finally showed up at Tiananmen Square at half past one. It was an overwhelming and determined force. An intensive barrage of gunshots dispersed the crowd at the northwest corner first. A large tent that housed the Workers Autonomous Federation there burst into flame. Tanks and armored personnel carriers followed in. They lined up on Chang'an Avenue facing south with their guns pointing to the Square.

Almost at exactly the same time, another contingent of the military arrived from the south. This was the 15th Army, the only paratrooper unit in the People's Liberation Army. Their approach through the Qianmen district was another bloody one, second only to the 38th Army's advance along west Chang'an Avenue. The 39th Army appeared next on east Chang'an Avenue. Going through Jianguomen, they had met only token resistance along the route. Either for tactical reasons or under restraints from their commanders, they held fire and were not the first ones to reach their target position in front of the Museum of Chinese History east of the Square. Finally, all the front gates of the Great Hall of People swung open. A flood of soldiers charged out and down the long flights of stairs. In just a few short minutes, all of Tiananmen Square was tightly encircled. Civilians were permitted to leave but not to enter the sealed off area. With the first phase of their battle plan accomplished, soldiers settled down and waited. Some troops sang army songs in unison to maintain their focus. Civilians outside countered with powerful renditions of *L'Internationale*. The atmosphere was surreal.

The official loudspeakers came alive again. It was yet a new announcement:

> Tonight, a serious counter-revolutionary rebellion has hap-

pened in the capital. Rioters attacked the People's Liberation Army, looted weapons, set barricades, and kidnapped soldiers. They want to overthrow the People's Republic of China and overthrow the socialist system. The People's Liberation Army has tolerated them for days but now must fight back against the counter-revolutionary rebellion. The citizens in the capital must follow the rules of martial law, help the People's Liberation Army, defend the Constitution, the safety of the great socialist motherland, and the capital. For anyone who chooses not to follow this advice, their safety will not be guaranteed and they will bear all responsibilities for all consequences.

It was the first time the term "counter-revolutionary rebellion" was used, meaning that the situation had been further escalated from "turmoil" or "riot." The martial law troops were now fighting against enemies of the nation. This latest announcement was broadcast repeatedly for a long time, raising the level of threat.

To withdraw or not to withdraw, the debate raged on among the student leaders at the Monument to People's Heroes. Chai Ling was crying again. Her tearful voice came through their own loudspeakers, "Classmates, please be calm! Classmates, please be calm! Those who wish to withdraw can do so now. Those who do not wish to withdraw can stay here with me. We will live and die with Tiananmen Square, . . . This is the final moment! This is the final moment!"

The Four Gentlemen were only more than one day into their hunger strike. For most of the night, they had stayed quietly in their tent. But now they were worried. If part of the students took up Chai Ling's offer and left, it might create havoc among them in an already uncontrollable situation. Fortunately, very few did. Liu Xiaobo wrote a note that was broadcast to a round of applause. The Four Gentlemen pledged that they would not leave until after the last student had left.

AROUND two o'clock, gunshots erupted in Tiananmen Square. Bullets whizzed over the heads of everyone at the Monument. The warning shots were fired by soldiers in front of the Great Hall of People. Then, a louder barrage of gunshots was heard near Chang'an Avenue which sounded much more terrifying. On a balcony high up the Beijing Hotel overlooking the northern edge of Tiananmen Square, *CNN*'s

Standoff At Tiananmen

Mike Chinoy was frantically describing the scene over a telephone line:[253]

> The troops are firing directly at the demonstrators! People are now running down the streets, bicycling down the streets as fast as they can. People are sprinting down the street. It's absolute panic, it's absolute panic! They're turning into side streets now, they're absolutely terrified. I can see someone carrying an injured person. There's an ambulance immediately in front of where I am.
>
> There are bodies, injured and dead all over the place.

After rescuing the three soldiers from their burning armored personnel carrier, Zhang Jian had made his way back at the northeast corner of the Square. There, he and hundreds of students and residents were in a standoff with soldiers on Chang'an Avenue. They were shouting slogans when a bus appeared from nowhere and charged into the no-man's land between the soldiers and civilians. Bullets immediately rained into the bus which came to a screeching stop. A bright search light illuminated the destroyed bus. Zhang Jian saw soldiers dragging a few people off. He recognized one of them as Guo Haifeng, the General Secretary of the Headquarters for Defending Tiananmen Square.

Guo Haifeng was one of the three students who had knelt down on the stairs of Great Hall of People during Hu Yaobang's funeral. On this night, he had ventured out to look for gasoline to make Molotov bombs. They found the bus and drained some of its fuel into a few bottles. They came under fire as they were returning to Tiananmen Square. He became the first captured student leader.

The soldiers tied down their captives and chained them onto a fence. The civilian crowd erupted with a chant, "let them go," "let them go!" Their appeal was answered by another round of gunfire. Several people fell onto the ground near Zhang Jian. Zhang Jian could no longer contain his anger. He tore off his shirt and stepped forward toward a commander and shouted. "We are all students. We have no weapons ...If you want to kill, shoot me first!"

He was only thirty feet away when the commander pointed his pistol at him. Three shots were fired. Two of them struck Zhang Jian's

260

legs. Zhang Jian was still standing, but barely. He stared into the commander's eyes and shouted "One more! You did not get me down. One more!" With that, he collapsed. As he was helped onto a truck, he saw three injured bodies already in it. Dozens of people pushed the disabled truck to a hospital where the other three were pronounced dead.[254]

At the Monument, the Four Gentlemen knew it was time for them to assert some adult leadership. Liu Xiaobo came out to give a speech on the importance of non-violence. He was barely into it when he was informed that a machine gun was spotted within their own ranks. They rushed over to the southwestern corner and found the gun set on a stone fence and trained in the direction of the Great Hall of People. A ring of workers stood by with knives and clubs to protect the weapon. They declared that they had seen too many deaths first-hand. It was their right to fight back.

Hou Dejian used his famous name to get close to the emotional youngsters and calm them down. After much persuasion, the workers gave up the machine gun along with another automatic rifle they had been hiding. Liu Xiaobo summoned the few reporters still on site. With a video camera recording, he destroyed the guns by smashing them on stone fences.[255]

It was past three o'clock. Shao Jiang found Zhou Dou and appealed to him to find a way for the students to withdraw. The Four Gentlemen had a quick meeting. Among them, only Liu Xiaobo was against the idea. But the other three talked him into agreement. The four of them then sought out Chai Ling, Li Lu, and Feng Congde and found the three still vowing never to withdraw. Too many people had already died for them to run away now, they argued. A student claimed that Zhao Ziyang and Yan Mingfu had passed in a message for them to stay till daybreak. Liu Xiaobo was angry. He shouted that they could not afford thousands of lives for a gamble based on a rumor.[256]

Feng Congde told Hou Dejian that they could go ahead and seek a negotiation with the army. But they could not represent the Headquarters for Defending Tiananmen Square. Even the Headquarters could not make the withdrawal decision anyway, he added, as it should be up to the student body.[257]

Standoff At Tiananmen

Time was running out. The Four Gentlemen decided that they had to take the matter into their own hands. Zhou Dou volunteered to go out and seek a negotiation. He reasoned that he was the calmest of the four and could use his scholastic look. But he needed Hou Dejian with him. If there was a name that the young soldiers might recognize, it would be Hou Dejian. Two doctors volunteered to accompany the pair. Their hospital overalls could help to prevent troops from shooting indiscriminately at them.

So, at half past three o'clock, Zhou Dou, Hou Dejian, and the two doctors walked down the stairs at the base of the Monument. They waved white shirts as they slowly entered into the no-man's land. Several student marshals followed along. They had sworn to protect the lives of the Four Gentlemen. The small troupe spent some time in front of the Great Hall of People and then got on an ambulance and headed to Chang'an Avenue.[258]

As they exited the ambulance and approached the military line, they heard the unsettling noise of rifles being loaded. They stopped. One of the doctors identified himself and shouted that Hou Dejian was with them. Hou Dejian could hear murmurs in reaction to his name. He could not decipher their meaning but he felt that it was not all hostile.

A commander walked out with a few soldiers. He was a man in his forties with three stars showing his rank. The commander shook hands with each of them and spoke in a calm and polite manner. He asked them to stop their hunger strike first, to which Hou Dejian and Zhou Dou replied they had already done so. The commander then told them that he had to consult his superiors and walked back into the troop formation.

It was an anxious moment. As they waited, Hou Dejian remembered that the commander's hand felt thick, soft, and warm. But suddenly, all the lights in and around Tiananmen Square were turned off. They were not sure if this was a signal for the military to take its final action. Even the soldiers on the other side were becoming restless. Some were yelling and others were posturing with their weapons. The two doctors stayed calm. They told everyone to stand absolutely still.

The commander walked out again after several tense minutes. He told the civilians that their request to withdraw had been granted. The

commander gave them his name and rank and instructed them to lead
the students out from the southeast corner. They had to be out of the
Square by daybreak, one way or another. Shaking hands again, he told
them that if they could successfully persuade the students to withdraw
peacefully, it would be an honorable achievement. Hou Dejian thought
the commander was sincere.

IT was four o'clock when all the lights went out in and around the
Square. In this moonless night, sudden darkness and terror gripped ev-
eryone. Almost spontaneously, students at the Monument to People's
Heroes sang *L'Internationale* once again at the top of their lungs.*

> *Arise, starving and freezing slaves,*
> *Arise, all the suffering people in the world,*
> *All our blood is boiling,*
> *We will fight for the truth!*
> *Let's totally destroy the old world,*
> *Arise slaves, arise!*
> *Don't say that we have nothing*
> *We will be the masters of all!*

In all the glorious movies for generations growing up in the People's
Republic, *L'Internationale* was played or sung whenever communist
heroes were facing their martyrdom. For this new generation, now
it was their turn although they were facing the tanks and guns of the
very communist government. Regardless, they sang *L'Internationale*,
the anthem of communism, loud and proud. The lyrics was ironically
fitting.

> *This is the final struggle,*
> *Let's unite till tomorrow,*
> *L'Internationale,*
> *Will become the reality!*

The rousing chorus seemed to have defeated the fear that came with
the darkness. Thousands of students sat on the stairs, holding hands
together. They found peace and strength. A couple of small bonfires

---

*The lyrics of Chinese version of *L'Internationale* were not a literal translation
of the French original but an interpreted one from a Russian version.

were lit with trash. The tiny flames, opposite the burning armored personnel carrier in the distance, created a ghostly image.

In the darkness, Zhou Dou and Hou Dejian made their way back. They rushed over to brief Chai Ling, Li Lu, and Feng Congde. They urged the students to take the deal with the troops and withdraw immediately. The student leaders could not reach a decision.

T HE lights came back on as suddenly as they had gone out. It was now half past four o'clock. Wu Renhua surveyed the territory again. During the half hour of darkness, a great many people had left the area. Outside of the base area of the Monument to People's Heroes, there was not a single civilian in Tiananmen Square. The number of students at the Monument had also shrunk to half of its previous size. Wu Renhua estimated that five to six thousand students were still sitting on the stairs as determined as ever.

Over the official loudspeakers, a succinct announcement was broadcast:

> The clearing of the Square will commence now. We agree
> with students' appeal to withdraw from the Square.

It was followed by a lengthier announcement which ordered everyone to leave the scene immediately. It was the ultimatum.

From a distance, platoons of soldiers with automatic assault rifles snaked through the tent formation toward the Monument as if entering a battlefield. Some stopped to examine the inside of the tents. Behind them, tanks and armored personnel carriers started their engines to push into the Square in a formidable row. It did not take long for the Goddess of Democracy to tumble down under the weight of a tank.

There was no more time to waste. Hou Dejian took the microphone himself and informed the students of their negotiation. He spoke apologetically and framed it as his own personal initiative. But because the bloody crackdown was continuing, he begged the students to withdraw for the purpose of preserving the seeds of China's democracy and future.

The reaction from the student body, who until now were unaware of the negotiation, was immediate. They erupted in anger with boos and curses. Some students rushed in and threatened to beat up and eject this traitor. Li Lu had to mobilize student marshals to keep the mob out of the little area reserved for the headquarters.

Liu Xiaobo and Zhou Dou followed up and each spoke to support Hou Dejian. The three of them took turns to painstakingly persuade the emotional crowd. All of them reaffirmed their own pledge that they would not leave until after every student had left. Shao Jiang read a statement in the name of Beijing Students Autonomous Federation calling for a withdrawal. He had scribbled the statement in a hurry himself as that organization no longer had a real presence. Someone who claimed to be from the Workers Autonomous Federation also spoke in support of withdrawal.

Critical minutes were ticking away. As speeches and debates raged on, advance soldiers were closing in. Within dozens of feet from students, they set up a row of machine guns on the ground. Another row of soldiers, half crouching, were right behind with their automatic assault rifles trained on students. The rest of the soldiers stood behind with their weapons ready to fire. Tanks and armored personnel carriers backed them up. A formation for a mass execution was in place. Facing so many gun barrels at such close range, students did not panic. They looked at the soldiers almost indifferently. In the front row, they raised their hands with V-for-victory signs.

The armored vehicles cranked up their engines to create an unbearable, intimidating roar. In an awkward display of force and impatience, soldiers in the far distance broke into a rhythmic clapping and chanting: "Hurry up Withdraw! Hurry up Withdraw!" The combined noise threatened to overwhelm the few loudspeakers the students had.

At the Headquarters for Defending Tiananmen Square, Commander-in-Chief Chai Ling remained quiet and incapable of making decisions. Feng Congde, the twenty-three year old graduate student, felt that it was his time and duty. He took the microphone and announced a voice vote. When he counted to three, he explained repeatedly, everyone should shout together, either "withdraw" or "stand fast." A decision would be made by the loudness of each response.

There were about six thousand present, occupying an area larger than the thirty thousand square feet of the Monument base. It was impossible to have everyone's voice heard, not to mention equally. Half of the students were on the north side facing the brunt of oncoming soldiers but far away from where Feng Congde was. Yet there were no alternatives. Feng Congde counted over the loudspeakers, "One, two, three," everyone screamed at once.

Over on the north side, Wu Renhua could hardly hear any "withdraw" voice, as students there proudly shouted their determination, "stand fast," practically in the face of heavily armed soldiers. At the opposite southeast corner, however, it was hard to discern any difference. Li Lu heard a stronger voice in "withdraw,"[259] while Feng Congde thought the two sounded the same. Without hesitation, however, Feng Congde announced that the "withdraw" vote had carried the day. In the cold morning air, his voice was clear and crisp, "Students, we have always wanted to learn and practice democracy. We now must obey the principle that the minority follow the majority. We will withdraw from Tiananmen Square in an orderly fashion."*

I T was already twenty past five. Dim morning twilight was peeking through the eastern sky. As the students in the southeast corner were standing up slowly to move out, those on the north side protested profusely. They believed that they were the true majority and they should hold on until after daybreak when they could effect a turning point in history.

The military was not going to wait. Bands of special force units charged into the student formation from several directions. As they advanced up the stairs, they fired their rifles into the sky and barked orders for students to remain seated and not move. No students did move. They sat there quietly, offering not a slight hint of resistance. Even so, some of them were hit by soldiers' rifle butts as the brigade cleared out a path leading to the top level. Once there, they shot up the loudspeakers on the Monument with a blast of bullets and smashed the broadcasting equipment. There would be no more speeches, debates, or votes.

---

*Feng Congde later justified his decision, reasoning that the "stand fast" voice might be exaggerated under the circumstances because the choice was perceived as morally stronger, intimidating those who were voting "withdraw."[260]

Other than beating out their path, these soldiers left the students alone. They made no attempts to capture leaders or arrest anyone. When students shouted at them, they answered with rounds of warning shots aimed at the sky. With their headquarters destroyed, Feng Congde, Li Lu, and Chai Ling started to organize the withdrawal. Students in their vicinity gathered around various flags. Student marshals lined up on each side, hand-in-hand. Together, they slowly walked down the stairs toward the southeast corner. Everyone was crying.

As soon as the first contingent of students stepped outside they came to an immediate halt. Feng Congde, Li Lu, and Chai Ling rushed forward together. To their greatest horror, they found their path blocked by rows and rows of soldiers pointing their weapons right in the students' faces. Just as they approached to reason with the soldiers, however, the soldiers split apart and left an opening of a few yards wide. Underneath a forest of assault rifles and bayonets, the three leaders led their formation through. They decided to stay at the front to lead students back to the campus area.

After the departure of the student leaders, the Four Gentlemen came around the Monument to the north side. They found thousands of students still sitting tight and refusing to withdraw. Soldiers hit them with rifle butts and kicked them with army boots. Other than occasional excruciating screams of pain, students kept their silent defiance.

Wu Renhua found the commander of this brigade right behind him. The thirty-something captain was calm and collected. He never participated in the violent acts of his fellow soldiers. Rather, he kept talking to the students, almost begging them, "You guys hurry up. Get out of here. If you stay, there won't be anything good. We have our orders. We must clear the Square no matter what." Out of the corner of his eye, Wu Renhua caught a glimpse of another soldier who had tears coming down his face.

Daybreak was slowly coming. The twilight was struggling against a heavy cloud cover intermixed with smoke from burning barricades and debris. There was not going to be sunrise on this fateful morning. At the southeast corner of the Monument, withdrawing students were moving at a very slow pace. On the north side, hundreds of students still stood their ground as more and more soldiers came up the stairs. The beating and kicking intensified. Most students were forced to stand up. But they still remained where they were, refusing to move. Ma Shaofang found himself on the outside row with fellow student leaders Yang Zhaohui and Liang Qingdun. Soldiers came right up to them and placed bayonets directly onto their chests. Seeing that students behind them had not yet started their withdrawal, the three stood firm. They pressed their own chests into the tips of the bayonets and stared down the soldiers, who backed away.[261]

Hou Dejian and Zhou Dou scrambled around and urged students to move. Taking advantage of his age and scholastic look, Zhou Dou was able to shout down screaming students and herd them into moving toward the southeast corner. All of a sudden, soldiers fired their guns in unison, again aiming at the sky. The barrage temporarily disabled the hearing of everyone. The remaining students finally started moving. They dragged and carried the few die-hard dissidents. It was an agonizingly chaotic process. They stepped onto each other and tumbled all over. Along their sides, soldiers continued firing into the sky to maintain the terrifying pressure. They also hit and kicked anyone who they deemed as moving too slow. In the midst of the student body, Zhang Boli felt a profound sense of humiliation. The Square they had occupied for fourteen days was now finally lost.[262]

The opening at the southeast corner was too small to allow the thousands of students to pass through. Debris on the ground and bushes nearby made it a horrible exit. Yang Zhaohui fell down and was immediately trampled on by many passing feet. His feeble cry for help could not be heard in the mayhem. Just as he was losing hope of survival, Liang Qingdun spotted him and, with the greatest effort, halted the stampede to drag him up.[263]

The students found open space after they rounded the corner of the Mausoleum of Chairman Mao Zedong, due south of the Monument to People's Heroes. Soldiers were everywhere. So were city residents who both greeted them as triumphant troops and comforted them as a retreating army in defeat. They took off their shoes and offered them to the many students who had lost theirs during the scramble. Several foreign reporters were dutifully recording this historical moment.[264]

At the front, Chai Ling, Li Lu, and Feng Congde marched together, leading their contingent turning west at Qianmen then north behind the Great Hall of People. From there, they entered Chang'an Avenue at Liubukou. Behind them, the procession of students stretched as long as a mile. This was where police had used tear gas to take back a bus-load of weapons less than twenty hours earlier. Li Lu had heard many reports of horrific fighting between the army and residents along Chang'an Avenue merely hours earlier. But he could not spot much residue of that bloody battle.[265]

As the main thoroughfare of the capital, Chang'an Avenue had four vehicular lanes in each direction. On each side, there was another wide lane designated for bicycle traffic. A green iron-bar fence separated the bicycle lanes from pedestrian sidewalks. Some of the fences had been taken off to make barricades but most were still intact. The student leaders led their procession across the avenue to the north side and then turned west. They chose to walk in the bicycle lane.

Near the very end of the procession, Wu Renhua was walking with some of his student marshals. As they finally turned west on Chang'an Avenue, they heard a threatening roar behind them. Looking back, they were stunned to see three tanks speeding toward them while shooting tear gas canisters. Once again, light yellow smoke filled the air. The orderly procession of students turned into a chaotic scramble. Yet the tanks did not slow down. One of them was right in the bicycle lane and plowed directly into the crowd. Dozens of students desperately scaled the green iron fence for the sidewalk. While most of them made it over to safety, some were left clinging onto the fence for dear life. As the smoke cleared and the tanks sped away, a most horrifying scene unfolded in front of their very eyes.

A section of the fence had been smashed into the ground and bent over under the weight of a tank. Several bodies were left sprawled over it. A couple of them were so badly mangled that they were barely recognizable as human remains. Red blood mixed with white brain flowed onto the streets. In that one instant, five had died and another nine were seriously injured.

One of the injured was Fang Zheng, a student at Beijing Sports College. The athlete was helping a female student who had fainted at the scene when a tank rushed in. At the last moment he pushed the

Standoff At Tiananmen

Now

girl away and barely had time to roll out himself. He did not get far when both of his legs were caught under the tracks of the tank. He was dragged forward a few yards when he grabbed the fence and pulled himself off the tracks and lost consciousness. Both of his legs had disappeared. He was rushed to a hospital and barely survived.[266]

IT was finally the morning of June 4. Tiananmen Square was a disastrous aftermath of a battle zone littered with destroyed tents and burning debris. Armored vehicles were parked side by side, sealing off the entire area. Helicopters hovered overhead. The only people remaining inside were soldiers dressed in combat camouflage. The traditional flag-raising ceremony commenced once again. To the rousing tune of the *March of Volunteers*, all the soldiers, who were the same age as the students they had just expelled, stood absolutely still, saluting the rising Five-Starred Red Flag.

> *Arise! All who refuse to be slaves!*
> *Let our flesh and blood*
> *Become our new Great Wall!*
> *As the Chinese nation faces its greatest peril,*
> *All forcefully expend their last cries.*
> *Arise! Arise! Arise!*
>
> *May our million hearts beat as one,*
> *Brave the enemy's fire,*
> *March on!*
> *Brave the enemy's fire,*
> *March on!*
> *March on! March on! On!*

This is Chai Ling. I am still alive.

Chai Ling

Epilogue

PROFESSOR Fang Lizhi had not been heard in public since the spring when his open letter to Deng Xiaoping helped ignite a political storm. He and his wife Professor Li Shuxian came under around-the-clock surveillance as the student movement emerged after the death of Hu Yaobang. Under watchful eyes, Fang Lizhi settled into a daily routine. He worked at the Beijing Astronomical Observatories in the morning, received various visitors in the afternoon, and wrote his scientific papers in the evening. He was aware that the government had already fingered him and his wife as "black hands," or conspirators, behind the movement. Therefore, he carefully kept his distance. Li Shuxian had been in contact with the students initially. Yet in early May, she was diagnosed with heart disease and quietly dropped out of the scene.[267]

Visitors kept showing up at their apartment, however. Liu Gang had sought advice in the early days of Beijing Students Autonomous Federation and urged Fang Lizhi to speak up. Other students and intellectual friends came with similar requests. Fang Lizhi dispensed advice when he could but declined any public appearances. As the glorious April 27 march was in progress, Fang Lizhi was chairing a seminar on pulsars, a deliberate arrangement by the Observatories to provide him an alibi.

The hunger strike changed the mood entirely. Fang Lizhi remembered that time in a later interview: "Once the hunger strike started, the movement went out of control, and I suspected that the government would use military means to end it. These students just did not understand. They grew up in the generation after the Cultural Revolution and had never seen the Party kill people on a large scale. The

271

students loved that line in *L'Intenernationale* about this being the final struggle, but I told those who came to my home that this was most definitely not the final struggle. They felt that if they just carried this struggle through, they would be victorious. I didn't think so."[268]

Along with those eager students, Fang Lizhi was also receiving many urgent pleas to use his influence to end the standoff. He remembered fondly the days at the end of 1986 when he engineered a peaceful ending of a student protest at his University of Science and Technology in Anhui. He was very anxious to give a repeat performance. Yet when he looked at Tiananmen Square from far away, he painfully concluded that it would be beyond his reach. So, in the heated months of that Beijing spring, Fang Lizhi buried himself in his research work. In late May, he left the city briefly for an academic conference and found himself closely followed. Li Shuxian was frightened enough to seek help from their friend Perry Link for the possibility of protection from the American Embassy.[269]

The fear was not unfounded. Despite their carefulness, they were publicly labeled as the "black hands" of the movement by the end of May. On the last day of that month, several government-organized rallies sprang up in the suburbs, with "angry peasants" burning effigies of Fang Lizhi. He was able to laugh it off at the time.

But it was the noise of tanks and gunshots during the night of June 3 that finally convinced him that his feeble attempt of avoidance would be in vain. Within hours of the massacre, he contacted the American Embassy and asked for protection. The couple, along with their second son,* entered the embassy the next day. They insisted that they were not political refuges but only there for physical sanctuary.

In an instant, "Wanted" signs with the couples' pictures were posted all over the city and broadcast on television. A long-lasting diplomatic standoff between China and the United States ensued. It was not until a year later that the couple was allowed to leave the embassy compound for exile to the United States.

IN the morning hours of June 4, the retreating students got back to

---

*Their first son was already studying in the United States at the time.

the northwest suburb and parted ways to their respective campuses. Strangely enough, there was no military presence in this area. Many students were busy setting up memorial stands and decorating the campuses in traditional mourning style. The mangled bodies from Liubukou, wrapped in white sheets, were displayed at the entrance of the University of Political Science and Law. At People's University, a tank and a truckload of soldiers arrived to surrender their weapons. Some students took the abandoned tank for a joyride.

At Peking University, the remaining student leaders gathered up in Shen Tong's room by The Triangle. Most of them collapsed as soon as they reached the bunk beds. Others talked quietly and depressingly about what they could do next. Outside, their own loudspeakers were repeatedly broadcasting the monotonously low and sad tone of a song by Taiwanese singer Luo Dayou:

> *The orphan of Asia is crying in the wind.*
> *On his yellow face there is red mud.*
> *In his black eyes there is white terror.*
> *The western wind is singing sad songs at the east.*
>
> *The orphan of Asia is crying in the wind.*
> *Nobody will play equal games with you.*
> *Everyone wants to take your beloved toys.*
> *Oh dear child why are you crying?*
>
> *How many people are chasing this unsolvable problem?*
> *How many people sigh helplessly in the middle of night?*
> *How many people wipe their tears silently?*
> *Oh dear mother why is this so?*

The Preparatory Committee was performing its last task. They decided to stop all open memorial and protest activities the next day and urge all students to leave the campus and go home. They also sent out dozens of student reporters to other campuses and hospitals to collect casualty data. Finally, they handed out cash from donated funds to the leaders, who would be on their own.

THE unsettling noise of gunshots could be heard in the city throughout the day of June 4, as if this ancient capital were involved in urban guerrilla warfare. Indeed, residents were engaging the martial law troops on the streets, but only with outbursts of "Fascists!" and occasional hurling of rocks. The soldiers were in a trigger-happy mood. They were shooting at anything that was coming close.

In late morning, an agonizing scene unfolded on Chang'an Avenue at the northeast corner of Tiananmen Square. Hundreds of civilians gathered there stretching across the entire boulevard. Rows of soldiers faced them a few dozen yards away, blocking their way to the Square. The civilians pushed forward slowly and were met with a round of fire from automatic assault rifles. Many fell to ground. The crowd dispersed instantly. The soldiers halted the shooting and allowed the civilians to retrieve the bodies, dead or injured. Then, the crowd gathered again and marched forward. Another round of shots were fired. Foreign reporters who had been confined to their rooms at the Beijing Hotel could not believe what they were witnessing. They recorded this horror as it repeated itself many times.

At other locations, civilians got the upper hand when soldiers found themselves alone. Along Chang'an Avenue, several charred bodies of soldiers were hung on buses or dangled from overpasses. They were labeled with blackened characters indicting them for having murdered civilians. At Muxidi, where the most intensive battle was fought the night before, a column of more than seventy armored personnel carriers was mysteriously abandoned on the street in broad daylight. Thousands of residents surrounded and burned them.

Acts of defiance were not restricted to the streets. In the afternoon of June 4, the *Radio Beijing* English Department quietly broadcast a brief message to the world:[270]

> Please remember June the Third, 1989. The most tragic event happened in the Chinese capital, Beijing.
>
> Thousands of people, most of them innocent civilians, were killed by fully-armed soldiers when they forced their way into city. Among the killed are our colleagues at *Radio Beijing*. The soldiers were riding on armored vehicles and used machine guns against thousands of local residents and students who tried to block their way. When the army convoys made the breakthrough, soldiers continued to spray their bullets indiscriminately at crowds in the street. Eyewitnesses say some

armored vehicles even crushed foot soldiers who hesitated in front of the resisting civilians. [The] Radio Beijing English Department deeply mourns those who died in the tragic incident and appeals to all its listeners to join our protest for the gross violation of human rights and the most barbarous suppression of the people.

Because of the abnormal situation here in Beijing there is no other news we could bring to you. We sincerely ask for your understanding and thank you for joining us at this most tragic moment.

In the morning of June 5, the same reporters confined in Beijing Hotel witnessed another shocking event: the man-against-tanks scene described in the prologue of this book. It took two more days before the shooting gradually quieted down. Even with the city completely under their control, the martial law troops were seen nervously moving around and establishing defensive positions. Rumors were rampant that a civil war, caused by a split within the military rank, was imminent. The rumors gained credibility when cannon fire was heard in the suburbs.

Massive protests and violent riots occurred in many major cities around the country. Students there laid down their bodies on railway tracks to block traffic for days. On June 6, a passenger train lost control and plowed into a sit-in crowd in Shanghai, killing six people. Protesters attacked the train and set it on fire. Ten days later, three workers were sentenced to death for participating in that riot. In Beijing, a dozen "hooligans" also received death sentences for attacking martial law soldiers or vehicles.

It was not until June 14 when the government published a list of twenty one "Most Wanted" student leaders. Wang Dan and Wuer Kaixi landed at the top of the list, followed by Liu Gang and Chai Ling. As the only non-student on the list, Liu Gang was derisively identified as a "jobless floater." Liang Qingdun, Ma Shaofang, Yang Tao, Feng Congde, Wang Chaohua, Zhang Boli, Li Lu, and Xiong Yan had all landed on the list, among others. By that time, they had all been in hiding or on the run. Out of the twenty-one, seventeen had direct connections with Beijing Students Autonomous Federation, founded by Liu Gang.

Another leader from that organization, Guo Haifeng, had already been captured at Tiananmen Square and therefore was not on the list. For the other four, Xiong Yan was active in both Peking University and the Dialogue Delegation and Chai Ling, Zhang Boli, and Li Lu led the various headquarters in Tiananmen Square. In contrast, the leaders of the more moderate Dialogue Delegation were spared inclusion on the list.

It turned gloomy in a hurry. Zhou Fengsuo, one of the leaders of Beijing Students Autonomous Federation who was on the Most Wanted list, was turned in to the police by his own sister shortly after he made his way home.* Within a couple of days, Ma Shaofang chose to turn himself in. Xiong Yan, on the other hand, was captured on a train in a remote western area.

Wang Juntao was staying at a hotel in a western suburb when the killing started. At the outskirts of the city, he saw a body on the main road leading to Chang'an Avenue with his skull smashed open. He felt a shivering cold come over his body knowing that a new date was entering the heavy calendar of Chinese history. He also regretted that he had not fully implemented his evacuation plan. Nevertheless, he spent a couple of days in the city to locate Wang Dan, Liu Gang, Bao Zunxin and place them in safe houses in the suburbs. Trusted resources within their Institute were mobilized to help them get out of the city with fake identification papers.

Liu Gang left Beijing in a couple of days. He disguised himself as a migrant laborer and planned to head to the vast grassland of Qinghai Province. He did not make it too far before his cover was blown. He was captured on June 19.

Wang Juntao, Wang Dan, and Bao Zunxin left the city together. They took a train traveling north. As it rushed through the vast expanse of the great northeast, two girls sitting next to Wang Dan were telling a gruesome story of how Wuer Kaixi was shot in the back of his head and Wang Dan was bayoneted in the chest in the final hours of Tiananmen Square.

The three of them then managed to fly to Shanghai, where Wang

Too dramatic ...

*Zhou Fengsuo later wrote that his sister had been deceived by the authorities.

276

Epilogue

Juntao was hopeful because of his many friends in the south. But his plan soon fell apart. Another list of "Most Wanted" was issued featuring intellectuals including Chen Ziming, Wang Juntao, Yan Jiaqi, Bao Zunxin, and Dai Qing. The three of them decided to go their separate ways. Wang Dan chose to return to Beijing himself. He was captured in early July after he made contact with a reporter from Taiwan. Bao Zunxin met the same fate in southern China. Wang Juntao fared a little better himself. With help from many of his friends, he hid on a lake island near Wuhan for months. In late October, he was lured out of hiding by a friend and was captured at a railway station rendezvous. Soon after, Chen Ziming, who had been on the run himself, fell for a similar trap.

THE good people of Hong Kong did launch a heroic effort to rescue the leaders of the movement. By the end of June, Wuer Kaixi and Yan Jiaqi were the first to resurface in Hong Kong. Others followed the same path. After staying in Beijing for a week in a failed attempt to organize an underground resistance, Li Lu took off and found his way to Hong Kong. Wang Chaohua and Cheng Zhen followed. Although not on the "Most Wanted" list, Xiang Xiaoji and Shen Tong did not take their chances and escaped safely out of the country.

Months later, in a freezing moonless night of March, 1990, Wu Renhua plunged into the ocean. He evaded patrol boats and survived the cold water to reach the safety of Macao and then Hong Kong.

It took Feng Congde and Chai Ling much longer. The couple spent ten months on the run, together but otherwise alone, to find their own way to Hong Kong. They found many sympathetic strangers who helped them along the way. When they emerged unexpectedly on the streets of Hong Kong in early April, Chai Ling was almost unrecognizable as she had had a facial operation. Appearing on television, Chai Ling could only whisper while Feng Congde wept silently. It was then they were finally convinced that their ordeal was over.

The voice of Chai Ling, however, had already preceded her own self. As early as a week after the massacre, while the couple was still on the run, they managed to smuggle out an audio tape of her testimony, made just days after the massacre:

Standoff At Tiananmen

> This is four o'clock in the afternoon of June 8, 1989. I am
> Chai Ling. I am the commander-in-chief of Tiananmen Square.
> I am still alive.

Blow by blow, her low but steady voice recalled the major moments
at and near Tiananmen Square during that fateful night, mixed with a
few exaggerated scenes that she had heard about but could not have
witnessed herself.

THERE were still longer journeys to freedom. After their departure
from Tiananmen Square in late May, the author Zheng Yi and his wife
did not stay at their home for long. After the massacre, his wife was
detained while he was on the run. The forty-two year old balding intellectual picked up a practical skill he had learned during the Cultural
Revolution and passed himself off as a carpenter who traveled from
town to town for work. It was three years later that he reunited with
his wife and they found their way to Hong Kong.[271]

Zheng Yi's author friend Zhang Boli took a road much less traveled.
He escaped from Beijing and headed north to his hometown near the
Soviet border. There, he evaded police and successfully crossed the
border. But there was no sanctuary. The Soviet government, worrying
about its newly normalized relationship with China, decided to deport
him back. But out of humanitarian concerns, they did not hand him to
the Chinese government either. In early January, 1990, Zhang Boli was
left, alone and discreetly, at the border, where he managed to survive
as a nomad in the Siberian forest. It was not until June of 1991, after
720 days on the run, that he found his way back south and arrived at
Hong Kong on a speedboat.[272]

After a media barrage against Professors Fang Lizhi and Li Shuxian, the government resigned itself to the fact that it could not do anything to the couple while they stayed at the American Embassy. They
needed to identify other "black hands" for the movement. Liu Xiaobo,
the professor of literature at Beijing Normal University, was the next
chosen target. The official media launched a full frontal attack on his
activities during the movement and focused on his connection to overseas organizations when he was in New York. But their case soon fell
apart as well. After twenty months in custody, Liu Xiaobo was even-

tually released without a formal sentence, partly due to his positive contribution in leading the students into a peaceful withdrawal from Tiananmen Square. Zhou Dou and Gao Xin received similar treatment.

Hou Dejian, the folk star and the last member of the Four Gentlemen took refuge in the Australian Embassy. After two months of harassment, he came out voluntarily with a written guarantee that he would not be punished. After giving a public testimony that he had seen no death in Tiananmen Square on that fateful night, the thirty-three year old musician was stuffed in a fishing boat and smuggled into Taiwan by fishermen under the orders of the mainland government. It was not a home-coming he had sought or expected. He faced severe punishment by the Taiwanese government for his earlier defection as well as his illegal entry back to the island, charges that were eventually dropped.

Dai Qing, the prominent journalist who had deep connections within the government, chose to stay put in Beijing. She was arrested on June 14 and released the following January, without a formal sentence.

But others were not so lucky. Starting in November, 1990, a year and half after the massacre, trials for leaders of the movement commenced in Beijing as the Gulf War commanded attention in other parts of the world. In a slew of quick decisions, several student leaders on the "Most Wanted" list were sentenced. Among them, Xiong Yan received nineteen months and Ma Shaofang got three years. Guo Haifeng, who was captured in a bus with Molotov bombs in Tiananmen Square, was initially charged with the deadly crime of attempting to blow up Tiananmen. The charge was later dropped and he was sentenced to four years. Wang Dan, the number one on the "Most Wanted," also received four years.

Compared to the death and life sentences that had been dished out to workers and residents, or "hooligans and rioters," student leaders had generally received lenient treatment. Even Liu Gang, a non-student who had demonstrated a defiant attitude during his detention, was sentenced to "only" six years.

As soon as Chen Ziming and Wang Juntao were captured, the "black hands" label was finally attached on them. Although they had only reluctantly joined the movement at its later stage, their rich history of dissident activities and their independent Institute provided a base for the government's charge of "a small clique of conspirators" with organized resources and premeditated actions. Courageously, the two chose not to defend their own individual actions but the movement itself as a whole. It probably did not make any difference as all sentences had been preordained. They were each sentenced to thirteen years.[273]

The images of armored vehicles roaming Chang'an Avenue with machine guns blazing at civilians were forever burnt into the minds of everybody close to the scene. Both the anonymous *Radio Beijing* reporter and Chai Ling had put the death toll in "thousands" in the immediate aftermath. They were echoed by Wuer Kaixi and Li Lu after their escape to safety. Filming on the streets of Beijing, *ABC News* caught a middle-aged man animatedly describing to them how twenty thousand people were gunned down by the army. A nationwide manhunt ensued and the man, by the name Xiao Bing, was arrested and forced to recant his story on television. For his rumor-mongering act, he was sentenced to ten years in prison, the same as Wang Dan and Liu Gang combined.

Student reporters from Peking University dispatched to hospitals and campuses tallied the death toll at two to three thousand, a figure agreed on by a couple of anonymous spokespeople from the Chinese Red Cross as well as Dai Qing, who had visited hospitals on her own. *The New York Times* was remarkably more conservative. On the day after the massacre, the paper put the death toll at "at least 300" but "may be much higher." On June 21, it revised the estimate to "400 to 800 civilians."

The government did not have its own story straight either. On June 6, the Spokesman of State Council Yuan Mu stated that about three hundred had died including both soldiers and civilians, twenty-three of them were students. He emphatically declared that nobody had died during the final clearing of Tiananmen Square.* By the end of June, the

---

*A controversy flared up from this statement as the interpretation of "within Tiananmen Square" was debatable. There were many deaths on Chang'an Avenue and the streets immediately surrounding the Square. Yuan Mu was perhaps referring

mayor of Beijing put the civilian death toll at more than two hundred including thirty-six students. There were also dozens of casualties in the military, who were hailed as martyrs and honored as "Guards of the Republic."

Professor Ding Zilin of People's University was the mother of Jiang Jielian, the high school student who was killed at Muxidi. As she mourned the loss, she was particularly angry with the vague numbers tossed around in this national tragedy. With fellow parents of victims, she founded the "Tiananmen Mothers" organization and, defying tremendous pressure and harassment from the government, painstakingly collected and investigated each individual case. Through years of labor, they had come up with a list of one hundred eighty-nine confirmed civilian deaths including seventy-one students. The numbers were expected to keep rising as their efforts continued.[274]

I⊤ took another half a year after the massacre for martial law to be lifted in Beijing. A reign of terror continued to grip the nation as dissidents were jailed and every citizen was forced into endless political study and self-criticism sessions. Deng Xiaoping's "Four Cardinal Principles" was the law of the land. Jiang Zemin, the mayor of Shanghai, was chosen to replace Zhao Ziyang as the General Secretary.

On the other hand, economic development screeched to a halt in the face of rigid policies and much reduced foreign investments.* It took two years for Deng Xiaoping to become impatient again. In the winter of 1992, he embarked on a dramatic tour to the south to reinvigorate his dying reform. With the nightmare of inflation out of the way, another boom followed, helped by an infusion of capital from overseas Chinese communities. It paved the way for a "peaceful rising" of this ancient nation. Ideology faded once more. By the time Deng Xiaoping passed away in 1997, the formal British colony Hong Kong had returned to

---

to the limited area around the Monument to People's Heroes, from which students had indeed made their chaotic exit without fatal casualties. In the years since the massacre, evidence has surfaced that at least two people died within the confines of Tiananmen Square itself near the giant National Flag Pole.

*In the aftermath, most western countries chose not to impose direct economic sanctions on China except for ones involving the military.

the fold of the People's Republic but retained most of its liberty. The "Four Cardinal Principles" had largely become a historical relic.

On June 4, 1989, the very same day of Tiananmen Massacre in China, the Polish Solidarity won a sweeping victory in an open election in Poland. In the ensuing summer and fall, revolutions swept across the entire communist landscape leading to the fall of the Berlin Wall in that November. Two years later, the Soviet Union imploded under the pressure of reform. The world entered a new era.

But in China, what happened in 1989 faded into a distant curiosity as newer generations of students passed through college campuses. The much less ideologically inclined students concentrated on their TOEFL, GRE, and economic betterment. There would be no significant student movements in the decades to follow. When students did take to the streets to blow off outbursts of emotion, they were protesting against foreign forces who had "wronged" China. These nationalistic upheavals were contained well within government control.

The subject of the Tiananmen Massacre itself remained a taboo with any hint of this part of history censored in public. In its immediate aftermath, Cui Jian, the star who had rocked the students in Tiananmen Square, went into hiding. But his performance was needed to raise funds for an upcoming Asian Games. So, in January, 1990, six months after the massacre, he was on the stage again. The place was jam packed by an eager and anxious audience. As usual, Cui Jian was wearing a faded army uniform and a red bandanna, just as when he visited Tiananmen Square. The stadium went dark. Suddenly, with blinding light pulses flashing and heavy metal blasting as if machine guns were blazing, he let out:

A stray bullet hit my chest.
Suddenly, memory swells in my heart.
I have tears, yet without sorrow.

If this were to be the last shot,
I would like to accept this magnificent honor.
Oh, the last shot.
Oh, the last shot.

Don't know how many, how many words I have yet to say.

282

Epilogue

Don't know how many, how many pleasures I have yet to enjoy.
Don't know how many, how many people who are like me.
Don't know how many, how many last shots there have been.

Lying peacefully on this warm earth,
With morning dew, sunset, and flowers blossoming,
Oh, I leave nothing but those words
To be with this world.

A stray bullet hit my chest,
Suddenly, memory swells in my heart.
Oh, the last shot.
Oh, the last shot.

His tour was shut down after only a couple of stops.*

Last Shot was written in 1988, a year before Tiananmen Massacre. Cui Jian had maintained that the song was dedicated to the martyrs in the 1979 Sino-Vietnam border war.

283

Bibliography

[1] George Black and Robin Munro. *Black Hands of Beijing*. John Wiley & Sons, Inc., 1993.

[2] Shen Tong. *Almost a Revolution*. University of Michigan Press, 1998.

[3] Li Lu. *Moving the Mountain*. MacMillian London Limited, 1990.

[4] Feng Congde *et al*. *Review and Reflections (in Chinese)*. Rhine PEN, 1991.

[5] Wang Dan *et al*. *Recollections of June 4 Participants (in Chinese)*. Mirror Books, 2004.

[6] Chen Zihua *et al*. *Transforming Totalitairan China (in Chinese)*. Mirror Books, 2004.

[7] Dingxin Zhao. *The Power of Tiananmen*. The University of Chicago Press, 2001.

[8] Hu Ping and Wang Juntao *et al*. *Open Up: the Documents of Student Movement in Peking University (in Chinese)*. Tianyuan Shuwu, 1990.

[9] Harrison E. Salisbury. *Tiananmen Diary*. Little Brown, 1989.

[10] Orville Schell. *Discos and Democracy*. Doubleday, 1989.

[11] Craig Calhoun. *Neither Gods nor Emperors*. University of California Press, 1997.

BIBLIOGRAPHY

[12] Bao Zunxin. *The Unfinished Phoenix (in Chinese)*. Fengyun, 1996.

[13] Mike Chinoy. *China Live*. Rowman & Littlefield Publishers, Inc., 1999.

[14] Richard Gordon and Carma Hinton. *The Gate of Heavenly Peace (Documentary Film)*. Long Bow Group, 1995.

[15] Human Rights in China. *Children Of the Dragon*. Collier Books, 1990.

[16] Zhang Boli. *Escape from China*. Washington Square Press, 1998.

[17] Timothy Brook. *Quelling the People*. Stanford University Press, 1998.

[18] Feng Congde. *Tiananmen Memoir (in Chinese)*. Mirror Books, 1998.

[19] Zheng Yi. *A Part of History (in Chinese)*. WanXiang, 1993.

[20] Chen Xiaoya. *History of the 1989 Democracy Movement (in Chinese)*. 1996.

[21] Dai Qing. *At the Juncture of Spring and Summer (in Chinese)*. 1993.

[22] Mikhail Gorbachev. *Memoirs*. Doubleday, 1995.

[23] Mok Chiu Yu and J. Frank Harrison, editors. *Voices from Tiananmen Square*. Black Rose Books Ltd., 1990.

[24] Philip J. Cunningham. *Reaching for the Sky*. 1999.

[25] Wu Renhua. *The Inside Story of the Bloody Clearance At Tiananmen Square in 1989 (in Chinese)*. Truth Press, 2007.

[26] Ding Zilin. *In Search of Victims of June Fourth (in Chinese)*. Open Magazine, 2005.

Notes

[1] See, e.g., [1], [2], [3], [4], [5], and [6].

[2] The government's operation during the student movement is still a state secret. There have been much speculation but little substantiation. The book *Tiananmen Papers* has been published by Public Affairs in 2001, purporting as a compilation of government documents smuggled out by an insider official. Its credibility has never been properly established, and that book was not used as a reference to this writing.

[3] For an excellent analytical work, for example, see [7].

[4] [7], p. 278, pp. 290–291.

[5] Based on various recollections and autobiographical essays by Wei Jingsheng.

[6] Many of the campaigning literature had been collected and published later in [8]

[7] [8], pp. 297–302.

[8] After the 1989 movement, Hu Ping wrote a series of essays analyzing and critiquing the movement in the Chinese magazine *China Spring*, which he edited and published in New York, USA.

[9] [9], p. 107.

[10] For a sampling of Fang Lizhi's speech, see [10], pp. 218–222.

[11] Based on various eyewitness accounts, including Fang Lizhi's own recollections.

[12] Based on various eyewitness recollections available on the Internet.

[13] The person running through the dormitories was a poet named Xue Deyun. See Liu Gang's recollection included in [6]

[14] Ironically, it appeared that Wang Ruowang was a case of mistaken identity for another outspoken intellectual Xu Liangying. A couple of months earlier, Xu Liangying, Liu Binyan, and Fang Lizhi had planned to organize a conference revisiting the history of the "Anti-Rightists" campaign thirty years ago, when they were expelled from the Party for the first time. The authorities promptly forbade the conference to take place since the subject was still taboo. The "Anti-Rightist" campaign, initiated by Mao Zedong, was spearheaded by Deng Xiaoping.

[15] Based on Liu Gang's own recollections.

[16] Winston Lord's speech during a panel discussion hosted by the National Committee on United States - China Relations in 2008.

[17] [7], p. 140.

[18] See [4], p. 10, 20 and [2], p. 135.

[19] In a letter to a Captain Butler dated November 25, 1861, Victor Hugo described the joint Anglo-French army as bandits and thieves.

[20] It was said that their list of trainees included Jiang Zemin, the mayor of Shanghai.

[21] The history of Chen Ziming and Wang Juntao's institute has been documented in [6] and, to a lesser degree, in [1].

[22] For a more thorough analysis of student life, see [7], pp. 90–94.

[23] [4], p. 10.

NOTES

[24] Shen Tong described his childhood in the first two chapters of his book [2].

[25] Two students, Li Dai'an and Zhang Xiaohui, who had no direct involvement in that student movement, were quietly arrested in its aftermath after they announced the formation of a "Young Marxist Faction."

[26] [2], pp. 80–84.

[27] [2], pp. 116–118.

[28] [2], pp. 135–145.

[29] [2], p. 148.

[30] [2], p. 150.

[31] According to Fang Lizhi's recollection articles on the Internet.

[32] After the crackdown, it was the copy taken by Liu Da that was displayed during a public exhibit as a criminal evidence for conspiracy.

[33] Fang Lizhi's personal recollection published on the Internet. Before Fang Lizhi's open letter, Ren Wanding, a veteran of the Democracy Wall movement, had already made a call for Wei Jingsheng's release in the preceding December. Lacking statue, Ren Wanding's call was not well known to the public. See [1], p. 143 and [11], p. 30.

[34] See, for example, [12]

[35] The essay was translated by Perry Link and published in *The New York Review of Books*, February 3, 1989.

[36] [4], p. 12.

[37] Orville Shell provided a vivid account of the incident in an article in *The New York Times* on April 16, 1989. President George H. W. Bush brushed aside the incident as just a blemish in the Sino-US alliance.

[38] *The New York Times*, April 6, 1989. The official inflation rate was cited as 7.3 percent in 1987, 18.5 percent in 1988, and 28 percent in the first quarter of 1989 in [7], p. 127. These official numbers tended to be underestimated.

[39] The activist was Zhang Ling, a graduate from Tsinghua University but with an active base in Anhui Province. Zhang Ling was later heard of organizing protests in Anhui to support the 1989 movement in Beijing and was arrested in the ensuring crackdown. Shen Tong recalled his encounter in his book [2], pp. 157–161 and [4], p. 14.

[40] [4], p. 14 and [2], p. 153.

[41] [4], p. 20.

[42] Chen Xiaoping and Wu Renhua each wrote about their activities at the time in [6].

[43] [4], pp. 1–2, 48–51.

[44] [13], pp. 184–185.

[45] The "Peking University Seven-Point:" 1. Reevaluate and praise Hu Yaobang's contributions; 2. Negate the "anti-spiritual pollution" and anti-"Bourgeois Liberation" movements; 3. Allow unofficial press and freedom of speech; 4. Publish government leaders' income and holdings; 5. Abolish "Beijing Ten-Points"; 6. Increase education funding and enhance the compensation for intellectuals; 7. Report this

movement faithfully.

[46] According to Ge Yang's interview in [14].

[47] [4], p. 51.

[48] Li Jinjin's recollections in [6].

[49] The representatives were Liu Yandong, Song Shixiong, and Tao Xiping.

[50] Han Dongfang, who would later become a leader of the workers movement, recalled being there to persuade the students in [14].

[51] [4], pp. 2–3, 20–21.

[52] [2], pp. 171–175.

[53] [4], pp. 51–52.

[54] Wuer Kaixi fondly recalled his earlier days in the leadership role in his interview in [15], pp. 48–49.

[55] [13], pp. 191–192.

[56] [4], p. 53.

[57] [4], p. 52.

[58] Wuer Kaixi's action was captured on film in [14].

[59] After his own investigation, Zhao Dingxin concluded that the so called incident was largely exaggerated, see [7], pp. 33–35.

[60] [4], pp. 5–7.

[61] [15], p. 53.

[62] See [1], p. 146. Very few, if any, students were aware of Wang Juntao's presence in the Square that night.

[63] [4], pp. 53–54.

[64] [15], p. 54.

[65] [4], pp. 34–36.

[66] [16], p. 37 and [4], p. 55.

[67] The scene in front of the Great Hall of People was described by many witnesses, including Liu Gang's recollection in [6], Ma Shaofang's recollection in [5], as well as many in [4]. Zhao Dingxin provides a description of the same events in his book [7], pp. 150–154.

[68] [15], p. 54

[69] [4], pp. 56–58.

[70] Shen Tong recalled his experience in both [2], pp. 186–191 and [4], pp. 18–19.

[71] Chen Mingyuan made the same speech on many campuses and in Tiananmen Square. One version of the speech was included in [15], pp. 54–60.

[72] In his recollection, [6] p. 153, Liu Gang stated that Wang Dan immediately demanded a built-in majority for representatives from Peking University to ensure its leadership position, which he declined on the principle of democracy. However, Wang Dan denies that he would or could ever have made that kind of demands. Wang Dan does not remember the details of that conversation.

[73] To this day, Liu Gang regarded that his failure in securing a more senior person for the leadership role as a critical factor in not being able to maintain a strong organization in the later phases of the movement.

[74][7], p. 155.

[75]During this early stage of the movement, Chen Ziming had offered financial support not only to Liu Gang, but also, at least, to at University of Political Science and Law. the exact amount he provided was not certain. see, for example, [1], p. 147 and [6], p. 157.

[76][4], pp. 25–26.

[77][4], pp. 39–40.

[78]The English translation was adapted from http://www.tsquare.tv/chronology/April26ed.html

[79][15], p. 61.

[80]Shen Tong recalled Wuer Kaixi's visit and Zhou Yongjun's hand-written note in his book [2] pp. 200–202.

[81][2], p. 196.

[82]See [2], p. 198 and [4], pp. 63–64.

[83]The beginning phase of the April 27 march was based on recollections by many participants, particularly Shen Tong in [2] and many other leaders in [4].

[84]During May, 1989, when the student movement had the potential to be recognized by the government, the official Museum of the Chinese History had contacted the makers of this giant board for the possibility of acquiring it. In the Chinese Constitution, there are three articles pertaining to the freedom of speech and assembly, which were all abbreviated on the board used in the march.

[85][17], p. 32.

[86]It was the 38th Army that was called into the city this day, see [7], p. 224.

[87]The symposium was organized by Ge Yang with the Beijing bureau of *World Economic Herald*.

[88]During many interviews, Wang Dan has expressed his feeling that the April 27 march was the most memorable moment throughout this movement, a sentiment that was echoed by many other leaders and participants. Wang Dan fondly remembers the time when he stood up the Jianguomen overpass and when he saw the old man crying in the cramped dormitory room.

[89][4], p. 68.

[90]Shen Tong was in the audience. He was impressed by the ease of Wang Dan and Wuer Kaixi in handling the reporters, see [2], pp. 208–209.

[91]The early struggles of the Peking University Preparatory Committee were documented by the leaders in their recollections in [4], pp. 7–9.

[92][2], p. 207.

[93][4], pp. 66–67.

[94][4], p. 68, pp. 109–110.

[95][2], pp. 213–217.

[96][7], p. 158.

[97][2], p. 218 and [4], pp. 78–80.

[98][2], pp. 200–222.

[99][2], p. 218.

[100]According to *The New York Times*, May 5, 1989.

[101][4], pp. 74–75, 114-116.

[102][2], pp. 225–229.

[103][2], p. 227.

[104]The five conditions are: 1. retract the April 26 *People's Daily* editorial; 2. recognize independent student organizations; 3. publish statistics involving official corruption and punish corrupted officials; 4. reinstate *World Economic Herald*'s editor Qin Benli; 5. review the Beijing Ten-Points regulation on demonstrations.

[105][18], p. 335, 444.

[106][4], p. 82.

[107][2], p. 234 and [4], p. 66.

[108][19]

[109][4], pp. 126–128.

[110]According to Wang Chaohua in [4], p. 94. Ma Shaofang would dispute this in his later collections. Nonetheless, the rumor of the "reform wing" needs students' help had been persistent throughout the movement.

[111][4], pp. 94–96.

[112][15], p. 65 and [4], p. 123.

[113][4], pp. 123–124. The initial idea from this group was to have the hunger strike on campus instead of in Tiananmen Square.

[114][4], pp. 94–96.

[115][7], p. 288.

[116]Although Chai Ling's speech was recorded that night, audio tapes had not been made available. There were many transcripts, some were based on the later polished *Hunger Strike Manifesto*. The quotes here was adopted from her own recollection in [4], pp. 90–91.

[117][2], p. 237.

[118]There would later be disputes on who was the real author of the *Hunger Strike Manifesto*. Bai Meng claimed that he had written it on his own after hearing Chai Ling's speech. But Chai Ling insisted that she had written the first rough draft. See [4], pp. 92–93, 119–122.

[119][4], p. 85.

[120][3], p. 93.

[121]Li Lu wrote about his earlier life in the first five chapters of his biography [3].

[122][3], pp. 97–99.

[123][3], p. 116.

[124][3], p. 124.

[125]The interaction between Chai Ling and Li Lu is based on Chai Ling's recollection in [4], p. 104. In his own book, Li Lu offered a different version of the same event. There was no mention of inside information. Li Lu said he was in the crowd crying when Chai Ling gave her speech that night. The next day, he was with the hunger strikers all the time in Peking University. Chai Ling had run over and asked him, "Are we going to die?" He told her that he had never been so moved by her

NOTES

speech. Then, with the entire contingent, he rode to Tiananmen Square on a bicycle with Chai Ling sitting on the back rack. See [3], pp. 133–134.

[126][7], p. 161.

[127][4], p. 85.

[128][1], pp. 170–171.

[129]*The New York Times*, May 14, 1989. The validity of the news could not be independently verified.

[130][20], p. 263.

[131][1], p. 136.

[132]The one who burst in was Zheng Naifu, a scholar in the Chinese Academy of Social Sciences. See [6], p. 164.

[133][11], p. 63.

[134]see and Wang Juntao's respective recollections in [6].

[135]This first meeting with Yan Mingfu was recalled by many. See, for example, [1], pp. 172–174; [2], pp. 240–243; [4], pp. 104–105.

[136]The *The New York Times*, which had been following the student movement closely since mid-April, failed to report on the hunger strike until May 15, when Mr. Gorbachev was already arriving.

[137][4], p. 130.

[138][4], pp. 100–101.

[139][4], pp. 96–97 and recollection articles by Wang Chaohua and Dai Qing.

[140][21].

[141]Wang Chaohua has written extensively on her experience with the intellectuals in her various personal recollections.

[142][4], pp. 101–103.

[143]In his book, Li Lu said that it was him who suggested to play the tape, see [3], p. 137.

[144][4], p. 105.

[145]Shen Tong described the scene in his book [2], pp. 246–247. Chai Ling's own recollection, however, seemed to indicate that they never had the chance to actually play the tape, which she regretted deeply, see [4], p. 106.

[146][4], p. 134.

[147]The failed dialogue session with Yan Mingfu were recalled by multiple sources. See, for example, [2], pp. 244–249 and [4], pp. 85–86.

[148][21].

[149][4], pp. 107–108, 132–133.

[150]Wang Chaohua later wrote several articles recounting her experience with the intellectuals.

[151]Wuer Kaixi's interview in [14].

[152][2], p. 253.

[153][4], p. 144.

[154][3], pp. 139–141 and [4], pp. 135–136.

[155]*The New York Times*, May 16, 1989

[156] [19], p. 93.

[157] [1], pp. 177–178.

[158] [19].

[159] [3], p. 145

[160] [4], pp. 137–138, 146–147.

[161] In his autobiography, [3], Li Lu stated that he had come to Beijing without any identification card. However, there were other rumors that he refused to show his card because it would have identified him as a member of the Communist Party.

[162] [3], pp. 146–150 and [4], pp. 147–149.

[163] [13], p. 211.

[164] Mr. Gorbachev had surprisingly little to say about his historical trip to Beijing in his lengthy *Memoirs* published in 1995. He did not mention Zhao Ziyang's fateful disclosure. See [22], pp. 487–491.

[165] *The New York Times*, May 20, 1989.

[166] [2], p. 243.

[167] [3], p. 153.

[168] According to Zhou Dou's later recollection, Yan Mingfu might have been forced into a vehicle by his body guards.

[169] [4], pp. 141–143.

[170] [2], p.281.

[171] [15], p. 83.

[172] [3], p. 152.

[173] According to later reports, Zhao Ziyang had proposed to rescind the April 26 *People's Daily* editorial in a Politburo meeting the night before. He offered to take the blame for the editorial himself and allow a public investigation into allegations of graft involving his own son. But he was overwhelmingly voted down.

[174] [2], pp. 278–279.

[175] [4], p. 163.

[176] [7], pp. 313–316.

[177] See [4], p. 246 and [1], p. 183. It was not clear whether the students actually received the money. Many of such large donations were held up by banks or the official Red Cross of China.

[178] [23], p. 151.

[179] [23], p. 151.

[180] [4], p. 163.

[181] [3], pp. 158–160.

[182] It was reported later that Zhao Ziyang had offered his resignation as early as May 17, after his proposal of rescinding the *People's Daily* editorial was thoroughly voted down in Politburo. His resignation was also turned down. Dejected, he took a sick leave.

[183] [6], p. 475.

[184] [6], p. 478.

[185] Wang Dan and Wang Chaohua were also included as deputies of the Hunger

NOTES

Strike Headquarters. But they rarely if ever participated in its activities.

[186][4], p. 195-196.

[187]It's probably unlikely that Yan Mingfu would have explicitly given out the information of the impeding martial law as it was a state secret at the time. But Liu Yan remembered the episode in [4], p. 201. News or rumors about the martial law had also surfaced in Beijing and other cities that afternoon.

[188]In his book, Shen Tong described how they decided to end the hunger strike at the United Front Department and that Wuer Kaixi was ready to assume the overall leader position after the end of the hunger strike.[2], pp. 287–289 and [4], pp. 201–203.

[189]Based on Feng Congde's own recounting of the event, which differs somewhat from a version presented by Zhang Boli in [4], pp. 196–198, 204.

[190]The process of ending the hunger strike was extensively discussed in [4], pp. 164–170 and 195–206. Li Lu also provided his take in [3], pp. 163–166.

[191]Chai Ling and other student leaders regarded the ending of hunger strike before the martial law as a significant tactical victory by the students, [4], p. 201.

[192][1], p. 196.

[193]Timothy Brook provides a vivid reconstruction of the troop movement during the night of martial law in his book [17], pp. 48–60. He also pointed out the importance of moonlight that night.

[194]Bernard Shaw recalled the moment on *Larry King Live* on March 8, 2001. Mike Chinoy documented the entire process in his book, [13], pp. 19–24, 220–224.

[195]*The New York Times*, May 20 and 25, 1989.

[196]citezhaodingxin, pp. 316–321.

[197]The signature drive was facilitated by the semi-private Stone Corp. and its CEO Wan Runnan and intellectual Cao Siyuan. After the crackdown, several members claimed that their signatures were either forged or obtained with false pretenses.

[198]See Gao Yu's recollection in [6].

[199][3], pp.173–175.

[200]The plan to escape was sometimes referred to a plan to go underground by some of the leaders involved. See [3], p. 172 and p. 175, as well as [4]. Feng Congde also claimed that it was Li Lu's idea.

[201][4], pp. 263–265.

[202]In later recollections, Chai Ling said she had spent a night in a friendly safe house. Feng Congde had traveled to nearby Tianjin to establish a secret communication station.

[203]Shen Tong mentioned in his book that he had also found more than fifty people in favor of withdrawing in a meeting attended by about seventy people. See [2], p. 302.

[204][4], pp. 207–209.

[205]According to Wang Juntao. This was his first meeting with Chai Ling and Li Lu. Neither of them knew him.

[206]The founding of the Workers Autonomous Federation by Han Dongfang and Li

Jinjin had been well documented in [1].

[207] [7], pp. 173–176.

[208] According to conversations with Wang Juntao and Liu Gang.

[209] [12].

[210] [3], pp. 176–177 and [4], pp. 219–220.

[211] The many activities of the May 23 were recalled by various people. Wang Juntao outlined his work in [6], pp. 125–126; Li Lu in his book [3], pp. 175–176; Other students remembered that day in [4].

[212] [3], p. 177.

[213] [10], pp. 215–218.

[214] For a limited glimpse of the chaotic financial situation in the Square, see [4], pp. 241–262.

[215] [3], pp. 178–179 and [4], p. 223.

[216] [18], pp. 163–164.

[217] [1], p. 363

[218] [1], p. 217.

[219] [4], p. 227 and [18], p. 162.

[220] See [3], p. 180 and [1], p. 218.

[221] [3], p. 180. In their book, George Black and Robin Munro described a scene in which Li Lu angrily confronted Wang Juntao, [1], p. 218. But Wang Juntao himself remembered that he was not at Tiananmen Square that day.

[222] According to Liu Gang's recollections.

[223] George Black and Robin Munro described the scene differently in their book [1], pp. 218–219. It said that Wang Dan handed in his resignation immediately after reading the statement. Wang Dan had no recollection on that act. In fact, he had no official position to resign from at that time. In his own book, Li Lu also incorrectly stated that Wang Dan had read a version with the June 20 withdraw date, see [3], pp. 180–181.

[224] This scene at the end of the press conference is based on Liu Gang's own recollection.

[225] [19].

[226] Philip Cunningham wrote about his first impression of Chai Ling on that day in [15], pp. 106–112. A more detailed, but slightly different, version was presented in his memoir [24]. Chai Ling's true intention at the time remained unclear as she has not openly discussed her plan or thoughts at the time. Her husband Feng Congde later wrote extensively on her behalf and stated that her plan was not to flee but to travel around the country and instigate nation-wide supports for Beijing, see [18]. However, Philip Cunningham's own memoir, [24], left no impression of such a plan. Rather, he was convinced that Chai Ling was ready to escape to Hong Kong and had already established contacts for doing so.

[227] [24].

[228] [14].

[229] This was a sentiment expressed by many people who were there at the time. For

example, [7], p. 285.

[230][18], pp. 168–169.

[231]Xiang Xiaoji left Beijing for his hometown on May 20, after the collapse of the dialogues, see [4], p. 87.

[232][2], pp. 313–314.

[233][15], p. 118.

[234]The exact intention of building the statue remained unclear. It was claimed to be commissioned by Beijing Students Autonomous Federation but Wang Chaohua had no idea about it at the time. There had been speculation that the statue was originally intended as a farewell gesture for the intended withdrawal date of May 30, [17], p. 87 and [15], pp. 116–122. Others thought it was precisely to forestall such a withdrawal attempt, [11], p. 110.

[235]Based on Wang Juntao's private conversation.

[236]This kidnapping attempt was led by Wang Wen, a student who had been involved in the hunger strike leadership from its inception. His proclaimed motive was the rampant corruption within the student leadership. He cited the money dispersed to student leaders when they secretly escaped from Tiananmen Square on the night of May 21. Li Lu described how he resolved the crisis in his book [3], pp. 187–190. Feng Congde wrote about his own experience in [18], p. 84.

[237]Liu Xiaobo gave a candid interview on his own experience in the documentary film [14].

[238][13], p. 247.

[239][17], pp. 94–107.

[240][3], p. 192.

[241][25], p. 30.

[242]Timothy Brook pointed out the importance of the moon phases during the nights of martial law and massacre, respectively, in his book [17], pp. 78–80.

[243]According to Ding Zilin's investigation, the first death of the night happened at Wukesong, further west from Muxidi. A thirty-two year old technician was shot on a sidewalk and later died in a hospital, see[26]. Wang Juntao, who was in a nearby hotel, also witnessed a dead body near Wukesong. See [6], pp. 129–130.

[244][26].

[245]Shen Tong gave a vivid account of his experience that night in his book [2], pp. 317–326.

[246]For a more detailed description of the military assault that night, see [17], pp. 108–150.

[247][4], pp. 308–309.

[248][4], p. 309.

[249][4], pp. 309–310.

[250][25], p. 67.

[251][25], p. 133.

[252][25], pp. 172–173.

[253][13], pp. 255–256.

[254]Zhang Jian told his story during an interview at *French International Radio* on June 4, 2001.

[255]The film of Liu Xiaobo smashing a gun survived and can be seen in the documentary [14]. In [4], student leader Liang Qingdun also remembered throwing a gun he had found into bushes. It was not clear if they were the same weapon.

[256][25], pp. 330–335.

[257][4], p. 318.

[258]The scene of negotiation is largely based on Wu Renhua's observation from the Monument and Hou Dejian's recollection, both of which can be found in [25].

[259][3], p. 200.

[260][4], p. 318.

[261]According to Ma Shaofang's recollection.

[262][16], p. 2.

[263]See [4], p. 320. There had been many recollections that involved student deaths during the final withdraw from Tiananmen Square. Some speculated execution of students left behind after the majority had withdrawn. This became a touchy issue as the government insisted that nobody had died during this process. So far, there was no clear and hard evidence of any deaths although numerous students suffered injuries from the beating and stampede.

[264][13], p. 259.

[265][3], p. 201.

[266]A picture of Fang Zheng hanging on the fence, without his legs, were published in the French magazine *Document Observervateur*, October, 1989, p. 117. Fang Zheng had become a handicapped athlete by 1994, when he was denied the right to compete in a regional Special Olympics.

[267][23], p. 164.

[268][17], p. 93.

[269][15], p. 116.

[270]The broadcast was transcribed and posted on the Internet by Erik Larsen from the University of Washington.

[271][19].

[272]Zhang Boli chronicled his story of escape in his book [16].

[273]A detailed account of the trials can be found in [1], chapter 19.

[274][26].

Index

INDEX

Chen Mingyuan, 89, 90, 96, 116, 218, 224, 288

Chen Xiaoping, 30, 60–62, 92, 108, 144–146, 201, 287, 289, 291

Chen Xitong, 197

Chen Zihua, 21

Chen Ziming, 15, 16, 21, 52, 84, 96, 108, 143, 144, 167, 191, 192, 198, 209–213, 242, 277, 279, 286, 289

Cheng Zhen, 157, 171, 180, 181, 195, 277

Chennault, Claire, *see* Claire Chennault

Children of Dragon, 244

Children of the Dragon, 243

China Women News, 87, 114

China Youth Daily, 15, 126

China's Despair and China's Hope, 57

China's Soul banner, 63, 64, 67, 69–71, 79

Chinese Academy of Social Sciences, 115, 291

Chinese Alliance for Democracy, 58

Chinese Central Television, *see* CCTV

Chinese Communist Party, *see* Communist Party

Chinese New Year, 45

Chinoy, Mike, *see* Mike Chinoy

Chiu, Fred, *see* Fred Chiu

Chopin, Frederic, *see* Frederic Chopin

Cixi, Dowager, *see* Dowager Cixi

Claire Chennault, 198

class boycott, 11, 42, 77, 86, 96, 108, 125, 127, 199

CNN, 75

CNN, vi, 63, 173, 200, 245, 259
 control room, 200
 Vice President, 200

College
 of Chinese Medicine, *see* Beijing College of Chinese Medicine
 of Economics, *see* Beijing Economics College

of Ethnic Minorities, *see* Central College of Ethnic Minorities
 of Sports, *see* Beijing Sports College

College of Aviation, 108

College of Posts and Telecommunications, 108

Columbia University, 27, 227

Communist Party, 6, 11, 25, 30, 32, 33, 40, 43, 44, 59, 75, 81, 83, 98, 101, 105, 114, 115, 138, 142, 172, 173, 186, 201, 219, 286
 Beijing city, 143
 Central Committee, 33, 70, 171
 Chief of Staff, 190
 flag, 83
 member, 82
 National Congress, 29, 115
 Polish, 59, 101
 Politburo, 44, 142, 143, 174
 support, 101
 the leadership of, 13, 20, 37, 98

Communist Youth League, 16, 25
 Central Committee, 16

Constitution, 49, 98, 99, 108, 289

counter-revolutionary, 14, 20, 75
 rebellion, 258, 259

Cry from Deep Lake Salon, 51

Cui Jian, 182, 183, 282, 283

Cultural Revolution, 5–8, 10, 11, 13, 14, 18, 19, 21, 25, 32, 34, 65, 71, 73, 74, 84, 90, 99–101, 110, 130, 138, 142, 148, 153, 168, 171, 176, 182, 199, 202, 217, 240, 271, 278

Cunningham, Philip, *see* Philip Cunningham

Dai Qing, 152, 153, 155, 160–163, 167, 277, 279, 280, 291

Dallas, 200

Dan Rather, 173, 200

death toll, 280, 281

Democracy or New Dictatorship?, 14

299

INDEX

Standoff At Tiananmen

INDEX

diff versions
    how the author selects one over another ..

Printed in the United States
215269BV00001B/31/P

9 780982 320303